Praise for *Deep Denial*

No one speaks to racism and its cure better than David Billings, a white southerner who has seen it all, but through a different lens...the lens of up close and deeply personal, but who has also been inspired by the positive lessons from past victories of others who fought and who even died for freedom and justice for all. And his is a voice that needs to be heard, especially during still another unsettling, uncertain period in our labored stride towards a more perfect union. It is a voice with perfect pitch.

Charlayne Hunter-Gault
Award-winning journalist and author

David Billings was one of the first white people I knew who talked about racism, who was willing to come in to the black community and build relationships. Over the 45 years I have known him, David has been an effective catalyst for multiracial, anti-racist work. His experiences and analysis will help all of us understand how deeply-rooted racial divisions are throughout our country, how deeply entrenched they are in each of us. This is a national story that we all must learn if we're ever going to heal our racial wounds. David writes from principles that are fundamental to building a movement for liberation. Because of the racial turmoil going on in our country, this is the right time to read *Deep Denial!*

Ronald Chisom, Co-founder and Executive Director,
People's Institute for Survival and Beyond

Deep Denial truly fills a void! David Billings focuses on the socially constructed racial divide in the United States and examines the implications of white people's anger, guilt and denial about the meaning of being "white." Further imbedded in this work are the intersections of gender, sexual orientation and age in relation to "whiteness." Billings skillfully documents a historical understanding of why the fallacy of white superiority, which is internalized and deeply embedded in both culture and psyche, is still very much alive and well today. This book is a must read for anyone seeking to increase their racial consciousness, interested in racial equity and social justice or having more successful outcomes in their work in human services, education and beyond.

Mary Pender Greene, LCSW-R, Psychotherapist,
Anti-Racist Organizational Consultant, author

Rev. David Billings, a white anti-racist minister, teacher, and organizer, and a long-distance runner for social justice, pulls the covers off the intricacies of white supremacy in this nation. His narrative is a brilliant fusion of personal memoir with penetrating and comprehensive historical perspective. *Deep Denial* is articulated clearly and plainly. Yet, it is not simple [but rather] profound in the honesty of the author's self-disclosures and in the historical lessons and strategic vision. The book inspires, and prompts protracted organization and action, for which Rev. Billings deserves effusive praise. Freedom-loving people should be grateful to him for his contribution.

Dr. Alan Colón
Eminent scholar in Education and African World Studies

Deep Denial is written from the point o
and again succumb to this evil Goliath
who are resurrected and re-strengthene
This book helps people understand wha
and to be better equipped for the long ter
Deep Denial is told with vivid descriptions,
importantly, with personal accounts reve
self-critique, and providing a detailed desc
being transformed in the process. Nobody d
Billings, and no one can read this book wit
ened for the next stage of the struggle.

Joseph R. Barndt, Lut
Understanding and D
Becoming a

Deep Denial is a superbly documented account f
point of a white southerner. In over two dozen suc
erfully written historical vignettes, Billings
demonstrating "how white happened and continu
today." From the legal construction of the white ra
colonial period to the renewing of white supremacy
the book exposes the processes and outcomes of a
structed to privilege whites, the only group expected to
and normalize racial superiority. Educators, scholars [a
agents such as community organizers and social activist
efit mightily from this cogent critique of the history of t
States.

Dr. Michael Washington, Professor of
Director of the Afro-American Studies I
Northern Kentucky U

Deep Denial

Deep Denial

The Persistence of White Supremacy in United States History and Life

David Billings

Crandall, Dostie & Douglass Books, Inc.
Roselle, NJ

Published by Crandall, Dostie & Douglass Books, Inc.
245 West 4th Avenue, Roselle, NJ 07203-1135
(908) 241-5439 www.cddbooks.com

ISBN 978-1-934390-04-7

Library of Congress Cataloging-in-Publication Data

Names: Billings, David, 1946- author.
Title: Deep denial : the persistence of white supremacy in United States history and life / by David Billings.
Description: Roselle, NJ : Crandall, Dostie & Douglass Books, Inc., [2016] |
Includes bibliographical references and index.
Identifiers: LCCN 2016032362 | ISBN 9781934390047 (alk. paper)
Subjects: LCSH: Whites--United States--Race identity. | Racism--United States--History. | White supremacy movements--United States. | Civil rights workers--United States--Biography. | Billings, David, 1946- | Civil
rights movement--United States--History--20th century. | United States--Race relations--History. | United Methodist Church (U.S.)--Clergy--Biography. | Mississippi--Social life and customs--20th century. | McComb (Miss.)--Biography.
Classification: LCC E184.A1 B533 2016 | DDC 305.800973--dc23 LC record available at https://lccn.loc.gov/2016032362

To Carla
without whom I might not have
begun this work;

To Stella
without your work, I might have not
continued this work;

and to Margery
without whom I most certainly
would have given up.

Thank you all.

Cover Images

Front cover, centered in frame

"Portrait family outdoors" by Monkey Business Images. Under license from Shutterstock.com. All persons depicted are stock photo models.

Front cover background collage, clockwise from top left

"Union pickets the Jewel Food Store" [Chicago]. Photo by Paul Sequeira, Aug. 1973. National Archives and Records Administration, No. 551939.

"Delano United" [Protest of the gentrification, West Harlem, NY]. Photograph [cropped], by jarito, 11/24/07. Flickr, (CC BY 2.0).

"Protest march in Rochester, Minnesota" Photo [cropped], by Rose Colored Photo, 12/06/14. Flickr, (CC BY 2.0).

"Newspaper headlines of Japanese Relocation." National Archives and Records Administration, No. 195535.

"First landing of Columbus on the shores of the New World." Painting [cropped], by Dióscoro Puebla, 1862. Library of Congress, No. 2001699099.

"Selma to Montgomery march, Alabama in 1965." Photo, by Peter Pettus, 1965. Library of Congress, No. 2003675345.

"Contrabands on Mr. Foller's farm, Cumberland, May 14, 1862," [group of enslaved people at the Foller Plantation, Pamunkey Run, Virginia]. Stereograph, hand colored [cropped], by James F. Gibson, 1862. Library of Congress, No. 2011646155.

"American progress: Westward the course of destiny." Painting by George A. Crofutt, 1873. Library of Congress, No. 97507547.

"Burial of the dead at the battle of Wounded Knee, S.D.," [U.S. Soldiers putting Indians in common grave]. Photo, with handwritten notation. Library of Congress, No. 2007681010.

"The KKK on parade down Pennsylvania Avenue." Photo, New York Times Paris Bureau, 1928. National Archives and Records Administration, No. 541885.

Back cover

"Elsie's Black Lives Matter Demonstration - Minneapolis" [Demonstrators gather at 8th and Marshall Street NE outside Elsie's, where a law enforcement fundraiser was taking place]. Photo [cropped, recolored], by Tony Webster, Minneapolis, MN, 12/3/15. Flickr, (CC BY-SA 2.0).

Table of Contents

ACKNOWLEDGEMENTS

Like all authors, I am indebted to more people than I will remember to recognize. To any I have failed to mention, please accept my apologies. Certainly I owe much to my parents, Charles and Joyce Billings, who never abandoned me, and who filled my head with stories about the life and times of the Billings/Hamn family that preceded me. I owe a great debt to my sisters, Bonnye, Patti, and Kay who have been as dedicated to family as I have been. To Peggy Billings who inspired me from an early age to join the justice struggle and to keep broadening my horizons. I knew she loved me, but at some point, she began also to respect me and my work. I saw it in her eyes. It was a special blessing. To my teachers, Vera Miller and Dr. Leon Boothe, in particular, who instilled in me a love for learning that has only expanded as the years have passed. To Nibs, my life-long friend and companion, who always set the bar high for both of us, and I followed his lead.

I owe so much to the People's Institute for Survival and Beyond, Inc. The trainers, especially those early ones, have instilled in me a commitment to understand race in all of its dimensions and to know what it has meant to be white. To Michael Washington and Dan Buford, who along with the great Jim Dunn, our co-founder, taught me history in ways that I had never dreamed possible. To Diana Dunn and Maria Reinat-Pumarejo, Shadia Alvarez, Margery Freeman, John Morrin, and Dr. Kimberley Richards whose influence on me has been profound. And to Ron Chisom and Barbara Major whose charisma and humor never leaves me. You are in my head and heart.

Meredith McElroy, this is for you and to you, Sharon Martinas, Sandy Bernabei, Mary Pender Greene and Angela Winfrey, Jeff and Becky Conner and to all the saints in the movement. You have made me proud and I hope I have meant the same to you.

And to Jeff Hitchcock, my editor and publisher, without your gifts *Deep Denial* would be less than it is now.

Prologue

On January 4, 1962, my uncle Harry was murdered in McComb, Mississippi. The murder was brutal and senseless and it tore my family apart and also the family of the young man who killed him. Their lives were immediately in danger. It set off a wave of violence and revenge-seeking in town. We were living in Helena, Arkansas, by then and I remember when my father left the room to answer the phone and receive the news about Uncle Harry. He was quiet but clearly shaken when he told us the news and immediately retreated to the bathroom. My memory is that he stayed in there for a few hours. I don't know how long he stayed, but it was an eternity to me. My life would never be the same. My father would never be the same either. He was always reserved and self-contained to the point of seeming distant and aloof. He would be even more so after Uncle Harry's murder.

More than anything I remember the ride down to McComb after Uncle Harry's murder. The trip to McComb from Helena was some three-hundred miles of silence — five of us — two of my three sisters, myself, my mother and my father. Three hundred miles of grim-faced grief broken only by the sounds of the radio. I remember Marty Robbin's hit song, "El Paso," number one on the country charts. It played over and over. My father never spoke. He stared grimly ahead. My mother shushed us from time to time. My uncle — his brother — had been killed by a black man.

The murderer was a young man — seventeen or so. That's how I remember it. One year older than I was. In another time and place we might have been in high school together. We might have played football and gone on to Ole Miss. But not in 1962 and not in McComb, Mississippi. Willie Lee would pay the price of that act not much more than a year later. On the night we arrived, one day after Harry was killed, Willie Lee Anderson was already in state custody, bound over. He was caught with blood still on his hands. He had not even bothered to run. He was ap-

prehended at home. Harry Billings was dead, Willie Lee Anderson was caught, and McComb was gripped with racial frenzy.

The Klan came. They wore no sheets. There was no need — they made no attempt to disguise themselves. I recognized some of the names and some of the voices. From the ante-room where I was to sleep, I listened as they talked to my father and my uncles on the possibilities. "Do you want us to burn him out? His family is there. We know where they live." "We can run them out of here if you say so." I remember the silence. Six Billings brothers remained. Who would speak? I was terrified. I thought it could go either way. I think it was James who answered. James was not the oldest, but he was a war hero, career Army. Maybe that's why he spoke. He had seen death. He knew what death was all about. Who knows? After what seemed an eternity to me, he said, "No, that's not what we want. It won't bring Harry back. It's not his mother's fault. We are not that kind of family." I gasped unconsciously. "We're not that kind of family." I was glad. I wasn't sure. I was scared.

What kind of family were we? In Mississippi, in 1961? White — Southern — Christian — diehard segregationists — racist. We were normal. Like everybody else that I knew at the time. In McComb, 1962, Brenda Travis and Ike Lewis would lead a walk-out from the black high school, two miles through downtown to city hall. It was a courageous act on their part. It was the year Bob Moses would relocate to McComb the first time, upon invitation from C. C. Bryant and E. W. Steptoe. Herbert Lee, Bobby Talbot, Curtis Hayes (Muhammad), Hollis Watkins, and many others would begin planning for a voter registration drive and Freedom House would be opened. Herbert Lee would later be killed and become one of Mississippi's early civil rights martyrs. He would not be the last. Churches would be burned by night riders. McComb would be known ignominiously for a while as the "church-burning capital of the world." But I didn't know anything about that. Bob Moses, Brenda Travis, Ike Lewis, Alene Quinn, Herbert Lee, Curtis Hayes and Hollis Watkins would be names I would later learn about, and some I would learn from. But at the time they had no names. "N----- agitators" is all I ever heard, although not at home. My parents didn't talk that way. Troublemakers, not martyrs. That is what they were. Looking back, there were many martyrs. Maybe Harry Billings and Willie Lee Anderson were martyrs, too, in that twisted time and place.

What kind of family were we? We were churched. My aunt was a missionary recently returned from Korea then working in New York. One of my uncles had gone to seminary in Atlanta. Another was a church lay leader in Memphis. All of us were Baptist or Methodist or in-between. At the funeral Harry's favorite hymn, "The Old Rugged Cross," was sung. I had never heard before nor since such piercing wails of grief and sadness and pain. Did Willie Lee Anderson go to church? I bet he did. I didn't know. The old rugged cross — "a symbol of suffering and shame" — it burned bright that winter of 1962. In front yards sometimes, in cow pastures, in church sanctuaries. "For a world of lost sinners was slain." Yes, Lord. Like Herbert and Harry and Willie Lee and…me?

What kind of family were we? We were a walking set of contradictions, as the Temptations song would say. My mother took me aside not long after it happened. We never had long talks about it. Her references were often oblique. "David," she would say, "there are a lot of things in this life we can't begin to understand, but I don't want you to lose faith. God has a way of making sense out of these things. Your father is very hurt, but he loves you very much. Be patient with him." From 1962 to this day I carry the memories; the contradictions inside of me are as much a part of me as life itself. The old rugged cross — Jesus' cross — the Klan's cross — "a symbol of suffering … and shame."

Time passes. In spite of itself. In October, 1962, the Russians approached Cuba. James Meredith entered Ole Miss. I did, too, in 1964. With my suitcase of contradictions, I watched as the first black women students on campus had snowballs hurled at them and two were knocked down. I watched as a panty raid prior to the LSU game turned violent and the black students were evacuated from campus. I watched as the first black athlete — a Tulane baseball player — stood silent in left field as the crowd chanted out "N-----" and cheered as a ball went through his shaking legs. And I later listened to the silence that fall as Houston's Warren McVea returned a punt for a touchdown. Barriers were being broken and quickly repaired. I was at Ole Miss. Where was Willie Lee Anderson?

Willie Lee Anderson was dead. In June of 1963 he was put to death in Mississippi's gas chamber. A small clipping in the Jackson and McComb newspapers was all there was. In the larger scheme of things, I guess it was no big deal, but it was for the Billings family and, surely, for the Anderson family. It read, quite simply, that Willie Lee Anderson, Negro male, convicted of the murder of Harry Billings, in McComb, in January, 1962, was to be put to death. Willie Lee had been in Parchman little more than a year while I was still in high school. We were two young Southerners who had grown up near each other and partly in the same town, yet we grew up worlds apart. The murder of my uncle and the execution of Willie Lee Anderson were the turning points in my life and ministry. I would never forget them. From that day on I began anti-racist work that would take me all over the United States and even to other parts of the world.

What kind of family were we? I don't know. Still don't. We were — still are — full of contradictions. Later I, too, would be sentenced to Parchman, but that's another chapter in the story. Did I ever forgive him for murdering my uncle? I don't know. As a Christian, I was supposed to forgive, but one thing was for certain, I never forgot it.

I played Willie Lee Anderson's death over and over in my mind so many times that I began to imagine I went to his appeal hearing and asked that the killings stop. I never did. I lived with the contradictions. I still do.

"We are not that kind of family." That is what Uncle James said. I guess we were not. I owe that to Harry, and in a strange way, I guess I owe it to Willie too.

Introduction

For the past fifty-four years I have been working against racism. The last thirty-five years of that time, I have crisscrossed the United States and a few other nations as a core trainer with the People's Institute for Survival and Beyond. Through its "Undoing Racism®/Community Organizing" workshop, I have interacted with thousands of people who were drawn by the vision of "undoing" racism. Some wanted to become more effective in their work, while others came simply because someone had mandated them to attend as a job or course requirement. At least half of the workshop participants have been white; the rest, people of color representing the wide spectrum of people not considered to be white in this nation.

In this book, I focus primarily on white people like me. How did we become racialized in the United States over the past 400 years? I ask, what does the designation "white" mean in a race-constructed country where racial inequities still dominate our homes, churches, schools, court rooms, and workplaces? What will it mean for our future, given the changing demographics of the nation? If we think race is no longer a primary indicator of our identity and status, how do we explain the systemic outcomes in wealth accumulation, physical well-being and structural dominance in institutions that still control American society? Is it just rich white men who benefit from racism, or do each of us as white people, men and women, old and young, gay and straight, reap the benefits of being white?

All of my adult life I have studied our history as white people and the cultural phenomena this history has produced. I have met and taught and learned from whites. I have heard and felt our anger about being white, our need to apologize for being white, but most of all, our denial of its importance to us. Thus the title of this book, *Deep Denial: The Persistence of White Supremacy in United States History and Life.*

This book is partly a memoir. It is also a guide, demonstrating how one white person, and by implication the rest of us who are white, can understand how being white happened and continues to happen today. This process is kept from us. In my experience interacting with thousands of white people over the years, most us never think about being white much less how we became white. I believe that only as we understand the impact of race on our lives will we be effective participants in building a movement to undo racism. In this twenty-first century United States, being a white person still constitutes a way of life. To deny this reality as a white person is naive and even dangerous.

I am often asked, mostly by people of color, "Why would you give up the privileges that go with being white in this country?" "What's in it for you?" These are tough questions. In this book I attempt to answer them not just in a personal way but by setting these questions in their proper political context. For race is a *political* construct; it must be "undone" politically. I can't — or won't — give up being white, with all of its privileges and benefits, until I am forced to do so by a radically transformed culture that includes a new racial morality. If any of us think we can make these transformations individually, on our own, we have not tried to do it. Not here. Not in the United States of America.

In Part I of *Deep Denial,* I set race in its historical context. Some of us who work against racism and call ourselves "anti-racist" may know this history. Most of us, white people in particular, know virtually nothing about our history because we are taught a history that excludes most of us. We have no idea that *white,* like *black, Asian, American Indian,* and *Hispanic,* are political terms, neither scientific nor biological. I am indebted to Dr. Y. N. Kly for introducing me to the phrase "the anti-social contract" to describe the relationship people of color have with the United States. Kly explains that whites have a "social contract" that a race-constructed society made with us.[1] None of this just happened. It was no accident that race became the bedrock of our nation's stratification. It is no accident that the realities of race continue to play out in our society.

Part I also introduces the concept of "Internalized Racial Superiority" — IRS. I first learned about IRS from the People's Institute workshop leaders, especially Barbara Major, Dr. Michael Washington, and the Rev. Daniel Buford. It made sense to them. Their analysis of the multigenerational impact on people of color being seen as "less than," of the process of internalizing a sense of racial inferiority, led them to recognize that where there is racial inferiority, there must also be, over generations, internalized racial superiority. After denying IRS for some time, I came to recognize its reality in my own life. Stories and analyses of IRS are woven throughout this book, demonstrating that IRS, and its flip side, Internalized Racial Inferiority, have enabled the race construct to survive for generations, for centuries.

Race is the Rubicon we have never crossed in this country. Even in the twenty-first century, everything in this country is touched by race, from where we live or choose to live, go to school, go to worship, go to the movies, or walk at night. School segregation is a reality much as it was 60 years ago. Housing patterns are deeply racially segregated. Wealth is white. A 2014 study by the Pew Research Center calculates that white people on average have thirteen times the wealth of blacks, ten times the wealth of Latinos.[2] Wall Street is white. So is most of corporate America.

The United States entered the twenty-first century much as it did the twentieth century, with its color line very much intact. Just as in 1900, the New Millennium sees people of color, especially blacks and Latinos, at the bottom of every national measure of wealth, health, and well-being. Even in the years since the Civil Rights Movement, power — real power — has remained in white hands. Blacks and Latinos are more likely to be poor, less likely to graduate high school, and are incarcerated far more than they have ever been when compared to whites. A white person still lives much longer on average and is deemed more credit worthy, is less likely to be stopped and frisked by the police, or go to jail, or be homeless. White people own our homes at much higher percentage rates than people of color, even in times of economic recession. Whites graduate from high school and college more often and are half as likely to be unemployed — even when white unemployment itself is at unacceptable levels. White babies are less likely to die in the womb and more likely to thrive in their first two years. Most of us can choose to live pretty much where we want to and go where we want to go. In some parts of the country we can go for days and never see or interact with a person of color.

Many people will point out that much has changed. The nation is far more integrated than in 1960. Particularly in the town square — at shopping malls and movie theaters, and at the banks and in restaurants and hotels — one sees a rich mosaic of diverse peoples of all ages going about their business. Sports teams at the collegiate and professional levels are an international mix of ethnicities and cultures. Most large companies now have added some color to their workforce even as the top echelon of these companies remains white and largely male.

Yet today in the largest of American cities, the word "public," when used as an adjective, increasingly means black and Latino and poor. We have public schools, public housing, public transportation, and public health. All of these descriptors are now euphemisms for color. Many of our cities' public schools have largely been abandoned by whites. Although some say housing patterns are changing, suburban housing — except for those first-ring suburbs outside our big cities — still remains rigorously segregated. Take Westchester County, New York, a primary destination point for whites leaving New York City for generations. Viewed as a whole, Westchester County appears quite mixed in its racial demographics. But a closer look shows that the overwhelming number of blacks and Latinos in the county live in the cities that border New York City: Yonkers, New Rochelle, and Mount Vernon. Except for a few pockets, the rest of the county is exceptionally white. Or look at the demographics of San Francisco today and ask, "Where have all the black people gone?"

In every realm of society, racism abounds. Mainline churches, civic clubs, and many professions, including law, finance, medicine, and media are overwhelmingly white. The vast racial disparities between those professionals and the constituencies they serve remain largely unnoticed by the general public. When there has been racial mixing, it has rarely been voluntary on the part of whites, but has resulted from years of struggle, litigation, and organizing on the part of people of color. During the Civil Rights Movement, advocates for racial equity were opposed by the overwhelming number of whites, especially in the South. Had it been up to white people, none of those civil rights acts would have passed. People of different races move past one another in the United States like ships in the night. We rarely stop and board one another's vessel.

It's true the nation has moved. The signs are down: There are no more "Colored" and "White" entrances. One does not see "No Chinese here" or "Mexicans — Take Out Only" or "No Japs." Certainly there are no longer posters offering bounties, plastered on boards at the town square, for anyone who brought in an Indian "Dead or Alive." Communities no longer announce their "sundown ordinances" on official placards at the edge of town as they did a few years earlier, warning people of color to leave before the sun sets.

Yet there are still towns that do not welcome blacks; real estate companies still steer people of color away from buying in certain neighborhoods; redlining is still unofficial practice among auto and life insurance businesses, loan companies, even funeral homes. Burials continue in segregated cemeteries, unabated, in small towns and cities across the nation. "Sundown towns" have barely modified their policies. Police in white towns and neighborhoods carefully scrutinize — and often stop — non-white travelers whether on foot or in cars.

In the midst of all these concerns, people still focus, sometimes almost exclusively, on the fact that some change has taken place. Bigotry is frowned upon except on talk radio or cable television. If the N-word is used by whites, an apology is necessary or a reprimand is in order, even if the forbidden word was spoken by Mark Twain's fictional "Huckleberry Finn" over a century ago.

There is something terribly false about all of this. When it comes to race, people in the United States are anything but neutral. We derisively call the niceties we perform with each other in the public arena "being politically correct." It is as if we, as a nation, know that, were it not for these freshly minted public standards, we would be free to say how we really feel and it would be nothing nice. Yet we are just one slight away from raving in public like Kramer of *Seinfeld* fame or pro-wrestler Hulk Hogan. Even in 2016 at political rallies, people are caught on video spewing racist epithets, and a presidential candidate can slander and criminalize Mexicans and Muslims. Thank heavens, then, for "political correctness," however insincere. This nation needs all we can get.

Our defenses as white people, when confronted about our white privileges, have been honed sharply over the centuries. What we can't outright deny, we are well-equipped to justify in a minute. "We" — meaning white people though never stated as such — really don't think people of color work as hard as we do. Most of us believe that white people earned all we have with no assistance from the federal government. This remains true to us because we have never had to turn the mirror around and look at ourselves. We are not taught about the three hundred years of "affirmative action for whites," as historian Ira Katznelson puts it, the legal exceptionalism that biased our laws in favor of white people since colonial times.[3]

So we have learned, through the media drumbeat, that when people of color dare to bring up race at a city council meeting or in a public forum, we can charge them with "playing the race card," or accuse them of living in the past, using race as an excuse or a crutch. We know how to dismiss them by saying "He is just an angry black man (or woman or child)." When a school teacher or university professor dares mention what the enslavement process was really about, or how "Indians" were really treated, or why the A-bomb was dropped on Japan and not Germany, or what "the growing number of Hispanics" in Texas really think about the Alamo, we know to charge them with being "revisionist" historians. Despite the recent swell of energy expressed through the Black Lives Matter movement, the white racial narrative, described by Juan Gonzales and Joseph Torres in their book, *News For All the People: The Epic Story of Race and the American Media,* is still the only "truth" we allow in most of our schools and universities.

I remember the first time, in one of our Undoing Racism® workshops, I heard Ron Chisom ask someone who was white, "What do you like about being white?" The mixture of silence, resentment, and confusion in the room was palpable. I had never heard a white person asked, and that included myself, "What do you like about being white?" I cringed. To have to answer in the presence of people of color was incriminating and intimidating. I would have rather been called a racist.

Because I had grown up in Mississippi and Arkansas, I was probably better prepared to answer the question than most whites in the room, but it was the effrontery I felt that stayed with me. "The question is unfair," many whites in the room said. Others felt it was a trick question and they had been set up. Ron Chisom, co-founder and director of the People's Institute for Survival and Beyond, answered "Oh, you have been set up alright, but we didn't do it. You were set up a long time ago."

Ron's response, and the whole process of the workshop, still fascinates me. Those of us who are workshop trainers spend hours asking probing questions of participants about how we all fit into the racially-biased structures and culture of the United States, even going so far as to say that all of us white people are beneficiaries of this white-dominated society. I am always taken aback like all the rest of the white people in the room. The emotional defensiveness stays with me. "Not me, not me!" is the refrain. Most of us would rather be called a liar than be called out as white. We cite our ethnicity and say, "I don't see myself as white." "I am Norwegian (or Irish or Jewish or Italian)." Anything but white.

What I realized in that early workshop, now years ago, and the hundreds of similar settings I have been in during the thirty-five years since I first heard Ron's question, is that most of us who are white have never had to think about what we like about being white. We have never examined our "race" from the psychological standpoint of internalized superiority. Even those of us who study history and have heard of "white privilege" have not, for the most part, explored the effects of being white on our psyche, our attitudes, and our deeply-held sense of place. We just have not done it. Yet if we are going to participate in the restructuring of our white supremacist institutions, we first have to examine ourselves and where we are as a nation.

This book seeks to understand the impact of racism on white people. For many years and with great insight and passion scholars and sociologists have examined the impact of racism on people of color. Yet there have been relatively few studies of the psychological impact of racism upon those of us who are white. What have been the messages we have received as whites over the generations that have us see ourselves, even unconsciously, as "better than" others? This journey of exploring Internalized Racial Superiority fascinates me. It is disquieting and yet liberating. All of our relationships and values have been cultivated within this framework in our race-constructed nation. Our hyper-individualism is but one example. The dominant culture in the US has always lifted up the nation's "rugged individualism" as key to understanding ourselves as a people. But not all of us have been allowed to be individuals. People of color have always been lumped together as a part of a group even when the grouping made no sense (Hispanic), was ahistorical (American Indian), or culturally insulting (Asian). Only white people are allowed to be individuals, first and foremost.

So what are the messages we receive as white people over the generations? How does white supremacy manifest itself as part of our psyche? What role has history played? Can we ever get past our racial legacy? Why are the feelings and attitudes of white superiority not examined in clinical settings? Why are they not a part of our professional training? Surely the impact of Internalized Racial Superiority is something that could be studied in school, not just as prejudice or discriminatory behavior, but as a psychological condition, perhaps even a disorder, among white people. We expect "white" to work for us, but we cannot admit it or study it. Our belief in white superiority has seeped into every facet of our lives in America. It's in our cultural DNA.

Nothing more crucial exists in this nation than understanding racism in all of its dimensions and then organizing as a people to "undo" it, as the People's Institute says. Such an effort requires a reconstructing of this country's structural arrangements — quite possibly a greater task today than in 1865, since today we think of racism as merely how we feel about one another, or what our intentions are. This denial by whites that racism still exists or that we bear any relationship to its past or present is a major barrier to racial equity. Our relationships with people of color are not only marginalized by this denial, but relationships across racial lines remain superficial, even disingenuous.

When Barack Obama was elected President of the United States in 2008, some said to ourselves, we have reached the mountaintop as a nation. Our mainstream media spoke of how we were finally beyond racism. Obama's election proved it. Then beginning in 2013 came publicity about a rash of police shootings of young black men across the country — shootings that had been happening all along but were finally getting attention in the mainstream press. The nation had to ask itself: Do those black lives matter? Would their deaths ever show up in history textbooks? Suddenly racism seems undeniable again.

This book rebukes the notion of a post-racial society. It revisits the past to better understand the present. My intent is both historical and empirical. Why do white people fare better in the arrangement than people of color, especially black and brown people? Why has this always been the case and why is it still? Why are even the poorest white people better off than most who are black and brown? Why is race a critical divide even among different dimensions of oppression like class and gender that would seem to mitigate against racism? How does a nation founded in white supremacist thought and worldview continue to function on that same premise even as the very words, "white supremacy," have been banished from the lexicon of proper discourse? Why, after all the attention given to race — all the attempts to eradicate racism through legislation, changes in the law, new ways of thinking about each other across race lines over the past sixty years — do the outcomes remain the same? White people still benefit. Black and brown people still catch hell.

I write as one born and grown older in white supremacist culture; my experiences are not just in the South but in all sections of the country and in every manner of institutional and personal settings. I tell the story as one who knows first-hand the dehumanizing effects racism has on all of us who live in the United States, especially on those of us who are white. I show how deeply-embedded notions of race supremacy meant that even radical reform movements, like Reconstruction and the Civil Rights Movement, ultimately depended upon white people's consent and the approval of white-dominant institutions and systems.

As a white person, even in my youth, I was taught that everything of significance that had happened in the United States had been accomplished by white people. I took this interpretation of history for granted so completely that I was not aware of the extent that this way of life must have shaped me as a person. I was brought up to think and see my white world as normal. Everybody else around me seemed to me to see the world in the same way. The enormity of the impact this would have on me as an individual never crossed my mind. My worldview, shaped by this internalized sense of racial superiority, meant that I saw history, morality, the will of God, and scientific truth as the special province of white people, usually white men. Why did no one ever speak about this narrow prism through which I was taught to see the world? More than laws or customs, my very understanding of myself was bound to the idea of white supremacy. There was simply no contradiction within me or with those around me.

What was the effect of all of this on someone like me? Did racial separation on all levels of society cause me to rebel later? Was it the reason I would be so obsessed with this country's racial dynamics? Or did it send another message about white superiority? Even when I later began to challenge racism, did I still function out of a sense of my white superiority? The messages I was receiving in every phase of my existence were "you're better than," "this is just the way it is," "this is God's will." I was in my teens before I ever met someone black who was said to be "smart" or "educated" or "successful." I was in my twenties before I admitted that black women were beautiful or sexy. It was as though white supremacy had infected me on a cellular level. It was the world in which I lived.

Segregation, and the seriousness with which it was enforced, made blacks in my mind appear innocent, acted upon. This was true of Indians also. I didn't have the words for it growing up. I did not understand the politics of white supremacy. Nor did I understand what it was doing to my psyche. The white supremacist state helped create a different reality for me. Had I gone to school with, played ball with, had to compete with black people, they might have seemed more three-dimensional to me and I to them. This was never the case. The messages were constant and the circumstances of my life were utterly different from those of black people.

Whites in my world were not self-reflective about race. There was little attempt to examine the morality of the Jim Crow South. We never used words like *white supremacy* or *racism* or even *racist*. We did not claim to be prejudiced against anyone, but had any number of explanations to justify the ways things were. The most empathetic statement one heard, usually from a preacher or a teacher, was something to the effect of "My people (meaning whites) are just not ready yet." Whites in my world thought blacks were pushing too fast and going about "it" in the wrong way. Whites also thought blacks wanted things handed to them. The most ignorant white person would be quick to offer suggestions as to what "Negroes" needed to do to earn his respect.

Fear associated with race shows up in all kinds of places: at town meetings on health care and gun control, on the front porch of one of Harvard's elite professors, hourly on cable news channels, or in night court in any large city or small town. This fear is multigenerational, reaching back to the country's founding. William Loughton Smith, South Carolina Congressman in 1790 (reported in the *Annals of Congress*) expressed this fear cogently:

> If the blacks did not intermarry with the whites, they would remain black to the end of time; for it was not contended that liberating them would whitewash them; if they would intermarry with the whites, then the white race would be extinct, and the American people would be all of the mulatto breed.[4]

After a lifetime in the Deep South, my wife Margery Freeman and I moved to New York City in 2004 where killings of black men by police occur all too often. It was the same in New Orleans where I lived half my life. I have since returned to live in my home town of McComb, Mississippi. White men chasing someone black in Harlem or Brooklyn or New Orleans or Ferguson, even McComb, is standard. We know it is a police action. Black men chasing anyone not on a football field or a basketball court, is a crime in progress. It is not surprising that white cops shoot their fellow officers of color. In any city or town in the US, we are a nation hard-wired by race. The stereotypical regional splits of North and South, urban versus rural have little efficacy within the larger history of systemic racism that is ingrained into every facet of American civic consciousness regardless of where we live in the United States.

I do not want to run away from my own comfort with this arrangement and my deep-down resistance to change. I want to face my complicity with and enjoyment of all that goes with being white. I want to resist granting myself a pass, believing I'm a different sort of white person. I do not want to get into how the dynamics of class, gender, age, politics or locale might intersect with the dynamics of race. I want to be white and stay white.

In Part II of this book, I have chosen to focus on the post-WWII era because it is the period of my own life. Even though the post-war challenge to white supremacy began as early as the 1930s, after 1954 a new generation of organizers was poised to dismantle "separate but equal." In this post-WWII period, forces for change would achieve traction in the struggle to bring down white supremacy. It would be different. Or so it seemed for a while.

The 1954 *Brown v. Board of Education of Topeka, Kansas* decision outlawing segregation in public schools was a seminal victory for civil rights. For a twenty-year period, 1954 – 1974, it appeared as if the forces fighting for civil rights had won or were winning. The battles had been for the soul of the nation and many felt that racism had been defeated in both the spheres of moral influence and legal sanction. Even Richard Nixon, who twice won the Presidency on a law and order campaign strategy, was more bark than bite when it came to dismantling the gains of the Civil Rights Movement.

The victories, however, provoked a powerful and influential counter movement characterized by political assassinations, imprisonment and exile of key civil rights leaders. A government-waged terror campaign against the Black Panther Party and the American Indian Movement was both deadly and unapologetic. Yes, the nation changed. The question remained, in the face of such resistance, could those changes be sustained? Would the white majority allow fundamental changes to its way of life? Would white dominant cultural systems and institutions be willing to move beyond symbolic change to structural equity?

By the end of the 1970s, the civil rights apparatus had largely been dismantled and in its place had emerged a massive social service industry throughout the United States. The emergence of the not-for-profit sector after 1970 as the primary vehicle to address long-standing needs created by the exclusionary racial arrangement was one of the most significant outcomes of the Civil Rights Movement. This was not the outcome intended by organizers who had faced down Bull Conner's attack dogs or the FBI's guns at Wounded Knee. This new social service industry adopted a needs-based strategy to mollify oppressed communities. It did not address historic grievances or collective patterns of inequity and marginalization. It did not support self-determination for oppressed peoples. It especially did not require institutional self-examination or an analysis of the connection between race and power in the United States. Persons who only a few years before would have migrated toward the "Movement" now matriculated through the universities to be trained as "case managers," "diversity officers," and "public policy advocates" rather than community organizers. "Movement" graduates would become professionals, licensed and certified, accountable to the very state-sanctioned systems that had necessitated their building the Civil Rights Movement in the first place. Social services replaced social change efforts. A host of government- and privately-funded "programs" rapidly disrupted and intruded upon organized communities of color that had transformed a nation. Non-profits proliferated, accountable more to counting numbers than to community outcomes. Once again, as in the past, the government would collaborate with private interests to define how those excluded from the social contract would be handled.

The myth of a colorblind nation replaced the myth of white supremacy when this nation outlawed overt racial laws. Colorblindness, however, is belied by the outcomes produced by all of our systems. Wherever one looks — foster care, juvenile detention, public housing, education, health care, the picture is the same. As the late NAACP Chairman Julian Bond said in 2003, "Whether race is a burden or a benefit is all the same to the race-neutral theorists; that is what they mean when they speak of being colorblind. They are colorblind, all right — blind to the consequences of being the wrong color in America today."[5] This book sees white supremacy. Our history as a nation demands it. Race is not only about the past, but also about the future this past creates.

Part I

Chapter 1

Creating a White Social Contract

My mind boggles. I knew the "slave trade" from school, but in my schooling there were never numbers or people attached to it. Faces were never shown or depicted by an artist's rendering. The moans of the captured were never made audible as a symbol of the brutality and inhumanity endured by enslaved women, men and children stolen from the African continent and trafficked from the Door of No Return in westernmost Senegal to God knows where in the Americas. The trade in Africans involved all of Europe and those Africans who facilitated the enslavement process. Those African and Arab traders had little idea either as to where the ships were headed or what was awaiting their cargo when they arrived. It is said that sharks followed the boats as they rocked and swayed their way westward to the Americas with so many dying en route that their corpses were merely pitched into the sea as a food feast for carnivorous fish.

I have often wondered as I grew older what the captors felt. Had they lost so much of their own humanity they could not recognize the humanity of the Africans below? What must it have been like to be the "keepers of the watch" as people suffered and died and met their God or the ancestors as fish food.

I had never heard the word MAAFA. I knew nothing of its meaning. In white dominant culture we were taught little about "the trade." What we were taught treated the calamitous trip as basically insignificant. It was never depicted with any of its accompanying horrors or the ghastly and degrading conditions those chained and tight-packed had to endure. After all, they had to get here someway, it was said. My teachers were quick to point out that Africans played a role in it. It was not just Europeans. Somehow, it even seemed to put the onus on the "slaves" themselves. As if it was somehow their fault. Or others of their same race for certain.

There are always those who collaborate in their own oppression just as there are always those of us who collaborate in the oppression of others. But in our school lessons the Triangle Trade had no personality to it. It was just a description. Slavery was started on the coasts of West Africa. "Slaves" were transported here in something called the Middle Passage. The slave ships landed somewhere along the Atlantic coast and slavery continued for two hundred plus years. This remained true until the war was over in 1865. President Lincoln freed the slaves. Now it is a historical reference point like the Civil War, like Jim Crow, like the Civil Rights Movement. That's it.

I was not ready for the MAAFA. Not one bit. I had been invited to preach at the St. Paul Community Baptist Church in East New York, Brooklyn. St. Paul was pastored by the Rev. Dr. Johnnie Ray Youngblood who was famous for building some three thousand affordable housing units in one of most beaten-down sections of New York City. He was also famous for being somewhat "outlandish" in the pulpit and unpredictable in his approach to ministry. What particularly impressed me was his ability to bring into the church those usually left out. Formerly incarcerated persons and those struggling with addictions were as much a part of the congregation as professors, city government workers and other middle class churchgoers. He had members called "Saints in Caesar's Household." These were people who worked in the jails and at juvenile court, in the hospitals and at the schools and who were expected to stand with others in the church who were caught up in the system. It was something to behold.

I had read his 1995 book, Upon This Rock, *in which he told the story of St. Paul Community Baptist Church. It was the most self-determined Christian congregation I had ever seen or heard of and it was there in vivid detail. It was an honor for me to be asked to preach at St. Paul's commemoration of the MAAFA. I prepared as best I could.*

My first indication that I was in for something unique was when I saw parishioners of St. Paul all dressed in white lined up around the block at 6:00 a.m. Some two thousand people packed the church as they would at each of three services that day. I remember thinking that at my small church in New Orleans we sometimes did not see two thousand people at church in an entire year. I was nervous, but appropriately so. My family was there. So were colleagues from the People's Institute.

My second indication that something was up was after some minutes when seated in the pulpit area, hands clasped and a prayerful countenance on my face, I noticed the sanctuary had been remade into a replica of one of the "slavers" as they were called. This replica was extraordinary, rounded at each end as a ship would be. There were posters advertising "Slaves" for sale and others for a "Runaway Negro." The MAAFA began to the sound of heart-wrenching cries of the tortured and maimed in the "hull" of the ship, with a procession of elders, holding the limp bodies of dolls representing children in their arms. They deposited the lifeless forms overboard into the sea (at the front of the church). Then the congregation witnessed what seemed to be a never-ending depiction of horror and violence, as men and women were raped, lynched, and bull-whipped across the stage. It was more powerful than I could imagine. I have never seen anything so dramatically depicted before or since. The commemoration ended not with resolution but with the appearance of the Sankofa bird looking back and yet facing forward. A huge banner stretched across the sanctuary that read: THE WAY OUT IS BACK THROUGH. *The MAAFA was a ritual healing process. Its message was that trauma unaddressed and unacknowledged leads only to the spiritual death and the internalized rage of a people. I can try to put it in words, but that's it. No way I can really know it or feel it.*

I turned to Rev. Youngblood at some point in the service and could only say "DAMN." He had a smile as wide as the sanctuary slaver. The notes I had carefully prepared had been rendered useless. The text I was to use seemed vapid and uninspired. What I said was hardly up to the moment at hand. I tried as best I could. I said my people (whites) were on the floor of those ships and that for whites, the way out was back through too. I could not lapse back into white-speak. I could not separate myself by ethnicity or nationality. I could not say that history does not know who was there. That audience did not want to hear that from me. It was clear who had been on the ships and where the ships were going. St. Paul's wanted to hear me "own it." They needed no explanation. I said even Jesus bowed to the gods of white supremacy. The MAAFA was hell.

Creating white people

No one really knows when the concept of white people came about. It could have been a descriptive term spoken in various languages dating back to European encounters with indigenous peoples of the "New World," especially those in what became South America and Africa in the fifteenth and sixteenth centuries. Members of the Wampanoag nation might have used a word that translated as "white" as English people stepped off the Mayflower and onto Plymouth Rock.

For Europeans, becoming white took more than 500 years. There were no white people when Europeans initially came to North America or South America. The first Europeans were Portuguese and Spanish followed by English, German and French. Some were Swiss and Scots, Scandinavians and Dutch.

Europeans in colonial North America were referred to by various names. In the first decades after the Jamestown settlement in 1607 (over 100 years after Portugal and Spain landed in South and Central America) persons were spoken of as "English and other persons" meaning other Europeans. Indians — and later "Negroes" — were non-persons under the law. This nomenclature evolved as increasing numbers of non-English Europeans arrived and became recognized in the law by their ethnicity or nationality such as "a Dutch man" or "a French man." All of these European ethnicities gradually conformed to Anglo-Saxon (English) cultural presumptions and dictates. English remained the national language. Over time, other Protestant Europeans gave up their languages in public trade and debate, conformed to certain manner of dress and decorum, and inculcated the story of the new nation as a history dominated by Anglo-Protestants. As European immigrants internalized this process of assimilation, they accepted the canon that constitutes what is fundamental to our nation's sense of self. Some literary critics, for example Barrett Wendell in his *Literary History of America* (1900), "argued that the greatness of New England letters in the period from 1830 to 1860 was to be attributed to the fact that the region was then almost racially homogeneous."[1] Others, such as Charles F. Richardson, "believed that the 'Saxon characteristics' of 'honesty, rugged independence, reverence for women and love of home and children' were ingrained in the early Americans."[2] As laws changed to reflect the changing demographics of colonial North America, English and Protestant Europeans were described as "Christian" or "baptized."

But this nomenclature created a dilemma once Africans were introduced into the Virginia and Maryland colonies in 1619. The Christian baptismal rite was used as a social control mechanism to bring "Negroes" under the precepts of the Church, especially to its dictates of subservience to one's master. Historian Winthrop Jordan concludes:

> From the first...the concept embedded in the term Christian seems to have conveyed much of the idea and feeling of *we* as against *they*: To be Christian was to be civilized rather than barbarous, English rather than African, white rather than black.[3]

Judge Leon Higginbotham's chronology in his book, *In the Matter of Color: Race and the American Legal Process: The Colonial Period,* uses the date 1691 as the first time the word "white" was used in the laws of Virginia to refer to the legal status of persons of European descent:

> Whatsoever English or *other white man or woman* (italics added), bond or free, shall intermarry with a Negro, mulatto, or Indian man or woman, bond or free, he shall within three months be banished from this dominion forever.[4]

In the century between 1691, when "white" was first used in the laws of colonial Virginia, and 1787, the year the US Constitution was ratified, "white" and "American" became synonymous. The difference between "white" and "Indian" or "Negro" is crucial. White confers legitimate status before the law so white people have access to the institutions sanctioned by the state. Whites were seen as full human beings. The terms "Indian" and "Negro" confer a status outside the protection of the law and without support from the institutions. Neither Indians nor Negroes were statused as full human beings in the US Constitution. Indians, not taxed, were not considered to be part of the body politic except as dependents of the federal government or as domestic foreigners subject to the Commerce clause. Negroes were 3/5 human, but only for purposes of determining Southern white representation in Congress. In the eyes of the law, in the emerging race-constructed society of the United States, Indians and Negroes were illegitimate — less than. Minority.

Historian Y. N. Kly calls this "the anti-social contract." He puts it this way:

> The anti-social contract is an unwritten, unspoken and unofficial agreement between the U.S. ruling elites and the remainder of the

> white ethny [*sic*] to maintain the minorities, particularly the African and Native American minorities, in a position inferior to that of the white ethny.[5]

This race-based nation had to be structured and legitimized. From the establishments of colonies at Jamestown and Plymouth Rock, in 1607 and 1620 respectively, until the civil rights acts of the 1960s — over 350 years — most judicial rulings handed down by the US Supreme Court or US federal courts upheld the preemptory rights of white people and discounted the rights of Indians and Negroes. Those few exceptional rulings that asserted Negro or Indian rights were ignored, circumvented or quickly rescinded.

The creation of the legalized "white person" with inalienable rights not granted to Indians or blacks presaged the end of indentured servitude in the US. Indentured servants had been present since the beginning of colonization. An indentured servant was a man or woman or even a child under some circumstances, almost always European and poor (although Africans also held that legal status for the first few years of colonial North America), whose passage to the colonies was paid by a bondholder in exchange for a prescribed number of years of work. The agreement usually lasted seven years. In addition to free passage to the colonies, an indentured servant was given subsistence shelter, food, and in some instances, a small amount of currency. It was a hardscrabble existence at best and at worst resulted in sickness, starvation, even death. But despite his or her lowly caste, an indentured servant was a human being who could become a citizen with some standing before the law even if such standing was rarely recognized. An indentured person's relationship with a sponsor was by individual contract. The contracts varied. Sometimes the agreement upon completion of the contract involved land. For example, Virginia, in 1705, passed a law requiring masters to provide white male servants whose indenture time was up with ten bushels of corn, thirty shillings, and a gun; white women servants might receive "fifteen bushels of corn and forty shillings."[6] Also, freed male servants were to get 50 acres of land. For white indentured women, receiving no land was an incentive to marry in many cases. Despite their lowly status, white female servants were privileged by law over their African co-workers. "A 1663 Virginia law prohibited English female servants from doing fieldwork, but allowed African women to work outside"[7]

Colonial administrators feared the continual prospect of indentured European servants making common cause with either Indians or enslaved Africans. Again, Kly says:

> The potential for revolt among impoverished Europeans, in combination with enslaved Africans, increased the necessity for ruling elites to emphasize white nationalism or the color line, to create a sense of community of interest among whites, an inter-class, interethnic solidarity to be exercised for the benefit of all whites (although to the greater benefit, naturally, of the Anglo-Saxon elites), and at the expense of the national minorities.[8]

Within a few decades of their arrival at Jamestown in 1607, indentured servants from northern Europe began to acquire a status — a stake in the evolving structures of the new world that was crucial to the creation of the concept of white people. In fact, "by the early 1660s white men were loudly protesting against being made 'slaves' in terms which strongly suggest that they considered slavery not as wrong but as inapplicable to themselves."[9] The theme of developing and maintaining a docile white working class has woven throughout the history of the United States. Many early European immigrants detested the social and economic hierarchies of Europe, especially those of England. However, in the New World one could, it was said, regardless of status or present circumstance, carve out a piece for oneself in the vast land. This opportunity became an indelible story of the new nation. Even in the twenty-first century, the United States white citizenry is represented as middle class despite the chasm between wealthy and poor white people, dating to the earliest days of the nation.

"White" also acquired moral underpinnings and a set of values that justified white control and inclusion and, to the contrary, subservience and exclusion of those deemed "colored" or non-white. This was, in part, because of the increasing status of scientists who attributed moral qualities to different races of human beings. For example, in 1738, Carolus Linneaus, the distinguished Swedish scientist, classified four races of human beings thusly:

Homo Americanus — Tenacious, contented, free; ruled by custom.
Homo Europaeus — Light, lively, inventive; ruled by rites.
Homo Asiaticus — Stern, haughty, stingy; ruled by opinion.
Homo Afer — Cunning, slow, negligent; ruled by caprice[10]

Yet becoming white, with all of the advantages of a preferred racial status in the new land, came at a price. To be included in the social contract required that white people relinquish ties to the old country — the languages and customs and ways of doing and living associated with Europe. Even one's name had to be changed, if necessary. White was no ethnicity. It did not embody history or a sense of place. White was not a language or a form of music or art. White did not come with a dance or a national literature. White was a political designation. It signified one's relationship to sanctioned state power. So did black or red, brown or yellow. White had to be assembled. It had to be molded. In the race-based nation still under construction, white people existed only in relationship to black people or to red people, and later to Asian people. Whites were included in the social contract; the others were not.

Gradually, white came to mean more than a legal status conferring economic opportunity and social possibilities. White began to mean "better than" just as being someone of color would come to mean "less than." This idea, that whites were smarter, more creative, trustworthy, more attractive, the purveyors of civilization, the guardians of the future of humankind and made in the image of God, became internalized and lived out. Whites became acculturated with a sense of superiority that gave them voice, assuredness, and mobility. As John Woolman, anti-slavery Quaker activist, wrote in 1762,

> White children, "born of Parents of the meanest Sort," were never considered candidates for a lifetime in slavery. "This is owing chiefly to the Idea of Slavery being connected with the Black Colour, and Liberty with the White: and where false Ideas are twisted into our Minds, it is with difficulty we get fairly disentangled."[11]

White became a "propertied right" like a copyright or the right of private ownership. White was seen as scientific, especially when biologists like Johann Friedrich Blumenbach, in his 1775 treatise, *De Generis Humani Varietate Native,* argued that the original type of man was Caucasian "based on characteristics such as stature, carriage, skull, hair, skin color, and so on...The white man was the 'primeval' type and stood at the center; but there was no indication that he was on top."[12] Subsequent natural philosophers developed the concept of the Great Chain of Being to create and refine racial groups into a hierarchy of mankind. Whites were said to be made in the image of God while blacks occupied the lowest rung of the great chain, closer to the animal kingdom than to God.

Creating a white nation

Racial policies of white supremacy, Indian genocide and African enslavement had been evolving for over 175 years by the time the nation won independence from Britain in 1784. One of the first acts by the new nation, the Naturalization Act of 1790, made clear the Founders' intentions. As historian Ronald Takaki explains in *A Different Mirror: A History of Multicultural America,* the Act affirmed the Founding Fathers'

> ...determination to develop a citizenry of good and "useful" men. Only the "worthy part of mankind" would be...eligible for citizenship...They also had to be "white"...The Naturalization Act excluded from citizenship not only nonwhite immigrants but also a group of people already here — Indians...As domestic "foreigners," Native Americans could not seek naturalized citizenship, for they were not "white."[13]

Why would this be one of the earliest legislative acts of the new nation? To understand, one needs to go back to a papal edict called the "Doctrine of Discovery," put forth by Pope Alexander VI in 1493. The Doctrine of Discovery played out in different ways in the Western Hemisphere. In the southern portion of the Americas, lands and people were set upon and conquered by European explorers. The conquering nations, in the main, did not seek to inhabit, but solely to plunder lands for their riches. The inhabitants of these lands were mere obstacles that got in the way of the conquerors' primary purpose. This conquest, first by Portugal and then Spain and later England, France and the Netherlands, impacted all of the Caribbean peoples and eventually included all countries in what is now Central and South America. This conquering strategy created a mestizo (mixed race) people throughout Central and South America, although it was achieved primarily through force of arms and the brute force of rape.

The Doctrine of Discovery empowered Columbus and his cohorts to claim all lands and peoples found by them in the name of Christ and His Church. This Doctrine was worldwide. It gave broad latitude to European explorers to use any means necessary to conquer the lands and their peoples. It included the right to claim the land's minerals, especially gold, silver, copper and tin. Indigenous artifacts, however precious or sacred to those whose lands were vulnerable to discovery, were there for the taking.

Even in Australia, organized by England as a penal colony in the 1700s, whites used *terra nullius,* a variation of the Discovery Doctrine, to declare the land unoccupied and therefore free for exploitation.[14] In the North American colonies, Europeans *settled.* Most who came decided to stay. Unlike the conquistadors of Latin America, they planned to establish themselves and raise families. Their labor was essential to the colonies' economic development. In some of these North American colonies importation of Africans to work the land was crucial because of the extreme heat and humidity to which poor whites were not acclimated. The use of Indians as laborers was not successful because of their familiarity with the terrain and thus their propensity to flee. English colonists did not see their efforts as simply reflecting a military campaign even though military might was a primary means by which the indigenous would be removed from the land. European women were colonists from the earliest seventeenth century.

The United States was to be a white nation, not mestizo. The Founding Fathers attempted to ensure its racial purity by federal mandate. As Benjamin Franklin explained in his 1751 *Observations Concerning the Increase of Mankind:*

> …the Number of purely white People in the World is proportionably [*sic*] very small…I could wish their Numbers were increased…Why increase the Sons of Africa, by Planting them in America, where we have so fair an Opportunity, by excluding all Blacks and Tawneys, of increasing the lovely White and Red?[15]

At the same time that colonial America was organizing itself into a United States, "race" was attaining a scientific status, with terms like Caucasoid, Mongoloid and Negroid invented to classify humankind and determine which peoples were from "civilized" nations and which people were thought to be "uncivilized," such as "Indians," or not even human, like the enslaved Negro. People in the emerging United States were color-coded—white, yellow, red and black — according to this new science. The system of racial stratification guaranteed that race would undermine any efforts to organize across class lines. Europeans, as they became Americans, might still be poor, but they would not be colored. White, as a legal and preferred status, would apply to any white person whether rich or poor, male or female, child or adult. Whites, in this racial pecking order, were considered full human beings. This social contract for white people was both an individual and systemic phenomenon. It came to be called the American Way of Life.

White was normative. White was universal in its application. Noted scholar and American culturalist Allan Bloom spoke of the Constitution, but without Kly's understanding of the "anti-social contract," when he wrote:

> The Constitution was not just a set of rules of government but implied a moral order that was to be enforced throughout the entire union...The dominant majority gave the country a dominant culture with its traditions, its literature, its facts, its special claim to know and supervise language and its protestant religions...The American revolution instituted this system of government for Americans, who in general were satisfied with the result and had a pretty clear view of what they had done.[16]

This was true, that is, if you were white and *ipso facto* part of the dominant culture. Bloom describes the social contract. It was between whites or Americans and their government. If you were "Indian" or "Negro," you were part of Kly's "anti-social contract."

The race construct in the United States originally was triangular, involving whites, "Negroes" and "Indians." After the Indian populations had been reduced to such numbers that they were no longer considered a threat to the peace of the nation, blacks occupied the outermost fringes of the racial construct. This racial hierarchy, as it evolved, would expand to include those considered to be of the "yellow" or "Asiatic" races. Chinese men, imported periodically in the nineteenth century as their labor was needed, were expelled when their work was done. After the Mexican War ended in 1848, the race construct would include Mexicans. Later still, after the 1898 Spanish-American War, it would include Puerto Ricans and Filipinos. But white would always remain at the top — to be protected and affirmed at all costs.

White was a way of brokering class privilege. The Naturalization Act of 1790 was not about social class but about race as class. It said that only free white persons might immigrate to the US and begin the process of becoming citizens. Time and again over the next century and a half, in a stream of court decisions and government regulations, the US would preference "white" over "colored" to such an extent that "white people" became synonymous with what it meant to be "American." Conversely, to be "colored" was to mark one's status as of minor significance in national law and thus in national lore.

The Naturalization Act of 1790 would remain law, with variations and exceptions, until the Immigration and Nationality Act (McCarran Act) was passed in 1952. The 1790 racial exclusionary act would be the primary reason the US would become an overwhelmingly white majority nation. Thomas Jefferson, envisioning the nation's future, wrote,

> It is impossible to not look forward to distant times, when our rapid multiplication will expand itself...and cover the whole northern, if not the southern continent, with a people speaking the same language, governed in similar forms, and by similar laws; nor can we contemplate with satisfaction either blot or mixture on that surface.[17]

Many whites — indentured servants, factory workers, prisoners, tenant farmers, poor women — in a nation "where all men are created equal," felt they were not treated as such. But "race" is a political concept and "white" a term used to create a contrast with those "less than fully human" — originally Indians and Negroes. As the new nation constructed and sanctioned its systems and institutions, people designated white had access to those systems and institutions. People of color did not.

CHAPTER 2

Expanding Whiteness

Had I been asked as a child growing up in either McComb or Helena, "Who lives here?" I would have responded, "Well, white people, colored people, Jews, Italians and a few Chinese." Had my children been asked the same question a generation later, they might have responded quite differently and said, "Well, white people, black or African Americans, a growing number of Latinos or Hispanic people, and some Asian Americans." What happened to the Jews and Italians one might ask? They had become "white." Had they been asked? No, at least not personally. But, they were now needed. Dr. Michael Washington, a People's Institute Core Trainer and a co-founder of the Black History Department at Northern Kentucky University was the first person I heard use the phrase "becoming white." This fascinated and intrigued me. This would have been in the early 1980s. By 1997 at U.C. Berkeley a conference on "The Making and Unmaking of Whiteness" attracted over 1,000 scholars and "white studies" was becoming a national phenomenon among progressives across the country. Well, really, just among academics, which is why it always frustrates me. Outside academia, white privilege had been studied for at least 25 years or even more. Maybe it is because I am not considered an academic and am jealous about their presumptive standard setting. Even among progressives there seems to be this phenomenon that something is not real until it is validated by those teaching and researching in higher education circles. At this same conference I remember long-time activist and leftist Sharon Martinas challenged those at the head table about this, saying if they were organizers they would have been studying whiteness and that there were groups like the People's Institute out there doing it. Nothing ever changes in this regard. Academia still gives its blessing on what is real and what is not, which is why when writing, one has to cite an academic as verification on any claim or statement made. Actually, academics are a bastion of white supremacist thought and practice, in my experience. Ask any person of color who is teaching in one of our great universities. I was there as an observer, sitting among those listening to the professors and other notables, but at the same time bristling a bit on not being recognized as one of those about whom Sharon Martinas spoke. She was also one of those long-time movement members who organized continuously around issues of white supremacy, white hegemony and how we, as whites, intrude on movement-building led by people of color. I had met Sharon only a few years before, but we bonded over our similar experiences organizing on the left and in other white radical circles. We stay close today.

The quixotic and ever-changing nature of whiteness came clear to me a number of years ago when I applied for work at an historically black public university. I thought, somewhat ironically, that my being white would be to my advantage. What else is new, you might ask? But it turns out that this advantage would not be for the usual reasons. I was eager to check the box marked "white," hoping to add to their "diversity" statistics. Here is how I found "white" defined on the employment application: "A person from any of the original nations of Europe, North Africa, or the Middle East." "Whoa!" I thought to myself. "From North Africa? The Middle East? What was this about?" A colleague clued me in. She said, "It must be like this in order for white supremacy to be faithful to its claim that white is the highest form of humanity. North Africa is white because Egyptian pyramids are one of the greatest wonders of the world. The Middle East has to be white because the Tigris and Euphrates rivers flow through this 'cradle of civilization' and, of course, Jesus was born and lived there all his life." Race has always served as a hierarchy establishing who is superior to whom in this world. There are two constants, however. Whites are always on top and blacks are always on the bottom.

This is changing in the aftermath of the destruction in 2001 of the Twin Towers in New York City and the rise of militant Islam. The census people are considering "MENA" as a category. MENA stands for Middle East/North Africa. This race stuff continues to be tricky and malleable. It changes shape as it needs to and always to the benefit of white supremacy.

Left out of the contract

African enslavement in the Americas is unique in historical annals. It represents for the first time a people removed from the context of humankind and made chattel. It differs from historical forms of slavery enforced through warfare over the generations where one might eventually find release and sometimes even assimilation into the society of one's captors. The status of Africans in North America and thus in what became the United States was permanent, lifetime servitude. It was not subject to change for it was God-ordained. It was a "peculiar institution," one that theologians, economists, politicians and scientists would deem "natural." It was not debatable. At the time of the ratification of the Constitution in 1787, enslavement was such a permanent fixture in the minds of those who framed the nation's foundational laws that those who opposed it and predicted its ultimate destructive power lost the political debate. The Constitution did not prohibit nor outlaw slavery. It took almost another century to finally end it.

African peoples captured and enslaved in the Americas would die in the millions during the European transatlantic trade between the mid-sixteenth century and the end of the nineteenth century. The enslavement of Africans would not end in Brazil, where vast numbers of Africans were transported, until 1888. Death tolls were enormous prior to the Middle Passage as many Africans were murdered or died from other causes like tribal warfare, religious struggles, illness or exposure to the elements as they were kidnapped, driven, then crammed together on the death vessels called "slave ships." Millions more Africans and African Americans were sold "down the river" to enrich the expanding plantation economy even after the international slave trade was abolished in the US in 1808. Most enslaved Africans were young people in their teens and early twenties. That fact constitutes yet another lesson, so obvious once told to me by my colleague Monica Dennis, but one never mentioned to me and generations of children. Stolen young people were just entering their adulthood. Teens, especially boys, who had not yet reached their full physical strength, were ripped from their families and cast into the abyss. If they survived the voyage, they might survive a year or ten years, depending on the nature of the work they were compelled to do. As they reached puberty young men and women would become mothers and fathers to other workers. By thirty years of age, most were dead. Thirty was old. The movies depict enslaved Africans as old. Maybe they just looked old.

The legal status of white, Indian and black people determined how the United State constructed its social mores and built its national systems. For example, as historian Jordan explains, "In 1806 Virginia restricted the right of masters to manumit [free] their slaves. [It] effectively prevented benevolent masters from providing manumitted slaves with the one endowment they most needed—land."[1] "Might the poor Indian warrant standing before the law?" The answer was NO! Indians, not taxed, did not count. "The only good Indian is a dead Indian," as General Phil Sheridan boasted and Americans came to understand. "What about the Negro?" many lamented. "Is a Negro not a human being?" Again, the answer was NO! Negroes were but 3/5 of a human being for purposes of representation only, Congress concluded. The fundamental question was: If blacks are 3/5 human, then who is fully human? The answer is implicit in the social contract. Only white people (men, women and children) are full human beings. In 1857, Supreme Court Justice Roger B. Taney reaffirmed this point in the famous Dred Scot case. Taney declared in *Scot v. Sanford* that Dred Scot, an enslaved African, had "no rights a white man need respect." The personhood of Dred Scot was found to not be legitimate. This white supremacist ruling did not say Dred Scot could be disrespected only by rich white people, but rather used the more inclusive racial category "white" — men, women and children included. Regardless of the Declaration of Independence, with its statement "All men are created equal," Chief Justice Taney reasoned that black people were "not intended to be included" because they formed "no part of the people who framed and adopted this Declaration." According to Taney, only white people were ever protected under the Constitution because only white people "would have represented the Founders' make-up and intent." The social contract existed between the United States government, its Constitution, and white people.

The wealth created by the enslavement policies of the United States helped finance the East Coast banking system, fueled the great western advance of the nation and undergirded its manufacturing/industrial revolution. America's twin pillars of wealth — free land from Indian nations and the free labor of enslaved Africans — produced great riches for the nation's white citizenry. Most of the profits from the export of cotton around the world in the years between the ratification of the Constitution and the end of the enslavement period would eventually find their way into the Northern financial centers of Philadelphia, New York and Boston, although the ownership class in the South included far more millionaires than the Northern part of the country. "[It is] estimated that slaves accounted for about 15% of all privately owned assets in the United States before the Civil War, totaling over $3 billion in 1860. Another calculated the value of slaves' unpaid wages as $1.4 trillion, adjusted for inflation up to 1990, or $56,000 each if divided among twenty-five million African Americans."[2]

When history is understood in this light, the argument for reparations — "repaying" African Americans in some measure for their centuries of unpaid labor — becomes indisputable. One often hears from whites, "My people didn't own slaves." Yet there is no piece of land or labor that anyone owns today in the United States that can't be traced back to those who did. The wealth created by subjugation of black labor and the expropriation of Indian land is less than "six-degrees of separation" from every American.

As enslavement of Africans expanded and took root, the cruelties of slavery inevitably produced a sense of disassociation:

> To the horrified witness of a scene of torture, the victim becomes a "poor devil" a "mangled creature." He is no longer a man. He can no longer be human because to credit him with one's own human attributes would be too horrible.[3]

Black and Native American men were treated as prey in the new nation. It was not until the Indian was near extinction that the Indian warrior was romanticized and memorialized in the nation's mythology. Prior to the 1880s, the Indian was often hunted like buffalo and elk. Similarly, the fear of the black man has been central to the white psyche since the first ship of enslaved Africans docked in the Americas. Far from enjoying privileged status as males in the United States, black men have had to survive the most heinous forms of degradation and dehumanization at the hands of white people. The looks of almost sexualized rapture on the faces of whites (men, women and even children) in photographs of black male lynchings were not exclusive to poor whites or just white males. Race was the one unifying factor among the white populace. And it existed only in relationship to its opposites — red and black.

Such manifestations of a "hunted" people lasted well into the twentieth century. James Weldon Johnson described a 1917 Memphis lynching thus:

> Early on the morning of May 22, a mob of men boarded the train outside of Memphis, took the prisoner [Ell Parsons] from the deputies and brought him to the place that had been prepared for the lynching. The press reported that a crowd of fifteen thousand — men, women, and children from counties throughout Tennessee and in Mississippi — gathered after daybreak. They tied Parsons to a tree, doused him with gasoline, and lit a fire. His body was consumed by flames as onlookers "fought and screamed and crowded to get a glimpse." A woman protested, "They burned him too quick!" and the complaint echoed across the mob. Two men hacked off the ears of the burnt corpse, another severed the head, and others pinched souvenirs from the remains.[4]

Africans were enslaved in the United States one hundred sixty-eight years before the Constitution was ratified and two hundred forty-six years before the Thirteenth Amendment was passed. They were kept in "slavery by another name," as newspaperman Douglas Blackmon names it, for another 100 years. Thus, Africans in America were ruled by legally sanctioned white supremacy for three hundred forty-six years before the Voting Rights Act of 1965 was signed by President Lyndon Johnson.

Creating white people was possible only in contrast to and comparison with people of color, especially red and black people. White was created to bond people from the European nations together in a way that produced wealth and social status for them.

Legitimizing whiteness

This country's social contract was between its white citizenry and its Constitution as interpreted by the courts, the Congress and the President. To those who protest that these racial categories have been consigned to the dustbins of history, the disproportionate outcomes speak for themselves. Each of the systems that undergird the nation's social order is rooted in the 360 years of legalized white supremacy (roughly 1607 – 1967). Each of these systems is rooted in the institutional worldview and ethos developed during the centuries when Indians were "removed" and Black people were enslaved and then separated as "unequal."

The Irish represented an interesting challenge to the myth of white superiority when they began to immigrate to the United States in the early nineteenth century. The historic enmity between English and Irish — rooted in 700 years of warfare, mistrust and hatred — meant that English saw the Irish as a mongrel race, boorish and slovenly in their habits. The "paddy" wagon would be so designated since it was used nightly to round up Irish men and women and throw them in jail for vagrancy or public drunkenness. But by the 1850s, as they continued to migrate by the hundreds of thousands to the United States, the Irish were becoming white. Ironically, given their long history of animosity with the English, many Irish would become buffers between white Anglo Protestants and all manner of other, less desirable white people as well as Indians and blacks. Irish would be laborers for the most part in America. Risking their hearing and even their lives, they would take jobs building the great bridges and subways of New York City and levees and canals around New Orleans. It was the Irish men who laid track along the eastern portion of the intercontinental railroad, meeting the Chinese who were building from the western slopes of the Rockies. This buffer role made the Irish natural civil servants, especially in the developing city police forces. The Irish cop and later political ward heeler as well as the Irish priest would be keepers of the status quo, prominent gatekeepers maintaining the country's racial arrangement.

Within communities of people designated as white, where no race designations were in play, whites divided along many different dimensions such as gender, class, ethnicity, religion, even region of the country. White women's role in the race-constructed nation would be a complex one, encouraged by the 1790 Naturalization Act which allowed "only free white persons," even women, to become citizens, albeit second class ones. White women had privileged status when compared to both men and women of color dating back to the origins of the nation. Yet poor white women lived lives of brutal drudgery, especially if they were immigrants and unmarried. Their lives were a never-ending round of hard work, child rearing, and white male domination. Their wages were meager. Benefits such as holidays and maternity leave were unheard of, and chances of advancement were a pipe dream. Conditions were so bad for most that many would jump at an opportunity to move westward with a husband to set up stakes, although life on the "frontier" was often back-breaking, dangerous, and emotionally starved. Marriage in the early stages of nation-building was often the result of economics and required hard work from both partners. Children became extra hands around the farm, in the mill or wherever they could be used to help support the family.

All the while institutions were being developed, which both shaped and defined persons' lives in the United States. Textbooks, though making scant mention of anyone beyond white male presidents, adventurers and military leaders, still describe a society whose white people were fully human. Poor white men could aspire to become President and white women could inherit Africans held as slaves and all were guaranteed due process of law under the Constitution. Whites could own property, move wherever they could afford, cross state lines without a pass, move westward and be granted 160 acres of land, and get paid for services rendered. And whites could own other people — people of African descent. White men were rarely charged with rape of any woman and never for the rape of a black woman. White women and men could accuse black men and women of a crime and black people could not defend themselves in court in most jurisdictions in the United States. White women could not vote for the first one hundred thirty years after the ratification of the Constitution, but could nurture their white sons to do so knowing that they would grow up to defend the white supremacist society. This pattern follows whites throughout the history of the United States into the present day. Whites are the real Americans. Others are mere add-ons. This is our country.

Whiteness as Manifest Destiny

Jim Dunn used to say, "Being white is like the American Express card. You never leave home without it." And the wealthier you are and the more degrees you have, the more freedom of movement one has as a white person. We are like the TV character Kung Fu: We walk the earth. Poor white people leave home less often than those who possess credentials, but at home we are protected most of the time even when we don't see it out there. When I was working in the St. Thomas Housing Development in New Orleans or visiting the Lafitte Projects in Tremé, many eyes were on me. I felt them. What I know now is that those eyes were looking out for me, not following or threatening to me. What the residents knew that I did not at first was if something happened to me, they would be held responsible for my actions, not me. This has happened to me time and again.

One evening I was speaking to a white church congregation in Metairie in a suburb of New Orleans and doing my usual spiel about my work in New Orleans and how I was called by the Lord to do this type of work and how this was the true mission of United Methodists and try as I would to not make me the center of attention, it always came back to me and I developed a reputation as a minister to the poor and oppressed. That's how I saw it anyway. On this particular evening some members of a group called Black Men United for Change came with me and on the way back I was chastised for this. I feigned ignorance, but I knew what they were saying: "You made it appear as if you were Tarzan saving black folks at the risk of your own life." "You're the safest person in St. Thomas. If something happened to you we would all have hell to pay." I knew this and I had been caught. It was not the first time and probably not the last time either. An elder in the Tremé community asked me to come speak to her early in my career as a community church person and she asked me point blank, "Why are you here?" I told her because Jesus had called me to serve the poor. She said back to me. "I knew you were going to say that." "Tell me," she said, "Why doesn't your Jesus ever call any of us to go wherever you came from." Touché. She had me. I could go with institutional backing and cultural support wherever I chose; she could not. The thought was ludicrous. I was white and she was not. It was not my degrees or expertise, or even Jesus that called me, but Manifest Destiny.

In July 1845, the New York newspaper editor John L. O'Sullivan coined the phrase "Manifest Destiny" to explain how the "design of Providence" supported the territorial expansion of the United States.[5] Millions from across Europe emigrated to the United States between 1800 and 1920. Even as white women, poor whites (both men and women), immigrants from eastern and southern Europe, and Jews from all over Europe faced persistent discrimination and marginalization in every aspect of their lives, they were given citizenship — made white.

The concept of Manifest Destiny gained popularity as the country continued its westward push to the Pacific. It was a term that evoked God's blessings on removing the Indians from the land and seizing more than half of Mexico. It explained white supremacy as a civilizing force as the white nation increasingly interacted with peoples of color. Those persons who agreed to "settle" wherever their wagons brought them became the backbone of America. In the mid-1850s, as differences over slavery engulfed the nation, the struggle over "free soil" in the West came to prominence. White farmers opposed the extension of slavery into Western territories for fear of competition from large plantation owners with enslaved blacks. In 1857, the US Land Office denied public land grants to African Americans. Yet in 1862, during the Civil War (thus without the Southern states), President Lincoln signed the Homestead Act offering 160 acres of land to any qualified homesteader. The term "qualified" was key. Only citizens or those persons applying for citizenship were eligible. Since black people did not become citizens until the Fourteenth Amendment was ratified in 1868, few were able to take early advantage of the Act. Historians at the Homestead National Monument in Beatrice, Nebraska, estimate that 93 million Americans living today are beneficiaries of the Homestead Act.

Poor white men and white women were dirt farmers and assembly line workers, small town haberdashers or store clerks. They populated the factory and mill towns of rural America as well as big cities. Small town preachers and teachers, the family doctor and the town's attorney blessed and certified the ongoing racial arrangement. While some white individuals took umbrage at the way "Indians" were treated, or decried how "Negroes" were forced to bow and scrape before white people, such doubts were sidelined by the immediate need to make a living. The assumption that "that's just the way things are" became part of the racial vernacular of the United States. "Things" meant black people or Indians in one part of the country, Mexicans or Chinese in another, Japanese and Puerto Ricans on the coasts. Nowhere in America did people live with equity across lines of race.

Whites and Indians could cohabitate and their offspring could still be white, although only as an extremely marginalized and much-despised "half-breed" version of white. Whites and Negroes, on the other hand, were forbidden by law in much of the nation from marrying. Offspring of whites and blacks were almost always statused as black. The law varied slightly from state to state. In fact, in the popular mindset white could not prevail if even a drop of "Negro blood" was determined to be present by the guardians of white racial purity. This is the infamous "one drop" rule. This arbitrary and capricious method of determining "Who is black?" remains a social control mechanism even today. It is neither scientific nor logical. Race cannot be determined by blood quantum.

As recently as 1977, a Louisiana woman named Susie Guillory Phipps sued the State of Louisiana because her birth certificate was marked with a "C" for colored. She said she was white and always had been. Phipps declared "I am white. I was raised as a white child. I went to white schools. I married white twice." This was to no avail. By Louisiana standards a check of her genealogical records found her to be 3/32 "Negro," dating back to an Alabama liaison between a white slave owner and a black woman enslaved on a plantation in the mid 1770s. By Louisiana's "one drop" rule, Phipps was "Colored." The US Supreme Court refused to hear the case, ruling that "race" was a matter of state law![6]

Chinese immigrants had been in America since the early nineteenth Century. Yet all Asian peoples were collectivized as "other" in America, their many ethnic and cultural differences erased by the dominant white culture. Chinese and Japanese laborers, admitted to the US on work visas in the mid-nineteenth century, were regularly expelled as the need for their labor ended. All Chinese were banished by the Chinese Exclusion Act of 1882. Ultimately, in 1924, Chinese, Japanese and all other "unassimilable Asiatics" were barred by federal law from immigrating to the US

This combination of citizenship for whites only, the expression of God's will through Manifest Destiny, and the race-constructed and color-coded racial pecking order, solidified the white supremacist state, even after our nation fought a calamitous war over slavery.

CHAPTER 3

The Contract Proves Binding

White folks is white folks, honey.

— EILEEN SAN JUAN, NEW ORLEANS

In 1985, a group of us in New Orleans associated with the People's Institute for Survival and Beyond met to take on Ron Chisom's challenging question: "How many of you (whites) have ever spoken out against racism with no people of color around? How many of you think you could organize 100 whites to speak out against racism?...50?...20?"

The People's Institute was founded in 1980, so some of us had heard him ask this question for years. Now we were determined to do just what he had been challenging us to do: Speak out against racism with no people of color around. It wasn't easy back then — or now for that matter. White people have always wanted people of color around to validate our anti-racist actions. Some of us, like myself, were not comfortable meeting by ourselves as white people. Even the great Anne Braden balked at the notion. She would say, "I have always worked to bring whites and blacks together. Now you are asking me to go back where I started?"

Not really. But there was that anxiety felt by some of us, that our credibility wobbled when we were by ourselves, just white folks.

When we did begin to meet as whites, all the trip wires exploded. We competed with each other on who would lead the meeting or who would teach and who would learn. We argued about whose history, even unspoken, would be acknowledged and be afforded a more revered role. What would we call ourselves? How would we get to know each other? There was a long list of arguments.

We spent two years telling our stories to each other. It took a while but we were the stronger for it. We learned from each other and about each other. Joey was our working class hero from Yonkers; Meredith had been a member of WWAR (White Women Against Racism) in New Orleans; Diana knew David Chappell whose parents were part of HUMAN (Help Us Make A Nation); she also knew Mamie Mobley Till, mother of Emmett Till and she was married to People's Institute co-founder Jim Dunn; Anne Romaine shared the stage with Doc Watson and the Carter Family; Margery had been a presidential elector in 1972 on the Socialist Workers Party ticket; during our storytelling, she discovered that both she and Lavan, another member of the group, had been cowgirls out West. I loved country music when country wasn't cool.

Gradually we emerged from our private conversations and went semi-public. We decided to call ourselves "European Dissent," because, as we explained in a public Accountability Statement, we dissented from what has been done in our name as people of European descent. We invited other whites to our meetings. We began to take the teachings of the People's Institute back to our agencies, our churches, even our families. We went to each other's weddings and family reunions. We attended the christenings of our children or other rites of passage that rose as alternatives to the more traditional rituals for some of us. Before Lavan died — she was a nurse who had inadvertently been stuck by an AIDS-infected needle when AIDS was just emerging as an epidemic — she brought her hand-made quilt to one of our meetings. "I have woven all my female ancestors into this quilt," she told us. "I was looking for anti-racist sheroes, and what I found was heroic women making their way out West." We buried her, shed tears, held hands, and celebrated a life now complete.

We learned how to ORGANIZE using anti-racist principles against David Duke and against the gentrification of the Lower Garden District and Tremé. We organized the Louisiana chapter of Jesse Jackson's Rainbow Coalition to support his candidacy for President. Since the GOP was holding its Republican convention in our city, we organized a counter-convention, the P. B. S. Pinchback Convention, to honor Louisiana's one and only African American governor who had been elected during Reconstruction. We joined the battle against the New Orleans Housing Authority as it drew up plans to destroy public housing (succeeding, finally, only after Katrina). We also organized several book signings for white anti-racist authors such as Nibs Stroupe, Tim Wise, and Joseph Barndt, attracting sometimes several hundred white people.

After the post-Katrina man-made floods devastated New Orleans, European Dissenters organized day and night, with dozens of other groups, to demand the right of return for the thousands displaced by the floods. As well-meaning volunteers flooded into New Orleans, European Dissenters worked with People's Institute organizers to lead orientation sessions, emphasizing the historic culture of New Orleans and challenging volunteers to learn about how racism has shaped the decisions about the city's past and future. More important, these same volunteers were urged to bring their analysis home, to look at how racism has shaped their own neighborhoods and towns. Today, European Dissent groups are organized in Seattle; Duluth, Minnesota, New Jersey and New York City. Sister anti-racist white organizations meet across the nation in places as diverse as Greensboro, North Carolina; Austin, Texas; Ithaca, New York; San Francisco and Los Angeles, California, to name a few. Anti-racist white groups are helping to break this country's silence about racism. Inspired by a variety of local and national events, they work against police violence, organize anti-gentrification campaigns, challenge city and state "criminal justice" systems, and demand that public schools are accountable to families and communities.

Re-constructing whiteness in the South after the Civil War

After the Civil War, the South's former slave owners, now penniless and often landless, commanded a non-militarized fighting force with poor whites as an ever-ready citizen army that could be mobilized to fight to defend white supremacy. The poorest white cast his lot not with freed blacks who were even poorer, but with the standard bearers of white supremacy. The idea of a "white Southerner" was a psychological state that embodied race and economics but encompassed more than mere financial well-being and white skin privilege. It developed as a sort of theological, even ontological world view that captivated poor whites within a veil of race superiority. Rather than vote economic self-interest, white Southerners supported the culture of white supremacy. As victims, they felt pitted against an onslaught of moral condemnation, editorial denunciation, and political subordination. White culture in the South was a curious combination of collective mental lockstep, racial self-justification and a dynamic of an individualism that was internalized and acted out by the vast majority of white Southerners. Scots-Irish, who largely peopled the Southern hills, brought their long warrior history of resistance to elite authority and distrust of outsiders. These were people born fighting, according to James Webb.[1]

W. J. Cash in his classic work, *The Mind of the South,* wrote of the mindset of the poor white in this way:

> Robbing him and degrading him in so many ways, it yet, by singular irony, had simultaneously elevated this common white to a position comparable to that of, say, the Doric knight of ancient Sparta. Not only was he not exploited directly, he was himself made by extension a member of the dominant class — was lodged solidly on a tremendous superiority, which, however much the blacks in the "Big House" might sneer at him, and however much their masters might privately agree with them, he could never publically lose. Come what might, he would always be a white man. And before that vast and capricious distinction, all others were foreshortened, dwarfed, and all but obliterated.[2]

For emancipated black people, slavery was dead but racism was not. Black was still wrong and white was still right. White supremacy was etched into every facet of American life. Black people were as oppressed by their race status after their emancipation as before. There was no section of the country where whites welcomed blacks into their midst. Not in schools or churches or neighborhoods were they seen as desirable, much less as equals. This was true in both the North and the South. Prejudice against black people followed the westward move of the United States. For example, from 1844 to 1926, Oregon's laws prohibited blacks from living in the state.

Dissonant claims to equality or civil rights faded from legislative debates and court arguments. The nation was weary of the South and its black people. Citizens of the North and the emerging West had more pressing issues at hand:

> Most ominous was how plainly the record showed that in the face of the rising southern white assault on black independence…the vast majority of white Americans, exhausted from the long debates over the role of blacks in US society, conceded that the descendants of slaves in the South would have to accept the end of freedom."[3]

By the end of the nineteenth century, white supremacy reigned across the nation, manifesting itself in the surge of lynching as a racial social control mechanism; the institution of Black Codes and a system of convict leasing throughout the South; and the rise of the Ku Klux Klan as a paramilitary force, not just in the southern US but in other parts of the country as well. As Thomas Gossett explains:

> The extreme racism of the early twentieth-century South was the chief evidence of the failure of the North to change the South's ideas concerning the Negro. The scales were, in fact, tilted in the opposite direction. So far as the question of race was concerned, the South appeared to be more successful than the North in getting the whole country to adopt its ideas. The task of elevating the Negro from slave to citizen was the most enormous one which has ever confronted the country, and by 1900 it was doubtful whether it would ever be accomplished.[4]

Blacks became an afterthought, doomed to live out their destiny in the southern US where by the end of the century white men's rule was unquestioned and unchallenged. White people as a group, men and women, rich and poor, North and South, even new immigrants from eastern and southern Europe enjoyed their God-given perch atop the racial arrangement. Jim Crow segregation worked both overtly and covertly. It was blatant to blacks and "Indians" as well as to Mexicans and Chinese. Signs proliferated across the country. In the South they read "Whites Only" or "Colored Entrance" with an arrow pointing to the back door. In other parts of the country, the signs declared "No Indians Allowed" or "No Chinee Welcomed Here." Towns all across America did not allow "Negroes" on the streets after sundown or even to walk the road to town without a pass. Historian James Loewen in his book, *Sundown Towns: A Hidden Dimension of American Racism,* defines a sundown town as "any organized jurisdiction that for decades kept African Americans or other groups from living in it and was thus 'all-white.'"[5] These towns were prominent across the American landscape. They numbered in the thousands. Embedded in the warp and woof of American culture, the practice continues — albeit unofficially — to the present.

This was America. As the late Dr. Frances Cress Welsing quipped, "America," when the letters are scrambled, makes the phrase "I Am Race." Eric Foner concludes:

> If racism contributed to the undoing of Reconstruction, by the same token Reconstruction's demise and the emergence of black people as a disenfranchised class of dependent laborers greatly facilitated racism's further spread, until by the early twentieth century it had become more deeply embedded in the nation's culture and politics than at any time since the beginning of the antislavery crusade and perhaps in our entire history....An enduring consequence of Reconstruction's failure, the Solid South helped define the contours of American politics and weaken the prospects not simply of change in racial matters but of progressive legislation in many other realms.[6]

From almost-white to white American

From the 1880s until the 1920s, eastern and southern Europeans immigrated by the millions to the US. The numbers were astounding. Upwards of 28 million persons, including Italians, Poles, Greeks, Lithuanians, Russians and Slovaks, joined the continuous stream of Irish to the United States. Forty percent of white Americans today can trace their ancestry through Ellis Island which opened its doors in 1892 and finally closed them in 1954. These new immigrants were not just passive adherents to the race arrangement. They changed the ethnic character of white so it no longer meant just the original whites of northern Europe, but included darker-skinned whites, what Matthew Frye Jacobson called "whiteness of a different color."[7]

These immigrants, while European, were not the nation-builders the founders envisioned. Debates about such "swarthy-skinned" and "Slavic" peoples abounded, particularly as they brought "foreign ideologies" and cultures with them and became stalwarts in the emerging labor movement. But white they would become, for even the lowest class white person had a status higher in the race-constructed United States than any colored person. As Lui et al. note,

> Widespread prejudices never translated into a prohibition of voting rights or naturalized citizenship. Italian immigrants, like the Irish, used municipal jobs to get ahead at a time when a private sector limited them to menial, low-paid jobs.[8]

The impact of immigration in the United States had two crucial distinctions. For Europeans, immigration since 1790 was the way they became white. The other impact is what sociologist Donald Noel hypothesized nearly fifty years ago in 1968:

> "If two or more groups come together in a contact situation characterized by ethnocentrism, competition, and a differential in power, then some form of racial or ethnic stratification will result."...If the contact situation has all three characteristics, some dominant-minority group structure will be created."[9]

Noel's hypothesis was evident by the 1860s as the Irish were becoming "white" and interacting with newly-arriving eastern and southern European immigrants. Since the Irish dominated certain occupations like police as well as local urban politics in major Eastern cities, immigrants from Poland and Lithuania had to get in line — wait their turn both for jobs and influence. This stratification would determine what neighborhoods, industries and unions eastern and southern European immigrants would be attracted to and what status they would enjoy in the nation's race construct. Italians and Jews, for example, would not become white until the mid-twentieth century. Both would occupy a sort of nether region in the racial construct — not exactly white, yet not exactly "colored" — much like Mexicans. And if they chose, they could always move west and take their chances on the "frontier."

David Roediger, in *How Race Survived US History: From Settlement and Slavery to the Obama Phenomenon,* uses the term "race suicide" to indicate those recurring periods in American history when alarms are sounded regarding the imminent numerical minority status of "white people" in the US. The period at the end of the nineteenth century was one such time. Roediger cites US census chief Francis Amasa Walker as among those sounding the alarm most stridently:

> Walker developed and popularized the enduring notion that the immigration of allegedly inferior peoples such as the Irish brought with it a threat of racial degeneration in the US population. The sheer numbers in which they arrived contributed to the change Walker feared....Fond of making various projections of just when the national racial "stock" would be disastrously transformed, those terrified by the prospect of "race suicide" agreed that at some point a few decades hence the "alien" races of Southern and Eastern Europe would swamp the superior "English-speaking races," costing the nation its racial character.[10]

While race suicide is too bigoted and raw a concept to be used in the modern day US, similar dynamics are at work. The press regularly reminds us that white people will no longer be the majority population somewhere between 2032 and 2052. The answer will be the same today as it was then: The nation has to create more white people. In 1886 the new white people were Russians, Slavs, Poles, Jews and Italians. These new whites, joined with the Irish of a generation before, kept the nation's race numbers in place. In 1925, after all the quotas and restrictions on immigration, "the commissioner of immigration said that virtually all immigrants now 'looked exactly like Americans.'"[11]

In 1905, however, Theodore Roosevelt warned in his Fifth Annual Message:

> We cannot have too much immigration of the right sort and we should have none whatever of the wrong sort. Of course, it is desirable that even the right kind of immigration should be properly distributed in this country. We need more of such immigration in the South, and special effort should be made to secure it...provided, however, that a stricter effort is made to see that only immigrants of the right kind come to our country anywhere.[12]

Even as politicians, theologians and business leaders were debating who would be the "right kind" of immigrants, another phenomenon would have enormous implications for a race-constructed America: the dawn of American imperialism beyond its land base. In none of the "possessions" of the imperial nations of Europe and the United States did colonized peoples have rights equal to those of white colonizers in their midst. The nations of imperial Europe — Britain, France, Dutch Netherlands, Belgium, Germany, Spain, Portugal, and Italy — were linked by a common belief in the presumed racial superiority of the colonizing white nations and the racial inferiority of the colonized darker nations. The United States mimicked this pattern. Alaska had been purchased from Russia in 1867. Hawaii became a possession in 1893 when the US overthrew the legitimate government of Queen Lili'uokalani. Puerto Rico, the Philippines, the Virgin Islands, Guam, American Samoa and the Marshall Islands came under its "protection" after the Spanish-American War. All of the US possessions outside its "lower 48" borders were populated and inhabited by peoples of color. United States imperialism, not officially blessed by either royalty or pope, understood its ventures as coming from an even higher power, Manifest Destiny — blessed by God.

As Protestant theologian Josiah Strong wrote in 1885:

> It seems to me, that God, with infinite wisdom and skill, is training the Anglo-Saxon race for an hour sure to come...the hour of "the final competition of races"...If I read not amiss, this powerful race will move down upon Mexico, down upon Central and South America, out upon the islands of the sea, over upon Africa and beyond.[13]

How did immigrants from US colonies fit into the multi-ethnic mix of white America? As always the race-constructed US would assign them a racial status. Just as indigenous people and Mexicans had been consigned to "minority" status and African Americans to the lowest rung of the racial ladder, this same process now ranked citizens of colonized territories as something less than white. Robert Blauner hypothesizes:

> Minority groups created by colonization will experience more intense prejudice, racism, and discrimination than those created by immigration. The disadvantaged status of colonized groups will persist longer and be more difficult to overcome than the disadvantaged status faced by groups created by immigration.[14]

Blauner's thesis is key to understanding the race construct in the twentieth century. Immigrants from southern and eastern Europe would become white. Colonized people of color would not.

Filipino people were an anomaly in this othering process. The Philippines were made a US protectorate in 1898 at the end of the Spanish-American War. Significantly, the control of one country by another and the denial of rights of citizenship to the mostly-Catholic Filipinos were difficult ideas to reconcile with the Declaration of Independence and with American institutions.

> The argument of imperialists ran that some races are inherently incapable of self-government and that it would be a crime to saddle the Filipinos with the burdens of citizenship. "Fitness [for self-government] is not a God-given, natural right," declared Theodore Roosevelt, "but comes to a race only through the slow growth of centuries, and then only to those races which possess an immense reserve fund of strength, common sense, and morality." "The testimony is absolutely overwhelming," argued Secretary of War Elihu Root, "that the people inhabiting the Philipine *(sic)* archipelago are incapable of self-government."[15]

Reform defaults to white supremacy

Many of the new immigrants soon became involved in the nascent labor movement which exploded in the years after the Civil War. By 1886, the Knights of Labor had hundreds of thousands of members representing workers from New York City to Chicago and growing. Samuel Gompers was elected the first president of the American Federation of Labor (AFL) in 1886. Branded a socialist, Gompers, once elected, chose not to push a socialist agenda. He headed the AFL for over 38 years, until 1924. The AFL's intent was to bring the various skilled unions organized by crafts and specialized industries into a political force strong enough to take on corporate power and workplace discrimination. Some argued for a more inclusive union that would organize both skilled and unskilled unionists and workers including blacks, Chinese and working women of all races. Rarely did that idea gain much ground.

Labor militancy grew in ways unprecedented in the US. Workers struck for some of the benefits of US industrial capitalism's profits and likewise from the enormous growth in US manufacturing. They struck as the wealth spread westward in silver, zinc and copper mines. For example, Big Bill Haywood and his Workers of the World "Wobblies" became legends and folk heroes as they fought the entrenched power of the mining bosses, lumber dynasties, and other bastions of capitalism. Railroad workers from engineers to porters organized for basic rights, livable wages, more leisure time and the eight-hour work day — finally won in 1916. Everywhere that there were wage workers someone was trying to organize them. New immigrants during this period often brought radical European class politics with them. Socialists, anarchists and communists organized their way into labor's leadership, providing both government and industry with further excuses to suppress the labor strikes.

So disruptive were the strikes and calls for boycotts that capitalist entities brought in private armies as well as state and local police forces and even federal troops in attempts to squelch union organizing. Open class warfare broke out, with the nation's leading newspapers most often siding with Big Business over Big Labor.

Yet labor foundered on the shoals of white supremacy. Few unions actively recruited African Americans, Asians, and Mexican workers. Equity was non-existent. In the western US, Chinese workers were imported to carry out the dangerous work of blasting for mines and railroad lines; Mexican farm laborers worked with low wages, ghastly conditions and no benefits. Blacks rarely got above entry-level jobs and were slotted for those jobs that paid less and were most dangerous. Those were the jobs white workers did not want to do. Compared to enslavement and the convict lease system so prevalent in the South, of course, any type of work that paid wages in a location bereft of "Black Codes" was preferable for most African Americans. In the twentieth century, several million African American men, women and children would relocate to the northern US, encouraged by the prospect of jobs, wages, and less onerous forms of racism.

Paralleling the labor movement, farmer-organized populist movements spread across the Midwest and into the South. The Populist era was propelled forward by the consolidation of wealth into the hands of a few silver barons, railroad magnates, and steel producers. These huge fortunes were being built during a period when farmers were attempting to eke out a living in the Great Plains and other parts of the American breadbasket. Populists formed their own political party in 1892 and supported the candidacy of William Jennings Bryan in the presidential races of 1896 and 1900 because Bryan supported "free silver" — a policy that would increase the amount of currency in circulation which many farmers' groups believed would lead to higher commodities prices.

Ultimately the Populists, like labor unions, could not overcome the persistence of a deeply-embedded racism in the country. Tom Watson, the charismatic organizer and spellbinding orator of the early Populist movement pushed early on for blacks and whites to come together around common economic conditions and pressures. By the turn of the new century, Watson had defaulted to a rabid form of white supremacy, using the same skills he employed for Populism now turned against African Americans. Watson would be a role model for twentieth century racists with a similar populist appeal such as Theodore Bilbo and James K. Vardaman in Mississippi and later George Wallace in Alabama.

Ironically, this same period was one in which some great strides forward were made in reforming some of the nation's most egregious practices. Calls for fiscal reforms became commonplace as opponents of the Gilded Age excesses sought to curtail and regulate the fortunes of the railroad barons, oil tycoons, steel magnates, and Wall Street financiers. The financial panics of 1887, 1895, and 1907 severely frightened common everyday people in the US who suffered mightily under the ebb and flow cycles of monopoly capitalism. Newspapers and books raised the alarm against big business with its unchecked pursuits of great wealth. Upton Sinclair books, especially *The Jungle* (1906) and *Oil* (1927), exposed the hideous conditions in meat-packing and the oil industry. Ida M. Tarbell's *History of Standard Oil,* first serialized in *McClure's* magazine in 1904, so castigated John D. Rockefeller that he spent the rest of his life attempting to change the public's perception of him as a man whose greed and avarice knew no bounds.

Yet the nation was ill-prepared for a post-slavery United States. The US racial cauldron was always boiling. If blacks were able to compete equally with whites for jobs, land, and basic human rights outlined in the Declaration of Independence and enshrined in the Constitution, what would become of the whites who had always, since the nation's founding, enjoyed special privileges and standing before the law? If white was no longer "right," would blacks still be willing to "get-back"? This had always been whites' greatest fear, one that permeated every systemic relationship in the country. African Americans had to be kept in their proper "place" at the bottom of the racial pecking order. White supremacy and black inferiority had to be reasserted as the essential fabric of the expanding American culture. Millions of "new white people" — ethnic Europeans who had not experienced Jim Crow and who had never interacted with black people — had to learn this.

How was this to be done? Christian theology was one way. In the white churches of America, Jesus was presented as white, and if Jesus was God incarnate, by implication God was white. The Catholic Church in the US, home base for most of the newly-arrived southern and eastern Europeans who were crammed into slums that abutted the emerging black ghettoes, was a crucial cultural mediator. It was not unusual for churches to speak the first language of their core membership for years until assimilation allowed for acculturation into English and what was called "the American way of life." In every part of the country, those churches that favored more racial equity walked a fine line balancing a sense of social justice for its immigrant parishioners with a firm recognition of the customs and laws that kept races separate and antagonistic towards each other. Black Catholic theologian Bryan N. Massingale, in his critique of the church's role in US racial reality, *Racial Justice and the Catholic Church* (2010), said,

> Notwithstanding the heroic witness of some, too frequently Catholics — rather than being agents of social change and cultural transformation — have conformed to the racial mores of our society and engaged in practices of racial denigration.[16]

This could also be said about virtually every mainline Protestant denomination in the United States.

For blacks, religion was either a coping mechanism or a survival tactic. As far as whites knew, black preachers presented Christianity in ways that reinforced white supremacy. Most whites really never knew what black people did with Christianity or how they saw Jesus. The black Christianity that would emerge over three centuries of oppression incorporated a totally different world view than its white counterpart. One could say it was an entirely different form of Christianity.

Mainstream Christianity, then, blessed the arrangement laid down in law and custom: White people were God's Chosen People. All that was needed was the voice of "science" to make them the light of the world.

Chapter 4

Defending the Contract

For most of my life I have taken white supremacy for granted. Not the ugly kind like the Klan, but the everyday kind that characterized life in the South and, as I experienced later, in the North and even around the world. Whites were the standard bearers for society so I assumed this was not only what God had ordained but that science backed it up. This arrangement was fueled both by racial stereotypes that I and other white people attributed to black people and by a racial mythology about our superiority that whites, often unconsciously, internalized. The greatest contradictions were probably those I was taught in church. I remember thinking to myself as a teenager that God had to be white because otherwise whites would not recognize his divinity nor follow his commandments. The opposite was also true. Blacks, in my racial world, accepted and recognized God as white because all authority was white.

When I first attended seminary in 1969 at New York Theological Seminary, Dr. Albert Cleage, senior pastor at the Shrine of the Black Madonna in Detroit, had just written The Black Messiah. *The very title shocked me. I was incredulous. I was afraid, at first, to even open the book much less read it. The world was shifting under my feet. It provoked another one of those internal discussions I had with myself about race. I wasn't just ignorant but also scared. I felt the same way about Dr. James Cone's milestone text,* Black Theology, *and over the next twenty years a host of other works by both North and South American liberation theologians, who argued that Jesus required Christians to have a "preferential option for the poor." I had not even heard the term "liberation theologian" in 1969. I realized that I depended both personally and psychologically on the institutions that undergirded the racial state (not a term I would have used back then) to either set the record straight or to marginalize those who threatened its premise of white supremacy. Liberation theology was a way of reading and interpreting the Christian texts that supported the push of the poor to liberate themselves from the yoke of colonialism and imperialism. It saw the Church as being a church of the poor and urged priests and theologians alike to stand with movements crying out and demanding justice for the masses.*

I, however, could question all that I was learning because neither I nor those who challenged the superiority of white people were in charge. This psychological defense of the arrangement allowed me also to feel free to explore leftist politics, even those calling for the violent overthrow of the government; I knew it was never going to happen. Those who protested and called for revolution were not in charge. My fears were not real, and I could thus pretend that I was willing to risk all for a new kind of justice and revolutionary new world order because it was a fantasy. Power will out. I was protected like a teenager rebelling against his parents. I knew I could come home whenever I chose to and all would be forgiven. This white supremacist worldview followed me everywhere I went, even to prison and exile from home. This is white privilege.

In 2001, I was part of a team of People's Institute organizers to attend the World Conference Against Racism, Racial Discrimination, Xenophobia and Related Intolerance in Johannesburg, South Africa. At the conclusion of the conference we went to Soweto where we led an "Undoing Racism®" workshop. At some point in the workshop, I asked a white South African minister, "What is it like being white in a new South Africa?" He answered: "In some ways, we have never had it so good. But I go to bed each night with a gun under my bed." What did he mean? He knew that the new Black South Africa needed white money and land, but it was a tenuous hold on privilege. "Yes," I said. I understood him precisely. Such is white supremacy. It is everywhere. Rock solid. But it can't last.

Eugenics: The Pinnacle of White Supremacy

Assimilation into the race-constructed nation was also abetted by the pseudo-science of eugenics. Darwin's "Survival of the Fittest" thesis was used by so-called Social Darwinists to prove the superiority of the white race. For over two centuries, noted scholars and scientists had been preoccupied with the urgent task of classifying humankind. By the end of the nineteenth century, racial phenotypes were an accepted scientific truth. Caucasoid (white) was the apex of humankind (most evolved — closest to the image of God) and Negroid (black) was the nadir (least evolved — closest to the animal kingdom). Scientists, reformers and professionals actively promoted eugenics. The American Breeder's Association, established in 1906 under the direction of biologist Charles B. Davenport, advocated for the removal of genetic "defectives" such as the insane, "feeble-minded" and criminals, and supported the selective breeding of "high-grade" individuals. Feminist reformers, including Margaret Sanger, advocated some forms of eugenic legal reform, though she rejected euthanasia.

Eugenics became part of the US mainstream culture: "Race betterment" would lead to the advancement of civilization. Many states enacted compulsory sterilization laws which, in 1927, were affirmed by the Supreme Court in *Buck v. Bell.* California was at the vanguard of the American eugenics movement, performing about 20,000 sterilizations or one third of the 60,000 nationwide from 1909 until the 1960s. Many eugenicists believed in the racial superiority of "old stock" white Americans as members of the "Nordic race."

These beliefs strengthened arguments against race-mixing and were used to justify the nation's many anti-miscegenation laws, both North and South. Not until 1948, when California's law against whites and Mexicans intermarrying was struck down in *Perez v. Sharp,* did state laws barring mixed-race marriage begin to be overturned. Only in 1967, in *Loving v. Virginia,* did the US Supreme Court rule all miscegenation laws unconstitutional.

Science and theology thus combined to create a double-edged sword that equated white with civilization. "Whiteness" was "burdened" with a special responsibility to civilize the world. European and American imperialism was, in the minds of most white Americans, both God's will and evolution's mandate. Virtually all US systems backed up this philosophy, including prominent philanthropic institutions like the Carnegie Institution and the Rockefeller Foundation.

Arguments to the contrary were brushed aside by most US scientists and social arbiters. As Thomas Gossett discerned about these leading scholars:

> When a physical basis of measurable race differences eluded them, [they] assume[d] immense innate psychological differences in any case. They did not really need proof for what they *knew* was there. When the evidence began to be overwhelming that none of their systems worked, why did the anthropologists not consider the possibility that there are no "hierarchies" of race? Some of them were bold enough to come to exactly this conclusion, but for others the idea of race was so real that no amount of failure could convince them that it might be an illusion.[1]

Despite a growing scientific consensus by the mid-1930s that eugenics had no basis in science, it continued to be supported well into the 1940s and 1950s. Franz Boas, often called the "father of American anthropology," spoke out vehemently against the notion of "scientific racism" from the early twentieth century. Yet not until the Nazi use of eugenics to create an "Ubermenschen" did the movement begin to be discredited in the public eye.

Jews made up a significant number of the European immigrants coming to the United States, where they were pushed into the emerging ghettoes and quickly became subject to anti-Semitism. Jews presented a conundrum for the racialists. Were they white? Were they colored? It would take until the mid-twentieth century and beyond for these questions to be answered. Their oppressed status in a race-constructed society made Jews frequently sympathetic to the plight of peoples of color. Jews would be disproportionately represented in the leadership of civil rights struggles throughout the twentieth century.

Violent defense of whiteness

The carnage of WWI, concluding with a worldwide flu epidemic that killed millions of young people, shook the social and cultural foundations of the Western World. The decade following the Great War was a wild ride in the United States. In a brief ten years, a League of Nations was created and US membership in the League was defeated by the US Senate; prohibition was mandated in 1919, then abolished in 1933; and the Nineteenth Amendment, adopted in 1920, guaranteed women the right to vote, although women of color were routinely disenfranchised by many states' laws.

The '20s also ushered in an era of unfettered racial violence and vigilante justice that struck terror among blacks, especially in the South.

This expanding violence, combined with new opportunities for work in the North, led to what is called the Great Migration. Isabel Wilkerson, in her prize-winning account of this massive movement, *The Warmth of Other Suns,* says over six million Southern blacks migrated north between 1915 and 1970, bringing with them their hopes for a better future in the urban centers of the Northern and Western United States.[2] This massive re-settlement of blacks in New York, Detroit, Chicago, Los Angeles and numerous other cities blossomed into a cultural and political ferment that exposed the lie of racial supremacy. The Harlem Renaissance, for example, became synonymous with the capacity of African Americans to produce great art, great writing, great intellectual and political prowess and analysis, all of which had been denied by the nation's white supremacist culture. These movements of black self-determination, demonstrating that the shackles of racist oppression could be broken, inspired a generation that later led the Civil Rights Movement. It also provoked even more widespread white resistance.

The cinematic triumph of D. W. Griffith's 1915 *Birth of a Nation,* a shameless caricature of the worst racial stereotypes of black people, became Hollywood's first true cinematic blockbuster. President Wilson helped arrange previews of the film at the White House for other elected officials, members of his cabinet, and justices of the Supreme Court. "'My only regret,' he reportedly said, 'is that it is all so terribly true.'" Griffith's glorification of the Ku Klux Klan led to a huge gain in Klan membership across the nation.[3] Fused with white supremacist ideology was a growing fear of communism which resulted in national paranoia and xenophobia. The Immigration Act of 1924 limited the annual number of immigrants who could be admitted from any one country to 2% of the number of people from that country who were already living in the United States in 1890, thus severely restricting southern and eastern Europeans. In order to preserve the ideal of white American homogeneity, it also barred entry to those ineligible for citizenship, effectively prohibiting most Middle-Easterners, East Asians, South Asians, and Africans.

With the calamitous Great Depression, fear of poverty, fear of black people, and fear of communism melded together as people of color began to challenge the white supremacist social contract. In the US, and again, especially in the South, to be for Negro rights was to be a communist. This association of communism with demands for racial equality was an oft-used subterfuge by government watchdog agencies. Blacks were thought to be unsophisticated politically, so protests by blacks were commonly portrayed as orchestrated from behind the scenes by white subversives — communists, anarchists, and sometimes unionists.

Labor organizing re-emerged with renewed vigor and violence in the late 1920s and early 1930s. White ethnic enclaves in the cities produced a ready base of workers collectivized in the slum neighborhoods of the great industrial and manufacturing cities. Labor powerhouses such as the AFL, the Congress of Industrial Organizations (CIO), United Mine Workers, and United Auto Workers built huge worker movements. As in an earlier generation, black unionists worked the most dangerous and difficult jobs in the plant and those that paid the least and had the fewest benefits. At home, black fellow unionists were not welcome in white neighborhoods, either as passers-by or certainly as prospective neighbors. The mere hint of a black family moving into a white neighborhood often led to furious outcries on the part of whites to their elected officials, school officials, and police departments. Black homeowners in white neighborhoods were met with chanting mobs of white citizens who shouted threats, threw firecrackers and cherry bombs on their roofs, harassed them with phone calls at all hours of the night, and in many instances forced black families to flee for their lives.

While the massive United Automobile Workers union led by the Reuther brothers was a consistent supporter and ally of black civil rights, unlike other big unions like the AFL-CIO and John Lewis' United Mine Workers, UAW rank and file workers were less than enthusiastic about cross-racial organizing. Isabel Wilkerson describes one instance in 1917 East St. Louis, IL:

> The colored migrants were flocking to the city at a rate of a thousand a month, some eighteen thousand having arrived that spring, and they instantly became the perfect pawns, an industrialist's dream: they were desperate to leave the south, anxious for work, untutored in union politics or workers' rights...Once the strike was over, the colored migrants, resented by the unions and unprotected by the plants that had hired them, paid the price. One union wrote its members that "the immigration of the southern Negro into our city for the past eight months has reached a point where drastic action must be taken."...[In the ensuing riot] thirty-nine blacks and eight whites were killed, more than a hundred

> blacks were shot or maimed, and five thousand blacks were driven from their homes.[4]

There were exceptions to the racial animosity that permeated working class America. The Southern Tenant Farmers Union (STFU) successfully organized sharecroppers across race lines between 1934 and the beginning of WWII. STFU was committed in both theory and practice to a racially-integrated union movement in the South. Accordingly, it was anathematized as "communist" by the dominant white society.

Another example of cross-racial organizing occurred in 1932 when some 45,000 WWI veterans marched on Washington DC to demand immediate payment of a bonus awarded by Congress in 1924 but not payable until 1945. For two months, this Bonus Army camped out in shantytowns, white and black living together side by side in the nation's capital, rallying peacefully to demand immediate payment of their bonus. Army Chief of Staff Douglas McArthur, assisted by Majors George Patton and Dwight Eisenhower, led a squadron of US Cavalry, accompanied by six tanks, to repel the marchers, many of whom were on crutches or were amputees. "The Bonus Marchers gave lie to the notion that black and white soldiers — ex-soldiers in their case — couldn't live together," wrote Roy Wilkins, then a rookie reporter for the NAACP's newspaper, the *Crisis*.[5] The Bonus Army, like the STFU, had to be soundly defeated. The power of race had to be reasserted.

The color line as federal mandate

A tidal wave of what would become "white flight" began across urban America as whites became convinced that blacks and other peoples of color were beginning to take over their neighborhoods. Fueled by the real estate industry, urged on by banks and credit and lending institutions, these fears were abetted by federal tax policies.

In the 1930s, President Roosevelt was determined to enact federal policies designed to bring relief to Americans who suffered from the effects of the Great Depression. To realize this "New Deal" as it was dubbed — to protect labor, older citizens, children, and to provide housing, farm assistance, and small business loans to distressed Americans — the Roosevelt administration required the support of Southern Democrats. These Congressmen, white men all and frequently senior members of both the House and Senate, were equally determined to maintain "their way of life." Ironically, as chronicled by Ira Katznelson in his 2013 book, *Fear Itself: The New Deal and the Origins of Our Time,* one of the most progressive eras in the nation's history required the unwavering support of Southern white supremacists to become law. For example, the Social Security Act specifically excluded agricultural laborers and domestics from its coverage. The Civilian Conservation Corps had to practice segregation in its efforts to rebuild the nation's infrastructure. This was the trade-off. The New Deal could have components quite progressive in nature, but not at the expense of white supremacy.

As Benjamin Rich writes, in his 2009 study, *Searching for Whitopia:*

> From 1934 to 1962, the Federal Housing Administration underwrote $120 billion in new housing. Less than 2 percent of that went to nonwhites. From 1938 to 1962, the FHA insured the mortgages on nearly one third of all new housing in the United States. Its Underwriting Manuals, however, considered blacks an "adverse influence" on property values and instructed personnel not to insure mortgages on homes unless they were in "racially homogenous" white neighborhoods. Under its eligibility ranking system, the FHA often refused to lend money to or underwrite loans for whites if they moved to areas where people of color lived. Some scholars now call the government's handiwork a "$120 billion head start" on white home ownership, on white equity, and on whites' ability to pass along wealth from one generation to the next.[6]

No sector of society was immune from racism. No systems, from education to health care, were exempt from racial bias. The outcomes of systemic efforts, regardless of purpose or stated intent, favored white people.

This bias was also true of reform movements. From the temperance movement to the fight led by women for voting rights, the bulk of the membership was white and certainly the leadership was. This is not to overlook the contributions of women of color in every struggle nor the efforts by certain white women to make racial justice a priority within their ranks, but it was difficult for women of color to have their voices heard and their numbers adequately represented.

Every justice movement in the history of the United States depended on the organizing skills and perseverance of women. The Abolitionists were largely women. Even as the fame usually accrued to men, the movement itself was kept alive by women. Their names, however, were often lost. For every Grimke sister, whose names have only recently become a part of the story, there are a hundred women organizers whose names we do not know. In the twentieth century women were key figures in the outlawing of lynching. Without the tireless efforts of women such as Ida B. Wells and Jessie Daniel Ames, both of whom used newspapers and church women clubs to keep pressure on men in powerful positions, who knows how long this vigilante form of injustice would have lasted? A generation later, women were essential in the Civil Rights Movement. Yet, with the exception of such luminaries as Ella Baker, Fannie Lu Hamer, or Angela Davis, few women appear in today's history texts. This lack of recognition of the role of women in the US liberation movements is a glaring omission that, with the emergence of feminist consciousness, was a weakness sometimes exploited to foment divisions in the freedom struggle. Even in the 2016 presidential campaign, debates about the role of women in positions of power have been heated.

The race construct has always been the nation's most fundamental flaw. From the writing of the Constitution of the United States to the present, the debate has raged: Whose nation is it? Who possesses inalienable rights? The great scholar and black organizer, W. E. B. Du Bois, called this the "color line." Du Bois said race would be the issue that defined the twentieth century. He was correct. It still defines us in the twenty-first century.

As a collective, people of color remain on the margins of US society. Undeniable progress has been made by individual African Americans, dramatized by the election of President Barack Obama and borne out in the lives of thousands of other black and brown people. Yet despite the Founding Fathers' hopes to ensure that the nation become "lovely white," in Benjamin Franklin's words, African Americans and Native Americans, Mexicans and Chinese, Puerto Ricans and Caribbean peoples have survived.

Chapter 5

Internalizing White Supremacy

I have always been white. In my family we never spoke of ethnicity or nationality other than American and, even more specifically, Southern, meaning white Southerner. I did not think of blacks as Southerners. I guess because they were held captive in the South. I now know blacks who say they are from the South. I guess because they were held captive in the North. It is one of the great ironies of the race construct that it robs us of a heritage that is tied to an ethnicity. This is not true of everyone. Many whites and some blacks are able to trace their lineage. But I have been white all the time. Always being white has worked somewhat to my advantage, given the work I have done all of my adult life. I can't say, "I don't see myself as white." Or, "I see myself as Irish or Jewish or Italian." This has meant that I have to get honest about this race thing. I cannot deny the advantages of being white because they have been pointed out to me all my life. I can't say "I don't see color" because I was brought up to see "color" in every interaction with black people, however benign. I certainly cannot say, "I never think about being white" because I think about it every day and always have.

I even see color where there is none. One of my earliest recollections after we moved to Helena, Arkansas when I was in fourth grade was a fight on the playground. It was between a white boy and a "colored" boy. But that was impossible. Our schools were segregated to the max. Turns out, it was between Dick and Ken Hatfield, two brothers, both white. I distinctly remember the empathy I felt for the "colored" boy in the fight. That boy was Ken, a rather dark-skinned white boy. Maybe this is why I became so progressive on the race issue — or maybe why I became so confused.

As a child, I would notice black people, but from my earliest memories it was as if we occupied two different planes of existence. I guess we did. I had a fascination with blacks. If I could aptly articulate my thoughts from those years, I would say I felt a certain judgment reflecting back on me. Not from blacks per se. I did not have a clue about how blacks saw me or the world around them. The judgment was ethereal. It was other-worldly. I was a part of something that I had no part in creating and was not given the words to explain my obvious involvement. Somehow I knew I was better. As far as I knew, white superiority was just a fact of life, like twenty-four hours in a day or the earth orbiting the sun. This is what I was taught. But, taught by whom exactly? I'm not sure. By everyone and no one in particular is the best response. At least, back then it was.

I knew white people ran things. White people, especially men, were in charge and were expected to take charge when necessary. Negroes served white people and did the work whites did not want to do. This was true in curious ways. For example, it was a source of pride for my uncles and father that they had picked cotton growing up. Even though picking cotton was something "colored" people (men and women) and only the poorest of white people did, saying that you once picked cotton was a rite of passage into full male adulthood for the white working class. It was always said in a "when we were poor" sort of way, but there was a respect that went along with it. Like something they could not admit to or say out loud.

There were various messages entwined in the stories: "We were poor, but we didn't let it define us." "We worked hard and learned that hard work can pull you out of poverty." "If you wanted to…" was the underlying message. Race was hardly mentioned, but the message was clear. Negroes worked hard enough (when watched), but didn't internalize a work ethic and thus were stuck in poverty. They were dependent on and expected to be taken care of by the government. White folks were independent. We didn't want to be taken advantage of by the government or anyone else. It was like Jim Crow didn't exist. It was like segregation was an excuse for laziness. It was as if Negroes had the same opportunities whites did. It was truly as if we lived on two different planes of existence.

It was a real shock to me growing up when my friend Nibs Stroupe pointed out that the reason so many black folks were sitting on their front porches during the day was because they were unemployed and could not afford air conditioning. The social custom or manners I was brought up with reflected the spirit of the Dred

Scot decision a century earlier that stated that a Negro had no rights a white man (or woman or child) need respect. This was reflected in my memory. I was taught to be polite and always respect my elders, but I should not call a black woman "Mrs." And never by her last name. I could direct black women and certainly men to the back door if they ever knocked on the front. Not only the back door but the back yard until recognized and permission was granted to approach the door. Thus instilled in me was the sense of superiority, of being in command of my world from a very young age. These cultural directions rarely had to be taught directly. You picked them up over time. You overheard them while listening to the old folks.

Individualism: Hallmark of Internalized Racial Superiority

Internalized Racial Superiority can be defined as a multi-generational process of racial entitlement and white privilege that gives whites a sense of special place in the United States. IRS is the thread that weaves through the generations for whites. It is often unconscious. White people rarely speak about their dominant white culture. Few books or articles have been written about it and those written have circulated among a narrow constituency of academics, social scientists and anti-racist activists. Yet for most of the nation's history, white supremacy was conscious and overt and, for whites throughout the nation, a certainty. It was not something for which the dominant culture apologized. Even the abolitionist, William Lloyd Garrison, and the Great Emancipator, Abraham Lincoln, did not question the superiority of white people. They opposed slavery, not white supremacy. To have questioned white superiority, for them, would have been ludicrous.

There are many manifestations of Internalized Racial Superiority. A sense of individualism is at its heart. White people are acculturated as individuals because the white dominant cultural institutions treat us as such. We are nurtured in a white culture that affirms our individual human worth. This makes interacting with people of color complicated because most of these institutions treat people of color as a collective. The dominant white culture does not affirm their individuality. In the workplace or church or neighborhood, where we gather across race lines, whites operate out of the "I" perspective and are acculturated to see people of color as a "they." We miss each other. The "all colored people look alike to me" is a result of this collective mindset. Racial profiling results. Since we see people of color as a collective, "if one black person steals, they all steal," to quote Ron Chisom. This is what race does to us.

The United States has always been proud of our "rugged individualism." This myth has been perpetuated throughout the history of this nation: that a self-sufficient, highly private individual is the apex of human development. Our belief in individualism is how white people in this nation can say, "Nobody ever gave me anything." "I worked hard for my money." "I've never been on welfare." This delusion is belied by the enormous historical and structural advantages whites have had in our accumulation of wealth. Over centuries, dozens of laws were passed intended "for whites only." Some resulted in white wealth accumulation, from the 1785 Land Ordinance Act that gave 640 acres of land at $1 per acre to citizens; to the 1862 Homestead Act that gave 160 acres of land to any citizen willing to build a dwelling and plant crops; to the 1934 Federal Housing Administration that loaned $120 billion in home loans, 98% to white people. The list goes on. These laws, which historian Ira Katznelson calls affirmative action for white people, are effectively used by groups such as the Racial Equity Institute of Greensboro, North Carolina to refute the pseudo-superiority of white individuals and to challenge the inequities of white institutional dominance.[1]

White people's belief in individualism makes us suspicious and untrustworthy in the eyes of people of color. Black people and other people of color know that white privilege is not about working hard. People from all classes, colors and conditions throughout this country's history have worked hard. What rugged individualism is really about is a myth of meritocracy, that white people got where we are today because we worked harder than anyone else.

Individualism promised opportunity for all — except the Indian, African and other peoples of color as they enter the nation's consciousness. This dichotomy between the individualized white person and the collectivized persons of color is foundational to the race-constructed society. History books describe a nation made up of white individuals who made it by their own grit, determination and ingenuity, with suitable conformity to established norms, and "colored" peoples in our midst whose work habits must be improved and enforced lest they slide into indolence and passivity. The dichotomy lends itself to dramatic contradictions, for it is the "indolent and passive colored peoples," along with the poorest of poor working white people, who do the hardest work. The degraded Irish in America along with the Chinese "coolee" provided much of the labor to build the Intercontinental Railroad. "Lazy" blacks picked the cotton and performed all manner of menial and demanding work that enriched the nation for centuries. Without Mexican vaqueros, who would have "tamed the West"? Without the ethnic white working class, who would have actually developed the industrial might of the nation?

This historical amnesia defies logic. Today, white supremacy protects itself not only by often denying that racism still exists, but by not discussing it. The most recognized authorities in the nation today can speak to issues impacting the country without ever mentioning race as a factor. Progressive whites espouse equity and inclusive intent even as we define the parameters of what constitutes appropriate behavior, action, style, credentials, and legitimate outcomes. People of color are usually called upon to validate, not initiate, the process of change.

Those whites who consciously and unconsciously resist racial equity have, ironically, adopted a denial strategy that proves quite effective for them: never mention race even when speaking about President Obama. Do not admit he is a racial being. Deny him the honor of being the nation's first black president. Decry any attempts on his part to assist the black community as racist or socialistic. Shout "Bias!" in every instance a policy or action might indicate that blacks face obstacles in this country that whites do not.

It is our acculturation as individuals that provides us as white people a cover for our continued investment in white supremacy. I can deny responsibility for anything I did not personally do or say. I am not accountable for the actions of other white people, all the while being unaware of the many ways in which I collectively hold people of color accountable, especially black and brown people, for the actions of a few.

White people's denial of racism can come across as naive and manipulative. To be oblivious to the impact of racism experienced by most people of color on a daily basis makes whites untrustworthy — even objects of hostility. Since whites as a collective wield inordinate power in the country through control of the institutions, people of color feel anger and constant frustration. This impacts interracial relationships in all facets of life in the United States. The different worlds inhabited by people of different racial status in America lead inexorably to racial tensions. In the workplace and in educational settings these tensions are fueled by the constant micro-aggressions experienced by people of color and a denial of their existence by white people. For example, a white person may ask an Asian colleague, "Where are you from?" When told "Chicago," she might follow the question with, "No, where are you *really* from?" When told that assuming Asians are "permanent foreigners" is racist, whites will cry in dismay: "I didn't mean anything by that!" Black people experience similar micro-aggressions when having to deal with white colleagues' enthusiastic "compliments:" "You're so articulate!" or "You're not like the others." Increasingly, white people's inability to understand the context of world events or our historical collective culpability for crimes against people of color is a form of mental dislocation. We absolve ourselves of blame while we absorb messages of worthiness and racial innocence. Such mental dislocation has profound psychological effects on white people. Winthrop Jordan explains it thus:

> Within every white American who stood confronted by the Negro, there had arisen a perpetual duel between his higher and lower natures. His cultural conscience — his Christianity, his humanitarianism, his ideology of liberty and equality — demanded that he regard and treat the Negro as his brother and his countryman, as his equal. At the same moment, however, many of his most profound urges, especially his yearning to maintain the identity of his folk, his passion for domination, his sheer avarice, and his sexual desire, impelled him toward conceiving and treating the Negro as inferior to himself, as an American leper. At closer view, though, the duel appears more complex than a conflict between the best and worst in the white man's nature, for in a variety of ways the white man translated his "worst" into his "best." Raw sexual aggression became retention of purity, and brutal domination became faithful maintenance of civilized restraints. These translations, so necessary to the white man's peace of mind, were achieved at devastating cost to another people set permanently apart because they looked different from the white man generation after generation. But the enormous toll of human wreckage was by no means paid exclusively by the Negro, for the subtle translations of basic urges in the white man necessitated his treating the Negro in a fashion which lacerated his own conscience, that very quality in his being which necessitated those translations. So the peace of mind the white man sought by denying his pro-

> found inexorable drives toward creation and destruction...was denied the white man; he sought his own peace at the cost of others and accordingly found none. In fearfully hoping to escape the animal within himself the white man debased the Negro, surely, but at the same time he debased himself.[2]

White supremacy has always been ugly and violence-prone. Over the centuries, individual white violence and mob actions against people of color have somewhat diminished, replaced by a more contemporary type of systemic violence that squashes the aspirations and sense of future for many people of color in the United States. This systemic violence, turned inward, crushes the spirit of those deemed to be the nation's "minority groups." Conversely, it creates a false sense of self-esteem among white people. We do not internalize the notion of a white collective. I'm just ME! This invisible individualism renders us unable to recognize the benefits of the racial arrangement. The concept of minorities describes not a numerical percentage in the population but a status in the racial arrangement. While it is often said that somewhere near 2050, "whites" will be a numerical minority, this obsession with numbers does not address the race-constructed nature of our society. Whites, even as we might represent a lower percentage of the overall population by 2050, continue to control the systems of power and cultural ways of life in this country.

Michael Washington and Barbara Major were the first People's Institute organizers to use the term Internalized Racial Superiority in their work. They demonstrated how whites define what is great American literature and music. White Protestant values and customs are the standard of what constitutes a well-brought-up American. From the earliest European immigrants to the twenty-first century, messages of superior status have been received daily and become a part of the nation's psyche. Internalized Racial Superiority has impacted white people regardless of individual politics or opinions and regardless of our morality or sense of justice. The images over centuries of white police forces, white teachers (even in all-black schools), white doctors, lawyers, judges, professors, store owners, lifeguards, grocery clerks, preachers, bankers and business leaders have been internalized and accepted as normal. This is why today some white people say, "I grew up in an all-white suburb and I never saw racism." This ability to deny that racism even exists is because the totality of white dominance is so pervasive as to make it invisible. As historian Wade Nobles might say, people who are white in a white supremacist society are like fish in water — not needing to know or understand the concept of wet.

Internalized Racial Superiority is a term rarely used in the dominant culture. Yet it helps explain the thought process of those who have been shaped by generations of white supremacy. Centuries of psychological myth making have made many white people indifferent or distant when it comes to the subject of race. People of color's historical memory of their collective trauma is difficult for most white people to comprehend. Thus, when black people react with deep rage and sadness to a police shooting of a young black man, many whites wonder at the "extreme" emotional response evoked by the event.

It is this myth-making that makes it difficult for white people to unite across race lines. Our sense of entitlement in being white has kept whites from making common cause with people of color to seek a more equitable social arrangement in this country. Many whites feel cut off from people not like ourselves. For centuries, "others" have been our maids, houseboys, gardeners, bell-hops, chauffeurs, handymen, tour guides when abroad, security guards and sexual conquests. We have demanded protection from others deemed less-than in the race construct. The pull of race has frequently caused us to vote against our own economic self-interest. It has made us complicit in our own class and gender oppression. Tea Party activists ("We want our country back") support xenophobic and racist political leaders. The fear of racial equity and the terror surrounding any perceived loss of race privilege make us bystanders as the world changes around us.

Our American culture is not imbued with a sense of history. Most Americans today are a-historical. When it comes to race, whites, in particular, are ill-informed; indeed, whites are frequently arrogant in our ignorance. We are rarely confronted with the nation's truths about the lingering impact of race on ourselves as the dominant culture in the US, or the devastating impact of racism on people of color. We are acculturated to think that past racial wrongs have been rectified and thus there are no excuses for blacks or any other "minority group" not to flourish. It is just a matter of individual will and application to the task. The novelist and playwright Toni Morrison, reflecting on our nation's racial history, wonders,

> What parts do the invention and development of whiteness play in the construction of what is loosely described as "American"?... One likely reason for the paucity of critical material on this large

> and compelling subject is that, in matters of race, silence and evasion have historically ruled literary discourse.[3]

Today's systemic disparities can still be predicted on the basis of race. In the New York criminal justice system, for example, according to the Drug Policy Alliance, 90% of the persons convicted and imprisoned for drug offenses are black and Latino. Whites are only 8% of those imprisoned.[4] Yet, a majority of the people who use and sell drugs are white. As Michelle Alexander explains in her 2013 book, *The New Jim Crow,*

> In the era of colorblindness, it is no longer socially permissible to use race, explicitly, as a justification for discrimination, exclusion, and social contempt. So we don't. Rather than rely on race, we use our criminal justice system to label people of color "criminals" and then engage in all the practices we supposedly left behind...we have not ended racial caste in America; we have merely redesigned it.[5]

Not only is racism the normal way of life, but the ideology of white supremacy has been replaced by an equally pernicious ideology of "colorblindness" that re-defines racism as racial prejudice. In ruling after ruling since the 1960s, the courts of this country have determined that, since white supremacy is no longer legal, racial discrimination is outlawed. Consequently, in an extraordinary catch-22, people of color who argue for laws that afford them relief from institutional discrimination are told that if an institution did not *intend* to discriminate, they have no recourse! This "institutions are colorblind" mantra was most succinctly stated by no less than John Roberts, Chief Justice of the US Supreme Court, who, when ruling in June, 2007 against using race to assign students to particular schools to achieve integration in Seattle and Louisville, KY (*Parents Involved in Community Schools v. Seattle School District No. 1*) stated: "The way to stop discrimination on the basis of race is to stop discriminating on the basis of race."

Today, the term "white supremacy" is confined to those who publicly and proudly advocate for white power — the Ku Klux Klan, the Militia, Aryan Nation, and other white supremacist groups — and who are ugly and violence-prone. Yet whiteness is supreme in America, for both men and women. In the institutional structures of the country it is currency, it has purchasing power. It is transferable to cash and it builds wealth. It can be traded upon. It has its own exchange rate.

Whiteness as currency is coded into the language of the society. The term "white flight" is one example. White flight denotes not only the physical movements out of a changing racial arrangement, but also the flight of resources that follow the movements of whites. "Changing neighborhoods," where youth are suddenly "at-risk" are racialized phrases used to measure the health of any given institutional or societal arrangement. To be living or working in any institutional setting that is "urban" or "inner city" often indicates the reduced resources one can expect.

A neighborhood is "predominantly white" when 90% of its residents are white and there is no more than 10% people of color — especially African Americans. White people structurally enhance the value of property disproportionately to our numbers. This is true in all institutional arrangements. In cities where whites are fewer in the public school system, that system will attempt to ensure their continued presence by offering special programs such as charter schools or magnet programs designed for "gifted" students, special arts schools or college-prep opportunities.

Mobility: Another hallmark

White people have always had options. They have mobility within the country and within institutional arrangements. This is the design. As long as whites remain stable in the institutional setting, situations seem normal. The normality is because the institutions are functioning as they were intended to function. In contrast, normality is threatened by people of color, especially black people. The institutional situation becomes unstable and can be targeted for transition when perception begins to shift. As economist Thomas C. Schelling hypothesized as early as 1971, whites see themselves as operating in a minority context when the percentages of people of color approach 25%; they move out of the situation by 30%. The setting has become de-stabilized.[6] White people can move about without fear of restraint, knowing they are backed up by their governments and professions and have their dominant culture's permission. This freedom of movement by whites is another foundational building block of Internalized Racial Superiority that is very much alive today. It can be understood not only in physical terms but through a psychology that permits whites to move when and where we please. Whites can move neighborhood to neighborhood or city to suburb and back again. White political activists can operate with the privilege of knowing we can move from issue to issue, choosing to deal with the implicit racism of our actions, or if we so choose, to not deal with it at all.

The Doctrine of Discovery gave whites access to colonized poor and oppressed peoples of color without their permission. Today, access to oppressed people's economic and cultural resources takes the form of professionalism. People with degrees, grants, and programs enter poor and oppressed communities and claim access to their lives "for their own good."

Whites who travel and visit indigenous lands and cultures enhance our sense of well-being as vacationers or tourists where we appropriate cultural icons, traditions, and symbols. Whites "discover" colonized, oppressed, and other "marginalized" peoples in ways that enhance our professional status or political position. White progressives can go abroad and be paid by institutions, then return having "met Fidel" or "gone to a sweat lodge." White volunteers who helped to rebuild New Orleans' infrastructure after Hurricane Katrina were often oblivious to the reality of life-long residents who themselves were blocked from returning home. The positive aspects of such humanitarian efforts are real, but they are countered by the psychology of whites who are accustomed to "going wherever I want, doing whatever I do and being whoever I choose."

This is Internalized Racial Superiority. It is the Doctrine of Discovery updated. The linkages stream unbroken through history with titles such as explorer, conquistador, soldier, invader, founder, militia, minuteman, missionary, priest, overseer, scout, trader, Indian agent, frontiersman, pioneer, prospector, teacher, one called by Christ, archeologist, professional, volunteer, student, intern, tenured, licensed, accredited, researcher, philanthropist, funder, grantor, grantee, ally, go-between, evaluator, and gatekeeper. As a result of the Doctrine of Discovery, even the most humanitarian white people become agents of social control and white supremacy.

Racism is a thing of the past in the United States. This is the mantra of most mainstream media and policymakers. The myth, that we are moving toward a "post-racial society," is belied by every systemic outcome indicating exactly the opposite. People who speak about racism are seen as "living in the past," "using race as a crutch," or "consumed by guilt." Even in recent years, as a "Black Lives Matter" movement has grown in response to racist police violence, most white people cling to the myths that black people are more likely to be criminals, that police are just doing their jobs, and "if you're not doing anything wrong, you won't be stopped" by the police.

We are still a segregated nation. We know little about each other beyond the forced politeness and niceties of the workplace. Most of us leave work to return to hyper-segregated housing. Residential segregation is as strictly maintained now as anytime in the nation's history. Our public and private schools are as segregated as they were in the 1960s. Our work forces are integrated, but most people of color are on the ground floor and the work force becomes more and more white and male the higher one ascends. Even as white mainstream media and policymakers have begun to acknowledge that many African American and Latino lives are in peril, Fox News and talk radio pound away at white America: It's not our fault!

Whites have been rendered incapable of connecting ourselves to a collective past. This appears disingenuous to people of color and makes interactions between whites and people of color fragile and dishonest. Genuine cross-racial dialogue is impossible without cross-cultural understanding and appreciation of historical experience.

White people's continued belief in Manifest Destiny is cast in its modern form as many of us protested, after the catastrophic September 11, 2001 bombing of the Twin Towers in New York City, "What have they got against us?" "What did we ever do to them?" That outraged innocence echoed a similar reaction 40 years earlier when Malcolm X, in his first response to the assassination of President John F. Kennedy, said America's "chickens are coming home to roost." Yet when we examine the US history of violence, or our contemporary drone- and cyber-war policies, we can better understand how the United States is viewed today by many of its citizens and the world's people. The internalization of superiority is not often recognized or admitted by whites. We are not made cognizant of it because in many ways we are unaware of it. In this race-constructed nation, now designated as "colorblind," state sanctioned institutions speak for us. We claim individual innocence because of structural advantage. We acknowledge racism only as individual acts of bigotry by others. This allows us the privilege of denial of intent when it comes to collective white advantage.

The extended network of white privilege is there even for the poorest of white people. We are much more likely to work even in periods of economic downturn. Not because of a greater work ethic but because of greater access to jobs. There is an economy that working class and poor whites are part of that is never seen in the want ads or hiring halls; entry point is word of mouth, town-to-town, family-to-family. These types of jobs run the gamut from small construction businesses to road repair that is out-sourced by city and state government. These independent employment sectors are disproportionately owned by whites. Job openings are rarely announced, but are passed on and around through family, church, and community connections. Because the individual opportunities are not acknowledged, working class whites today claim a more stringent work ethic. They insist that this is all done on the up and up. Such experiences seep into the white psyche that we've earned everything and "nobody has given us anything."

Internalized Racial Superiority is both an historical reality and a present day psychological state. It justifies my taking whatever I desire. The events of the past require nothing of me. Can't we just move on? Thus the dance continues.

Part II

CHAPTER 6

Post World War II and the Challenge to White Supremacy

My father returned from WWII to McComb, Mississippi, a small railroad town in the southwest corner of the state. He had enlisted in 1941 and returned in late 1945. My oldest sister, Bonnye, who was less than six months old when he joined the army, was five when he returned. By then she was accustomed to referring to her father as "my picture frame Daddy." Daddy went to war to defeat Hitler. So did his brother James. His brothers Aubrey and Norwood and Bobby joined the Navy after Japan bombed Pearl Harbor. Brothers Cliff and Harry were in essential industries like the railroad and stayed stateside. Sisters Fanny and Peggy did what they could, as millions of women did, to support the war effort at home. It was a fully-mobilized family within a fully-mobilized nation. It was also a fully-racialized nation.

McComb was as committed to racial segregation in late 1945 as it had been when my father left in 1941, Hitler notwithstanding. Housing, schools, colleges, restaurants, hotels and motels, public entities like hospitals and health clinics, court rooms, jails, state prisons, churches, city-sponsored recreation and youth sports, all zealously protected not only separation of the races, but a system of white supremacy that governed every facet of life. Crossing the boundary of race in personal matters, like anything remotely sexual or romantic, even friendship, except in the most patronizing of ways, could get you killed. Most white Southerners would have someone black in their family mythology. This mythical all-

caring, all-loyal black woman (it was usually a black woman) is said by literally thousands of white men and women of a certain age and era "to have almost raised me" and "we loved her like she was a member of the family." The myth of "the good black people" versus "the bad black people" was a staple of internalized racial superiority. Good black people served white people and did so happily and never said a word about civil rights or integration. They were "just fine" with the way things were. It was only "outsiders," often from "up North" and "bad black people" who ever said anything to the contrary. Whites insisted that it was always the "bad black people" who got on television because they were marching for equal rights. Those were the ones who were written about in the newspaper. "Bad blacks" covered a lot of territory from any "Negro" from "up North" to criminals who should be locked up to successful blacks like Congressman Adam Clayton Powell, Jr. or to groups like the NAACP, and certainly preachers like Dr. Martin Luther King, Jr. They were just trying to stir things up and were in it for themselves and were really under the control of "Yankees," "communists" and "Northern preachers."

My father had won the Purple Heart after barely surviving a bomb attack on his railroad battalion headquarters in Antwerp, Belgium where he was stationed. It became a part of family lore — how he would witness his partners in combat being blown apart and yet live to tell about it. He was part of what Tom Brokaw called "The Greatest Generation" in Brokaw's 1998 award-winning account by the same name. He was the soldier featured in a thousand different Hollywood movies, during and in the aftermath of WWII — good-looking, loyal, brave, patriotic, driven by the American Dream, hard-working. And white, especially white.

Growing up, I thought everyone was white — anyone of any consequence anyway. White people ran things because it was normal for us to do so. White people were smarter and stronger. White people made history and wrote books. White people invented things and discovered other lands. White people found cures for polio and one day would fly to the moon. Superman was white. So were Batman and Tarzan and Babe Ruth, the Lone Ranger and Flash Gordon. All presidents of our country were white men. It could not be any other way.

I knew some "historical" figures were black. "Uncle Tom" was a Negro as was "Jim" in Huckleberry Finn. Aunt Jemima was "colored" and so was "Uncle Ben." Great white people had "freed" the "slaves." This was on my good days. On my not-so-good days, "Yankees" freed the slaves, but most "coloreds" didn't like Yankees any more than we white Southerners did. They preferred the South, truth-be-told, even slavery when they were free to admit it.

To us, my father was the movie stars Audie Murphy, John Wayne, Robert Mitchum, Van Johnson, and Victor Mature all rolled up into one. In fact, I grew up thinking only white people fought in the war. It was easy. That is how it seemed to me. The news reels depicted only white soldiers. Even when the audience watching the news reels was panned, every audience, it seemed, was comprised solely of white people. This was true in fact for movies in general. The westerns showed Indians, but only as background for endless morality tales of the conquest of the West by white settlers and heroes.

In school my teachers didn't contradict these misrepresentations. There was never a mention of WWII veterans who were not white. Only we rarely got as far as WWII in class. In Mississippi and later in Tennessee and Arkansas, we spent an inordinate amount of time on the Civil War. Teachers perpetuated the myths, but not only teachers. The local American Legion chapter was all-white. So was the Veterans of Foreign Wars. None of the service clubs like Rotary or Kiwanis or the Lions Club revised the history. Certainly the churches did not. God must have been white. Jesus was always white. His disciples were white.

When it came to countering the white supremacist culture of post-WWII McComb to which my father returned in 1945, the state-controlled media rarely set us straight. The Enterprise Journal, *the local newspaper in McComb, was one of those exceptions. Although it didn't write of the heroic exploits of black veterans such as the Tuskegee Airmen or highlight the heroism of such units as the black-led Red Ball Express in its news sections, the editorial positions of Oliver Emmerich, father and son, spoke out against some of the most heinous of white supremacist violence throughout the post war era, continuing through the 1960s. The Emmerichs joined a group of courageous newspapermen and women who collectively were the most outspoken white critics of Mississippi's racial apartheid system, journalists like Pulitzer Prize winner Hazel Brannon Smith with the* Lexington Advertiser, *P. D. East, the highly controversial publisher of the* Petal Paper *in Petal, Mississippi, and the famous Hodding Carter whose* Delta-Democrat Times *waged war against segregation for over forty years from the small Delta town of Greenville, Mississippi.*

In the public sphere, veterans of color did not exist. Not to me. Not often in McComb's Enterprise Journal *and definitely not in the* Helena World. *Helena's newspaper made very clear in its layout who was to be honored and who was not. A news item concerning someone "colored" would be titled "Negro, Victim of Hit and Run, dies in West Helena" or "Negro jailed for Theft at Local Store." Even obituaries followed suit: "Etta Simpson, Negro, died Sunday." I asked my mother why the newspaper always said "Negro" and never "white." She said it would be assumed someone is white if it does not say differently. This was wise on my mother's part. This was certainly true in the history books, magazines, news reels and television news. One is to assume whiteness unless it is stated otherwise. That is a learning that I have kept close at hand to this day.*

My father, upon the 50th anniversary of D-Day in 1994, was asked by his granddaughter, Erika, to speak to the high school senior class in McComb about his experiences in the war. The school's makeup was not anything like the one he remembered from his own school days back in the 1930s. McComb High School had transitioned from an all-white student body to one almost entirely African American by 1994. While he graduated from a small white school outside McComb named Carter's Creek High School and not McComb High, the culture shock from the make-up of the schools would have been the same. I was nervous for him as he went to speak, afraid that he might misspeak or not be listened to by the young people, his being elderly and white. I was both afraid for him and afraid of what he might say. Afterwards, I asked him "How did it go?" "What did you say?" He told me, "I told them about the Red Ball *Express," as if he did this type of thing every day. "It was an all-colored troop." He went on: "I told them they took heavy losses. Without them we wouldn't have won the war."*

It was a proud moment for him and another one for me, too.

Even had the Enterprise Journal *or the* Helena World *written about the* Red *Ball Express, no one would have read it aloud to me nor talked about it on the front porch in the evening where reliving WWII was a topic of conversation among my family for the sixty-five years between 1940 and 2005. Suffice it to say, there was no veterans parade welcoming home the troops. Not all the troops.*

Black service men indeed could not walk downtown dressed in their uniforms. It might cause a riot or evoke hostility from white people, not all of whom had served themselves. The uniform commanded respect and the presence of a black soldier proudly wearing insignia implied an equity that did not exist and would not be tolerated.

Dred Scot still ruled Mississippi, not Uncle Sam.

The end of World War II ushered in a feeling of euphoria for those American families separated for so long, many for four years or more. The United States was justly proud of the role it played in defeating Hitler. The death toll was enormous. Russia had lost some 27 million soldiers and civilians during the war. Millions were executed and worked to death in Siberian prison camps after having been declared enemies of the new Soviet state. Britain, France and the United States had nearly half a million casualties each. Among the Axis powers, Japanese deaths were close to three million and Germany lost almost six million people. This, of course, did not include the six million Jews killed in the Holocaust.

Hitler's Nazi regime had not only exterminated Jews but many groups he considered the dregs of humanity. In all, another five million people killed in the Holocaust were non-Jews, commonly referred to as the "others": mentally and physically disabled peoples, Gypsies and Germans of African descent were rounded up and killed; others were forcibly sterilized. Close to 100,000 homosexual men and women were murdered.

Yet even as the United States had fully mobilized against Nazi Germany and imperial Japan, it had brought its own contradictions into the war effort, for the US was also a white supremacist nation. It could claim moral high ground against Hitler because Hitler was so blatantly racist and such an immediate and looming threat to the world order. But the US reeked of hypocrisy where race and racial supremacy were concerned. The great flaw of the American ideal was its treatment of racial groups within its borders. Black, Latino, Asian and Native American soldiers and sailors fought valiantly and with distinction in WWII, but only as part of a segregated armed services. Often serving under horrendous conditions and with little respect for the sacrifices they made, troops of color took up arms at higher rates of enlistment than did white inductees. It is difficult to explain why America's "minorities" would fight so valiantly in WWII as well as other wars before and after. Were they out to prove themselves worthy of being "real Americans"? Were they determined to "fight for freedom" as an ideal so worthy of respect that, even as they themselves were not free, they fought to make it so? Were they attempting to "shame" white America into doing the right thing?

War is said to be the great leveler. It is fought largely by the working classes. Like white soldiers, people of color thought military service would provide a path to full equality. Once again peoples of color expected to be treated as full citizens. Once again the nation's fixation on race awaited them. In the twentieth century, W. E. B. Du Bois and Gunnar Myrdal wrote about it. White supremacy was the stain on the "cradle of democracy" that would not go away.

On the world stage, US racial policies were being effectively used by the Soviet Union to place the US in a hypocritical and undeniable position with emerging non-white nations in Africa, Asia and Latin America. That the "arsenal of democracy" was not using its power to bring about genuine democracy at home played well with colonized nations in the midst of throwing off their oppression. In fact, the arsenal was more often used to control the discontented masses of people of color in its midst. To most US citizens, such accusations of hypocrisy were mere propaganda, coming as they did from "the communist enemy." Others were not so sure. How could the US present itself as a freedom-loving nation, given that millions of its citizens were not free?

In the fall of 1949, the Ford Foundation called together a group of scholars, business men and fellow foundation colleagues at its offices in Dearborn, Michigan. The group was commissioned to produce a detailed study of conditions impacting the future of democracy in the United States. They were well aware that for the second time in less than fifty years, working class whites and people of color had fought valiantly and died disproportionately to "make the world safe for democracy." They knew an "alien ideology" was threatening to recruit these veterans and laboring classes for another type of war — a war of competing ideas and conflicting ideals. Without ever mentioning the Soviet Union, communism, or the Cold War, the context in which the scholars came together was clear. The preface to the resulting Gaither Report, as it was called, stated:

> The people of this country and mankind in general are confronted with problems which are vast in number and exceedingly disturbing in significance. While important efforts to solve these problems are being made by government, industry, foundations and other institutions, it is evident that new resources, such as those

> of this Foundation, if property employed, can result in significant contributions.[1]

The Ford Foundation meeting was the opening of a national strategy to combat a perceived communist threat. Its purpose was to reduce communism's appeal to disaffected groups like blacks, Jews, and wage-earning workers. The Gaither Report called nobly and appropriately for a more open society and expansion of the democracy to all US citizens. While mentioning race as a "barrier" to the achievement of this goal, it went no further in acknowledging how race and racism permeated the society. This, at the very apex of "separate but equal" in the United States! How were the brutalities of the segregated systems of the nation to be eased? How were practices restricting labor organizing all over the country to be changed within the basic social and economic structures of the nation? The report called on sincere, but elite policy makers to act and change things — in ways that would keep existing social and political power arrangements in place. For blacks, and later, other peoples of color and for whites willing to engage the Big Taboo of race, the answer at the community level would be organizing, movement-building, and direct confrontation with power. This had long been Big Labor's approach. Labor and civil rights were beginning to come together. Things were about to change.

Chapter 7

Racialized "Communist Threat" Post-WWII

I, of course, knew no communists when growing up in the South, except for Herbert Philbrick, who was the star of the 1950s television series, "I Led Three Lives." This weekly dose of anti-communist serum injected into American living rooms chronicled Philbrick's adventures as a double agent. Philbrick personified the redemption story of a communist turncoat now working for the FBI. Communists were depicted as fearsome and duplicitous people. They replaced Nazis in my imagination as people to shy away from. But, like I said, I knew no communists.

Dr. Martin Luther King, Jr., was, of course, called a communist by most white people in the South, although I was starting to become suspicious of anything white people had to say about Dr. King. However, I still would not dare say anything out loud, though I suspected they were lying. It reminded me of a pamphlet that I, along with a couple of hundred other future leaders of America, were given at the 1963 Class of Arkansas Boys State. It was a list of the 200 most subversive organizations in the United States. They were scary and mysterious to me with names like Industrial Workers of the World and Veterans of the Abraham Lincoln Brigade. Most of the names have escaped me over the years, but I was grounded in the fear that communists really existed and they were not all in the Soviet Union. There could be communists in Mississippi or Arkansas.

Two other memories of Boys State have stayed with me. One of the speakers was a veteran of the Spanish-American War. I thought he was very old, and since it was some sixty-five years after that war, he must have been. What made him stick in my mind was that he was as exercised by the communist threat as anyone I had ever met, heard on television or read about in the newspapers. He urged us to leave Boys State that very day and join those patriots organizing in the US to run Fidel Castro out of Cuba. Even then I remember thinking, "This guy is really nuts."

The second memory is a recollection that came to mind only after I saw the picture of a young Bill Clinton shaking President John F. Kennedy's hand, wearing a 1963 Boys Nation T-shirt. That meant I was at Arkansas Boys State with Bill Clinton. Each state could elect two representatives to Boys Nation. Ours were Bill Clinton along with his best friend from Hope, Mack McLarty. Mack McLarty would become Bill Clinton's Chief of Staff during the President's first term in office. I remember at Boys State thinking that McLarty might be president someday. Almost, I guess.

Decades later, in 1982, when I was working for the National Division of the United Methodist Church, I was sent to my home state of Mississippi to attempt to quell the outrage among white United Methodists over the case of Mayor Eddie James Carthan, elected one of the first black mayors in Mississippi since Reconstruction in the tiny Delta town of Tchula. One of our divisions was involved in an effort to effect his release from jail. Meeting at an area steakhouse with local United Methodist preachers, the District Superintendent, D. S. Furr, opened the meeting and immediately pointed me out: "See him? He is a Communist." Welcome home. Suffice it to say that my homecoming was anything but. The national movement to free Eddie Carthan was in some ways the coming out party for the People's Institute for Survival and Beyond. Led by Jim and Diana Dunn for the most part, PISAB utilized the national network built up over many years to publicize the blatant racism that was at work in the case. Arnett Lewis and LeRoy Johnson were leaders in the United League of Holmes County, Mississippi with the able assistance and tireless efforts by two catholic sisters working in Holmes County. Carthan was freed, but not before the charges against Mayor Carthan had grown to include capital murder and drug trafficking. Carthan escaped a life sentence. Those of us with the People's Institute were witness to a "net that works."

Throughout the 1950s, any call for social change in the United States, whether from Big Labor, civil rights groups or Ban the Bomb efforts were blasted as communist-inspired. This fear of communism was pervasive and growing. In every part of the country, paranoia reigned. Under every rock there seemed to be Americans willing to undermine this nation's ideals and to subvert democracy. So we were told. In the South, the fear of communism was racialized. Anyone white who espoused civil rights or in any way called for a more fair and equitable society was a communist, subject to government investigation and personal harassment. The equating of work for civil rights with communism spread across the nation and lasted many years, well into the 1960s and beyond.

The Communist revolution in China ended European and American imperialist ambitions for an economic, political and military stronghold in Asia. The success of Mao's revolution led to outcries from the right wing in the US: "Who Lost China?" During the early 1950s, the specter of communists in the US government, especially in the State Department, of left wing professors "soft on communism," and of "reds" in media and the arts was sold to the American public as part of a worldwide communist conspiracy. No sector of the society was untouched. Millions of Americans bought the hype. Suspicion and paranoia, fueled by the venom spewed by the likes of Senator Joseph McCarthy (R. Wisconsin), Eisenhower's Secretary of State, John Foster Dulles, as well as FBI Director, J. Edgar Hoover and countless others exploded across the nation. Efforts to deal with racism and white supremacy were all painted "RED."

Despite grave consequences of being identified or suspected of being a communist, in the early years of the Russian Revolution and through WWII, the Communist Party USA enjoyed significant support among many progressive Americans. The newly emerging Soviet Union had a certain cachet, fueled by its heroic support of Spanish loyalists in their fight against fascism, and its extraordinary sacrifices as part of the Allied forces fighting Hitler, Mussolini and Hirohito. Many academics, artists and persons on the political left joined or supported the Party in the 1930s and only left after the German-Soviet Nonaggression Pact was sign in 1939 or when the extremes of Stalin's totalitarianism were revealed.

In the US, communist organizers in both industry and agriculture were a constant reminder of the flaws in the democratic ideal. Communist organizers found fertile ground among the most oppressed in the nation. Though their organizing rarely resulted in large increases in membership in the Communist Party USA, their critique of the capitalist system resonated with many workers and farm laborers. Throughout much of the early twentieth century, this critique found voice not only with those calling themselves communists but with progressives and socialists like Eugene V. Debs, the five-time candidate for the US presidency. Groups such as the Farm Labor Party, the Socialist Party of America and the Socialist Workers Party were determined critics of US social, political and economic systems throughout the 1920s and into the 1960s.

These cries damning capitalism as a system for rich people at the expense of working people were successfully countered, however, by ardent defenders of the American Way of Life. The US, they said, is the most open and democratic of any nation in the world. Demands for racial and economic equity were met with accusations of "communist." Anyone painted with the "communist" brush was hounded into oblivion or prison, often both. It took courage to adopt communism as a set of political and economic beliefs in the United States. It took even more courage to organize as a communist. To be so labeled was to ostracize oneself from the great democratic debate. This remained true throughout the twentieth century. The collapse of the Soviet Union in 1989 was interpreted in the US as the final death knell of a rejected ideology and the inevitable outcome of a failed social and economic system.

Still, no discussion about race in the United States and organized efforts to promote racial equity can omit the contributions of the communists, socialists and other political leftists. Paul Robeson is a powerful example of one whose place in American history has been marginalized and often ignored because of his affiliation with the Communist Party. Robeson, born in Princeton, New Jersey to a working class black family, attended Rutgers University where he was an All-American football player as well as an actor in the theater department and one of the most honored students in his senior class. When Robeson graduated he continued to perform in all of these arenas. He was a top-flight pro-football player, a movie actor and Broadway star on stage and screen. Robeson was a man on fire against racial and class discrimination. He relentlessly stormed the gates of American "exceptionalism," speaking out with vigor and energy against America's treatment of its black citizens and working classes. Robeson was untiring in his commitment to the cause of racial and economic justice in the US even as he pursued a movie career and a life on stage. Had Robeson been a non-communist white man in the United States, he would probably have been viewed as "Presidential material" or seen as one of the great voices of film and stage history. Instead, because he was both black and a member of the Communist Party USA, Robeson was hounded by authorities, shunned by Hollywood and Broadway, and relegated to preaching on the outskirts of the great American debate on race. Robeson, who died in 1976, was so tarred by the communist connection that even leaders of the civil rights, labor and peace movements could not publicly embrace and celebrate him for fear of retribution from state and national authorities. Like other radicals such as Rosa Luxemburg and Emma Goldman, Robeson is rarely mentioned in textbooks. Generations of school children have never heard of one of this country's foremost voices for freedom for oppressed people everywhere.

Lillian Smith, like Robeson, was a brilliant and radical social critic who has been left out of mainstream social justice history. Her best-selling novel, *Strange Fruit* (1944), dramatized the deadly consequences of interracial love and earned the distinction of being banned in Boston (and elsewhere). *Killers of the Dream,* published five years later, created a huge scandal both because of its psycho-sexual analysis of white supremacy, and perhaps more because the author was an upper-middle class Southerner. Smith was called communist, despite her strong anti-communist opinions.

Thurgood Marshall was one of the early voices to recognize the racialized nature of the anti-communist hysteria. In 1947, Marshall, then first Director-Counsel of the NAACP Legal Defense and Educational Fund, Inc. filed a friend-of-the-court brief in the appeal of the "Hollywood Ten" — the actors, directors and producers who had been convicted of subversion by the House Un-American Activities Committee (HUAC). Marshall argued,

> the writers involved were those among the writers in Hollywood who had been most friendly to Negroes...[They] have taken the position in their actual work in Hollywood in writing scripts of giving the Negro as fair a break as they could possibly do.[1]

Subversive indeed!

CHAPTER 8

The 1950s: GI Bill, White Flight, and Resistance to Integration

My grandfather was able to qualify under the 1935 Resettlement Administration to purchase twenty-five acres of land in an area outside of McComb, Mississippi in 1936. The twenty-five-acre parcel was located in a new rural subdivision called the Eleanor Roosevelt Homesteads. These McComb homesteads constituted one of 100 communities developed across the country in 1935 and 1936 under a short-lived Division of Subsistence Homesteads. With the federal government's backing, my grandfather was able to purchase the land and the newly-constructed house on it for $1,500, a sizable amount of money during the depression years. This Homesteads initiative was one of many New Deal programs designed to assist people in the US to build wealth equity and to move toward middle class status. However, because no federal agencies pushed for integrated neighborhoods, black people in McComb — and there were a few thousand — were not allowed to live in the Homesteads. As historian Paul Conkin writes, "Homesteaders would, in practice, have to be selected 'according to the sociological pattern of the community, at all times interpreting the facts as liberally as feasible, keeping in mind the success of the project.'"[1]

The Homesteads were made possible by the "means" test of income and employment. But had racial segregation not continued to be legal and enforceable and built into the language of the legislation, the New Deal initiatives would have never become law. It was an income-eligible act, meaning one's income could not exceed a *certain amount after adjustments for family-size and the local housing market were made. But there was a hidden, unspoken race test. My grandfather earned approximately $3,500 per year at his highest point as an engineer on the Illinois Central Rail Road. He qualified. He was also white and had nine children. This was fundamental. Some "coloreds" might have passed the means test, but the real test was always race. Agencies such as the Federal Housing Administration did not require states to alter the accepted "rules regarding race." The official stance of FHA was that neighborhoods were preferable and stronger when different races and ethnicities were not "intermingled." Similar to the GI Bill enacted in 1944, these federal guidelines effectively prevented African Americans, Mexican Americans, Puerto Ricans and Asian Americans from buying new homes in areas throughout the country where segregated housing practices were both commonplace and rigidly enforced. This was once again affirmative action for whites like the Billings family.*

My grandfather's purchase of his first home in 1936, backed by the federal government, significantly raised our wealth-quotient. The family has owned the "Homestead," as we continue to call it, for eighty years through an unbroken line of succession from one family member to another. Significantly, it has been the collateral or base from which different members of the family have built wealth for most of a century.

In 1953, my father moved his new post-WWII family to a suburb of Memphis, Tennessee called "WHITEHAVEN." Using the GI Bill, my father purchased a home near his new job. It was obvious that the name of the suburb was used effectively as a marketing tool. I did find out later that the town was named, in fact, for Colonel Francis White, an early settler and major property owner who was influential in getting a rail line in 1853 to run through what was first called White's Station, later White Haven and then Whitehaven. Nonetheless, I am sure he knew how his name would be understood throughout the Memphis and northern Mississippi area as whites became increasingly anxious about issues of "integration" and "civil rights." The move to Whitehaven, Tennessee, albeit for just a short time, would be yet another step toward the middle class, one that again was facilitated by federal affirmative action for white people. The terms of purchase of our Whitehaven home were similar to those my grandfather agreed to: a small down payment with 2% interest over a thirty-year span. The equity build up allowed us to move, just four years later, to Helena, Arkansas, where we bought a large house and where my parents lived for more than thirty years. When my father and mother retired they moved back to the Homestead and lived there until their deaths in 2007. The children of Charles and Joyce Billings inherited property worth over one hundred times what they paid in 1936. The nation had invested in our net worth as white people. These structural advantages were opportunities for which, had we been statused "colored"— black or brown or Asian — we would not have been eligible.

Home, regardless of our other addresses, would always be the Homestead. Originally, the Billings homestead encompassed some twenty-five acres of land, fifteen of which were forested with pine and oak and of course, a Magnolia tree near the house. The house was modest by today's standards and small, only 1400 square feet. My wife and I live in the Homestead today. The Homestead has always been more than an address. It is a "place" that roots us and nurtures us. The Homestead signified who I was and whose I was: Son of the South, a white Southerner. And once again a beneficiary of white affirmative action.

At the beginning of the second half of the twentieth century the United States was the richest and most powerful nation in the world. It was America's Century, no doubt. By 1950, most GIs had returned home. Americans wanted to enjoy life after many years of war and sacrifice. Time-saving home appliances like the electric dishwasher and other household gadgets were being invented almost daily, it seemed, by giant companies like General Electric, General Motors, Westinghouse, Amana with its self-cleaning oven, and Emerson with its television sets. New tract suburban housing was being built all over the country close enough to drive to and from work on a network of new interstate highways. These housing developments were clean, and sold with built-in appliances, modern kitchens and bathrooms with a garage, a back yard, and schools just down the street. All was made available to whites through low cost mortgages made affordable by the GI Bill.

Who could have asked for more? This was truly the American Dream. In the span of two generations, working-class whites who had toiled at factory jobs and on farms, as well as recent European immigrants, many of whom had arrived at Ellis Island with all their possessions in a trunk or knapsack, were now first-time homeowners with a new car in the driveway and a patio in the backyard.

"The fifties" conjures up for white people the era of tree-lined suburbs, *Leave It to Beaver* and *I Love Lucy* on Zenith television sets; of cars with four-on-the floor souped-up engines; sock-hops; teenie-boppers, crew cuts and James Dean. The fifties are depicted as an innocent time with two-parent intact families, sodas after school, and baseball as the national past time. This view of America in the 1950s was sold to the public by a growing advertising industry. Television commercials let us know what was important to buy and the six o'clock news told us what we should be aware of or worried about. The '50s saw the emergence of a youth culture. It was the first generation where "having fun" became an entitlement among young people, mostly white and largely middle to upper class.

This post war economic miracle repeated itself for millions of white Americans. It resulted in one of the biggest accumulations of wealth in the history of the nation, second only to the land grants whites had received in the settling of the western "frontier." The white middle class had arrived.

White progressives and even radicals have long wanted the problems and challenges of race in America to be class-based. Still today, one hears that intractable social problems are really about class, not race. Yet rarely do you hear the class argument from a person of color. Race trumps class in this country, historically and by design. Race doesn't disappear when you look through a class prism; in many ways it is exacerbated. White working class Americans have since the earliest years of the republic protected the racial construct as the foundation of the nation. "Free labor for free men" was a slogan early on as the nation moved westward. The phrase never meant freedom for those enslaved. It spoke of the demands by whites for free access to employment not undercut by those enslaved who worked for nothing, however unwillingly. "Free labor" forces opposed the expansion of African slavery into lands being incorporated into the United States. Slavery's expansion shrank the economic playing field. Both "freedom" for those enslaved and the expansion of slavery into the new Western territories of the ever-growing nation threatened free white labor.

There is no racial equity across class lines. A working-class white person has systemic advantages that a black person does not enjoy in the United States. These advantages are due to the nation's history of white supremacy. The racial wealth gap has only grown over the centuries. In every indicator of systemic well-being the racial differential is striking, from longevity to birth outcomes. Whites have for the most part not been exposed to this information or if so, don't attribute it to racial advantage but to their individual resilience and hard work. This, in part, is why it has been difficult to forge a class-based movement in this country. A working class white person, by definition, works to keep his racial privilege in place, to extend his or her racial advantage, even if unaware of it. This racial arrangement requires the racial disadvantage of those conversely statused as "colored." In the United States, to live "equal" to a person of color has never been something to which a white person aspired. Indeed, the phrase "reverse discrimination" is a telling one. It implies that discrimination against "colored" is natural, and to "reverse" it goes against the norm.

Class is mobile. We have class mobility in the United States. A white person might come from "working class" origins, but as s/he becomes part of the "professional class," with a certain educational attainment and employment opportunities, s/he leaves those origins behind except as memory of part of a cultural story. But whites remain white. Even after the 2008 Great Recession, most white people continue to benefit from institutional privilege, and therefore, continue to accumulate wealth, albeit at a lower rate than earlier in the century.

A black person, on the other hand, may reach the same professional status as a white person, but s/he remains black. White professionals experience white privilege while the person of color who is a professional experiences racism. Access to white privileged status by blacks *ipso facto* cheapens it. White privileged status has no meaning except as it stands in opposition to black.

Racial consciousness on the part of whites might be something one is aware of or it might take the form of denial. For example, small, private, white-owned businesses have been bastions of privilege that have excluded black workers since the end of enslavement. This is especially true in such businesses as family-run retail stores, construction and building trades and a myriad of small commercial interests from insurance offices to accounting firms. Whites miss this when the notion of "reverse discrimination" is discussed. Most small, individually-owned, private businesses are exempt from federal labor laws except for the minimum wage. Blacks are almost totally shut out of this huge sector of the nation's economy. Most people do not think of these white-owned small businesses when it comes to discriminatory practices and employment opportunities, but there are hundreds of thousands of such businesses across the nation. It is what historically allowed white men to leave school early to take employment in their father's business. Blacks have not experienced similar access to entrepreneurship, but instead, have been the subject of racial discrimination in the economic sector. The discrimination covered the gamut from start-up loans to bonding and licensing requirements.

White privilege abounded in post-World War II America. But it needed to be defended. White wealth accumulation was tied to race and to black people. A house was appraised higher if it was owned by white people who lived in an all-white neighborhood. Once this arrangement was "threatened" by the incursion of blacks, the housing appraisal went down and the home was worth-less. It did not matter if the neighborhood was white working class. Solidarity on the assembly line did not transfer to the neighborhood. White property values went up or down depending on where black people lived.

Protection of white neighborhoods from the threat of integrated housing was, for many years, official government policy. The well-known examples of the Levittowns, suburban communities outside New York City and in Pennsylvania, prohibited blacks and Jews from purchasing homes there. It not only was legal to bar certain groups from buying homes, but these policies had the backing of the federal government. The Federal Housing Administration had issued rules explicitly stating that racially homogeneous communities meant less crime, better schools and an increase in property values. These rules guaranteed home ownership possibilities for millions of white families, while denying the same to families of color. These policies helped create a wealth gap between whites and people of color that has continued to grow larger over the years.

White suburbs attracted not only white people but white resources as well. Huge malls making it possible to shop where one lived meant that many whites returned to the inner core of cities only to work, further depleting the city coffers of much needed resources. The American Dream was real and it was "for whites only." Or so it seemed. Times were flush.

The struggles of returning veterans of color mattered little to most of these GI families in their new homes. Black veterans could rarely use their GI bill to purchase homes even in the section of town reserved for them. "Red-lining" meant that real estate companies and financial institutions colluded to refuse mortgages or other types of loans or financing in communities labeled "at-risk" or "bad credit" areas. This would push blacks and other people of color to do business with high-interest loan companies — "loan sharks" who did business in the "colored section of town."

Although restrictive covenants were outlawed in a 1948 Supreme Court ruling, *Shelley v. Kramer,* discrimination in housing was rampant from the smallest towns to the largest cities across the country. A white person selling his home to a black family was likely to set off violent resistance from white neighbors.

Racial discrimination benefited real estate speculators. The process of "flipping a neighborhood" was commonplace in most parts of the United States. Real estate agencies and housing developers put the word out through a sort of dominant culture grapevine invisible to the untrained or naive eye that a given neighborhood was likely to be integrated over the next few months or certainly within the next year. The first "colored" family would be met with outcries and threats from taunting phone calls to rocks through a window to arson, intended to force the family to move. If these intimidations did not work, whites would begin to put their houses on the market and commence the process of "white flight." The unofficial but real 30% rule meant that whites would start to think about leaving as the percentage of black families in a neighborhood rose toward 10%. By 20%, whites would begin to leave and by 30% most whites were in the process of leaving. This 30% rule still pertains today, not only to housing but in other arenas like schools, churches and theaters. As "block-busting" was allowed to happen, city services became more sporadic and police patrols less frequent.[2]

The biggest fear, of course, was that housing integration would have a negative impact on area schools, since most schools were funded through property taxes. If property assessments went down, there would be fewer resources for the neighborhood school; if schools were resourced less, the value of nearby housing decreased. This circular pattern of interlocking systems, combined with a belief that white is more valuable, demonstrated the structural nature of racial inequities. In a time of greatest economic growth in the US, blacks, Latinos, Asians and Native Americans across the country were shut out by systemic racism manifested in rampant and comprehensive institutional discrimination. As Lui et al. conclude:

> Many billions of dollars of equity were accumulated by white people thanks to government help not available to people of color. These FHA and VA recipients are the parents of the baby

> boomers, and their homes form a substantial part of the record-setting $10 trillion in inheritance now being passed down to the baby-boom generation.[3]

The GI Bill not only allowed millions of working class white families to become homeowners, it was also crafted to support efforts by returning veterans to attend college or trade schools. The GI Bill did support veterans of color who desired to attend college. Again, there was a caveat: They would have to find a college that would accept them. In Mississippi, for instance, the only colleges that would enroll black students were historically black colleges and universities (HBCUs) or state "colored schools."

Policies and practices in housing and education which benefited whites were rarely acknowledged and never discussed. White children were not taught about them. These affirmative action policies for whites did more than create wealth. They re-enforced a sense of entitlement among white people. Whites were "legitimate." Whites were the real "Americans." Racial entitlement was both a psychological process and a cultural phenomenon. As ethnicity began to fade among most whites by the 1950s, the broader designation of race became the key to status, wealth accumulation and social class. In many ways white and American were synonymous. It had taken almost two hundred years to firmly root European ethnics in the United States race-constructed society, but by 1960 even Jewish Americans were becoming white. This did not mean that Jews did not face anti-Semitism in the United States. To the contrary, anti-Semitism was evident in every region of the country. Many neighborhoods would not sell to Jewish homebuyers, private clubs banned Jews, and Jews, in general, were victims of extreme stereotypes by the dominant society. Like Mexicans who were statused "white" by the census, but treated in everyday life as "colored," Jews and Italians and some eastern Europeans, especially Romanians, Poles, and Slavs were looked down upon by those Americans who felt that they themselves embodied a certain racial purity. Other whites were deemed swarthy, "oily," unpolished and crude.

Still, Jews were considered white; they were not classified as "colored" or given another racial designation. Like Italians and Greeks and other "almost-white" people, Jews were ostracized and put upon, but they were white. The board rooms of corporate America did not yet include Jews or Italians or Greeks. In many parts of the country, Catholics and other non-Protestants were also subject to discrimination.

The "WASP"—White Anglo-Saxon Protestant—was still the American ideal. But idealism needed help.

The "old world" with its demarcations along lines of nationality, religion, and ethnicities no longer formed white Americans' primary identity. For the peoples of Europe now in the United States, being perceived as white was what made one a real American. To be an American was to be white. Conversely, to be "colored" meant more than skin hues. It also defined one's status as being "less-than" or "minority." Colored people had less of a claim on the "American Dream."

By 2014, the Pew Research Center's Social & Demographic Trends demonstrated that such structural racism has resulted in white wealth in this country being *thirteen* times that of black people and *ten* times that of Latinos. The researchers conclude: "The racial and ethnic wealth gaps in 2013 are at or about their highest levels observed in the 30 years for which we have data."[4] So much for the American Dream!

CHAPTER 9

White Fear/White Violence

In 1955 Emmett Till was murdered less than 100 miles from Helena, Arkansas where I spent most of my years growing up and in the same state of Mississippi where I was born. Yet I never heard of Emmett Till until I was at least a young adult. The same goes for the lynching of author Richard Wright's uncle in West Helena in 1916. The story of the Elaine, Arkansas riot now being brought to light was never mentioned or studied or said to be a factor in the continued separation of the races in this country.

I was oblivious to these crimes and the many others like them. They were never mentioned. If something ever got out about some heinous crime, the white response was predictable. "Must have had it comin'," or "There is more to it than what you have read in the papers" was the refrain. This denial of racism is another cornerstone of Internalized Racial Superiority—"I didn't do it," "I wasn't there," "They had it coming," are phrases whites learned early on. Had Emmett Till's mother not insisted on the return of her son's body to Chicago and had she not opened the casket to the black citizens of Chicago, Jet *magazine would not have photographed his battered and bruised face and published the photos to the utter shock of every subscriber and reader. Some have said that the picture of Emmett Till's brutalized countenance sparked the Civil Rights Movement as much as the actions of Rosa Parks and the Montgomery Bus Boycott. The Movement had a million sparks dating back to the first enslavement of Africans in the seventeenth century. Few whites ever saw the picture of Emmett Till or read* Jet *magazine or ever knew he had been lynched. Not even the arrest, trial, and release of J. W. Milam and Roy Bryant for Till's murder excited much interest in the white press. Whites in the South were never convicted of a black person's murder. To do so would undermine white supremacy and this country's pervasive racial totalitarianism. Ironically, most findings of guilt when it came to judging a white man culpable in a black person's death happened during the enslavement era when such convictions were not for murder but for destruction of property.*

I remember as a teenager in Helena, Arkansas riding in our family car with my buddies and terrorizing black neighborhoods in Helena/West Helena. We thought nothing about crossing the levee to the "colored" section of town and throwing things through black people's windows, roaring through their streets at high speeds to frighten pedestrians, or just being loud and obnoxious. This type of racist behavior was as normal as hanging out at the local Tastee Freeze. We never expected resistance from terrorized blacks; it never crossed our minds that we might be caught and jailed by the police. After all, "we meant no harm and didn't mean to hurt anybody." The fact is that we don't know who was hurt. Still don't.

When I think back to those days I am ashamed to the point of stupor. Not, me. I could not have participated in such hate-filled, criminal actions. But I did. Did I throw a rock or a Coke bottle at someone's home or person? Did I shatter glass? I would like to say I never threw anything. I never hurt anyone, but how can I say that with certainty? The fact is, I don't know. Internalized Racial Superiority is in my bones, now layered over by several thousand books, three or four college degrees and a lifetime of anti-racist work. Does that make up for my actions? No, I am sure it does not. Not to me. I was no different from the Klan member who wore a sheet. I needed no sheet. There were no arrests. No retribution.

This nation has had many Emmett Tills. Some were the result of vigilante violence which characterized the many lynchings in the US in the sixty years after the turn of the century in 1900 until around 1960. Lynchings were so common that the NAACP office in New York City which published the Crisis *hung a sign out the window that read "Another Negro was lynched today." Very few whites knew these stories. For the most part they went unnoticed. Our racial naiveté was fed by our lack of understanding as to how white supremacy was operated and the extent to which this nation would go to protect it. This is not something just in our past. Today's epidemic of police shootings rips at the very fabric of black life in America. It is what bell hooks says in her book,* Black People and Self-Esteem, *constitutes "soul murder."*[1]

As all European ethnics became white after WWII, racism became an even greater part of the nation's culture. By the time the Supreme Court handed down the *Brown v. Board of Education of Topeka Kansas* decision in 1954, "civil rights" were being discussed not only in education, but in arenas like housing, voting rights, public accommodations and even diplomacy. Despite their enormous — though unspoken — advantages, whites were fearful of losing their "favored" status in the US white supremacist state and were fighting back. The term "white supremacy" is rarely used, then or now, when referring to white people's societal hegemony in the US. It has been relegated to usage only when speaking about race hate groups or overt racial bigotry, but white supremacist institutions still reign. In the aftermath of WWII, preferential treatment of whites was still the law, especially in the South. Discrimination against people of color — without exception — was rampant in all parts of the country. The term "dominant white culture" was also not used; indeed, it is still a term not used by most whites. But it adequately describes what was thought to be "at-risk" — what was usually referred to as "the American way of life." White cultural dominance was a given. Whites were the standard-bearers and collectively set the nation's agenda. Yet suddenly, in post-World War II America, white people felt under attack and it all had to do with "civil rights." The world was changing again, as it had 100 years earlier, and many whites were again prepared to resist those changes, violently, when necessary.

The term "riot" has always been synonymous with black people in the nation's white psyche, despite the historical reality that demonstrates just the opposite. "Black riot" became normal nomenclature after WWII. "White riot" would be an oxymoron. In some ways, this was because of television. Prior to the rapid growth of homes with television sets in the 1950s, white people's violence against peoples of color was rarely reported, or if reported would be blamed on others. But white violence against black people had been unrelenting. It had not stopped since the founding of the nation and had continued after the Civil War. Interpretations of white violence often turned reality on its head. For example, the 1873 Colfax, Louisiana riot, when over 150 blacks and three whites were killed in what historians Eric Foner and Nicholas Lemann call the bloodiest battle of the era, was interpreted in a 1950 state highway marker thus: "On this site occurred the Colfax Riot in which three white men and 150 negroes were slain. This event on April 13, 1873 marked the end of carpetbag misrule in the South."[2]

In the notorious "Red Summer" of 1919, blacks across the nation were lynched by the hundreds. In that year and throughout the decade that followed, black communities were ravaged in places like Rosewood, Florida; East St. Louis, Illinois; Elaine, Arkansas; and most notoriously, in the "Black Wall Street" of Tulsa, Oklahoma. Only the black press, both local and national, reported the events.

When veterans of color sought to challenge the continuing race-based laws and customs, they were "dealt with." In 1946, a mob of white men shot and killed two young African American couples near Moore's Ford Bridge in Walton County, Georgia, sixty miles east of Atlanta and lynched four other young sharecroppers, one a World War II veteran. This "shocked" the nation. Although the FBI investigated the crime, they were unable to prosecute.

Detroit would, in many ways, demonstrate most dramatically this nation's post-war racial dynamics. Detroit, with all its possibilities, was the bellwether of America's future, embodying the nation's potential as a society in which all peoples, regardless of color, lived and worked side by side. It was the home of General Motors whose president, Charles Erwin Wilson, believed what was good for General Motors was good for America, and vice versa.

Detroit was to race in the United States what Hollywood was to style and New York to finance — the leading edge. As early as the late 1930s, whites in Detroit had rioted over incursions of black people into white neighborhoods. Neighborhood riots were usually triggered in response to the perceived threat of blacks "taking over." This was especially true anytime a "Negro" family bought a house in a "white" section of town. White Detroit instigated some of the nation's most prolonged and vicious race-rioting throughout pre- and post-WWII America. But they were not called riots. Much of the violence went unreported in the pre-television era. Whites across the country could remain in denial. When word did get out, blacks were usually blamed for instigating "the riot." This type of violence did not bring a nation's censure but served to heighten the anxiety of white people across the country. For white people, a home was not a castle if Negroes can move in down the street.

The now well-known lynching in 1955 of fourteen-year-old Emmett Till exemplified white lawlessness. Till's death at the hands of two white men is well-chronicled. Young Till was only fourteen and his shocking and cold-blooded murder by two working class white men, J. W. Milam and Roy Bryant, occurred in the small town of Money, Mississippi. Bryant and Milam removed him from his grandfather's house in the middle of the night without fear of arrest or retribution. His "crime" was "whistling" at a white woman, Carolyn Bryant, Roy Bryant's wife. Others say he was guilty not of whistling but of "reckless eye-ballin'." "Reckless eye-ballin'" was one of those Black Codes that became the white South's method of enforcing white supremacy after the federal government ended Reconstruction in the South in 1877. "Reckless eye-ballin'" occurred when a black man looked a white woman "face to face" instead of with his head bowed, hat-in-hand, at a distance required by whites. Emmett Till was dead by morning, beaten, shot, and thrown into the Tallahatchie River.

Some argue that blacks should have resisted the violence that rained down on them. Most did in one way or another. But the full force of the state was against them. As evidenced at the trial of Milam and Bryant, when "More than one hundred reporters sat in the segregated courtroom where the sheriff greeted the black press — 'Good morning, N-----s' — and where the defense urged the jury, 'every last Anglo Saxon one of you,' to find the killers not guilty. The jury complied in just over an hour."[3] Even the eyewitness testimony of Emmett Till's grandfather displaying the courage required to testify in court against white men as he aggressively pointed out the murderers of his grandson was for naught. A "colored" man's testimony had no standing against a white person in a Mississippi courtroom. Till's murderers not only went free, but later would have the audacity to sell their account of the murder, in which they admitted killing Emmett Till, to *Look* magazine for $4,000. Milam and Bryant never served a day in jail.

Yet these many examples of white violence against people of color are not part of most school curricula, even today, for fear that describing this nation's brutal treatment of black people might damage the fragile psyche of school children. When in 1975, James Loewen sought to have his award-winning history of Mississippi adopted by the Mississippi State Board of Education, his "radical" textbook (it described some of the white violence in the state's history) was dismissed out of hand. (Loewen later won a First Amendment suit against Mississippi, though the text was never adopted.)

Instead, we are a nation that grows more and more a-historical as the years pass. This failure to educate children — both white children and children of color — about the nation's racial history further isolates whites from people of color and mis-educates everyone at the same time. For children of color not telling the truth leaves them unable to understand and explain the day-to-day discrimination that still occurs. This anger thus turns inward and becomes an internalized rage affecting both their own image of themselves and of others who look like them. White children on the other hand feel no connection to or responsibility for the many manifestations of white racial superiority in US history. If the history books absolve present day whites from any historical culpability in the nation's race-constructed society, cries for legal remedies such as affirmative action, much less reparations, come across as cynical and self-serving on the part of black people.

Most people in the US have little or no knowledge of such events as the destruction of Tulsa's Black Wall Street in 1921 or Emmett Till's lynching in 1955. These "race stories" are confined largely to academic historical records and even then only to certain historians interested in such matters.

Yet they are important historical markers that demonstrate how deeply embedded in the structures of the society is white supremacy. This is not erased just by the passage of time. This is no accident. Key to the internalized sense of superiority of white people is denial of responsibility for any actions against black people or other people of color. When confronted with incontrovertible evidence, powerful whites usually blame the unfortunate events on the thuggery of the lowest element of white people. "Trash," as they were labeled, allowed nice white people to remain blameless, unaware of the bitter edges of race in the US. But, Colfax, Money, Mississippi and Detroit, along with countless other outrages happened with the complicity of people at the highest level of government, media and the public's business interests.

Even today, few white people outside academia and those who might watch some PBS or History Channel documentaries know these historical events that are so seared into the minds of many African Americans and other people of color. Were it not for national black media outlets such as the *Crisis,* published by the NAACP, the *Chicago Defender,* the *Louisiana Weekly,* the *Pittsburgh Courier,* and New York City's *Amsterdam News,* or Los Angeles' Spanish-language press, these tragedies might have been overlooked as insignificant. *Jet* and *Ebony* plus weekly newspapers focused on the black community kept these stories alive. They were seen as unworthy of mention by most white publications. Even the *New York Times* and the *Washington Post* barely mentioned the racial violence sweeping the nation after WWI. In a review of *Life* and the *Saturday Evening Post,* each with millions of subscribers all over the United States during 1919–1921, no mention is made of the day-to-day white violence against communities of color.[4]

The *New York Times* did print an article about a Congressional committee meeting on the "race problem" on October 1, 1919, that called for action to prevent mob mentality. The articles that followed in the *Times* often blamed communists for "inflaming blacks" or for instigating "radical propaganda among Negroes." When it did make a report, the infrequent reporting by the mainstream white press used headlines such as "Race Riot in Texas: Whites Wounded, Retaliate by Burning Homes in Negro Section," or "Service Men Beat Negroes in Race Riot at Capitol: Civilians Join to Avenge Attacks on White Women."

By the time that Watts, a section of Los Angeles heavily populated by blacks, rebelled in 1965, followed by uprisings in Newark, Gary, and Harlem, white Americans could watch such outbreaks live on television and hear reports by trusted newsmen such as Walter Cronkite and Eric Sevareid on CBS and Chet Huntley and David Brinkley on NBC. When Detroit erupted in 1967 and the 101st Airborne was brought in to quell eight days of fighting between black citizens and white police, white Americans equated urban uprisings and race-rioting with black people.

"White race riots" in the minds of most white people was a contradiction in terms.

Chapter 10

Mississippi: Model for White Resistance

My love of history began early. Stories almost always are about history in one way or another. And I grew up in a story-telling family and culture. Whether on the front porch at the Homestead in McComb or in the living room in Helena, everything was woven around a tale or remembrance of some sort. Everything I knew about family, the war, sports, especially college football, was put in a context of history and within history, race. It was never called history. It was just how people talked and told the same stories again and again, so that family lore was a historical framework through which I learned about race and when I learned to put a name to it, the white race and "colored people." It was white and colored in Mississippi, Tennessee, and Arkansas. Mississippi was always my reference point, although I would spend more years in Helena, Arkansas, than I would in McComb, Mississippi. We were Mississippians in my mind. We lived in Arkansas.

I was raised on Ole Miss football. I knew all the great Rebels from Chunkin' Charlie Conerly and Eagle Day in the 1940s and early '50s to the great Ole Miss teams of the late '50s and early '60s. But, it was more than football to us. It was the clash of cultures that was played out on the football field. It was not so much what other Southern football team we were playing. We were competing against an ideology. We were fighting forces that we were taught were out to change our way of life, our culture. Sometimes this opposing force was referred to as the "Yankees," other times as the "North." Still in other situations it was "the government." But it was always about race. This was the threat to us. Whether Yankees, the North or the government, it was always about race and the destruction of a way of being that was near and dear to us.

On September 30, 1962, my father and I drove from Helena to Jackson to a football game of the Ole Miss Rebels. The stadium was packed and electric with a frenzy that was part pep rally and part call to arms. I was sixteen. I remember my father, normally a quiet man, reserved and courtly in demeanor, bolting from his seat at the kickoff, hollering, whistling "Go rebels!" I had never seen this side of him. I didn't know whether to be scared or just shocked, but I knew I liked it. At half-time with Ole Miss leading 7 to 0, the Governor of the State of Mississippi, Ross Barnett, spoke to the near-hysterical fans and opened his remarks with a long, drawn-out, Southern drawl of defiance: "I Love Mississippi!" He said it three times and each time the crescendo built on itself to the point of mob ecstasy. Barnett didn't have to say more, although he did. Everybody in the stadium, including the handful of blacks employed to clean it after the game, knew what he was saying. It was an anthem as clear in 1962 as it had been in 1862: Defend the homeland by any means necessary. Mississippi would fight. White Mississippi would draw a line in the sand. Regardless of what anyone else would do, White Mississippi would resist — integration, race-mingling, federal control of our institutions, and Yankee-cultural values and ways of being. The governor concluded this church-type religious, sexually-charged exercise in group psychology by leading us in a call and response: "I'm from Mississippi, born and bred, and when I die, I'll be Mississippi Dead," and again, three times, "I'm from Mississippi..."

It was as mesmerizing as it was scary.

Barnett was literally rallying the troops. James Meredith was to integrate Ole Miss the next day. The date had been set for October 1st. The football game, as important as it was, was a mere tactic in a much larger strategy of resistance. It was important for Ole Miss to be the national champion just as it was important for Mississippi to have crowned two consecutive Miss Americas, Mary Ann Mobley in 1959 and Linda Lee Mead in 1960. Mississippi represented the South at its full flower on the battlefields of football glory and in the beauty of white Southern womanhood.

Violence by white people toward peoples of color has persisted throughout American history. Yet far more pervasive and systemic in nature have been the everyday restrictions and humiliations of people of color. After WWII, everywhere and everyday there were reminders of whose country this was. Whites did not want people of color, especially blacks, to live near them, shop near them, worship near them, swim in their pools and certainly not go to school with them. Most whites feared that social proximity and interaction would eventually lead to intermarriage and "mongrelization" of the white race. It was the same everywhere. Integrated housing was rare. Only larger cities would have some areas of town where blacks and working class or poor white — usually newly arrived white ethnics — lived in proximity to each other. This was usually by economic necessity, not by choice among even the poorest white people.

This fear of blackness is ingrained, psychologically-speaking, in whites' racial DNA.

The late Dr. Frances Cress Welsing calls this phobia "the fear of racial genetic annihilation." She says that since whites have historically made up a tiny fraction of the world's overall population, and since the genetic variation of whiteness is a recessive quality (as opposed to the dominant genetic trait of color), instilling the dominance of superiority/inferiority is a genetic survival mechanism that is deeply ingrained over the course of the millennia. Racism, Welsing concludes, is a behavioral system for the survival of a white people.[1] The threat to white purity — whether or not one accepts it as biologically engendered — created an interesting psychological conundrum: Whites who so believed in their moral and intellectual superiority feared intermarriage. If, in fact, it was unnatural and repugnant to even think of equality among blacks and whites, why was intermarriage so feared by white people? One never hears a similar fear from black people either when looking backward to "the old days" or in the literature. It appears to have been the farthest thing from black people's minds! Yet in October, 1963 a *Newsweek* poll conducted by Louis Harris Corp, 90% of white people (97% in the South) said intermarriage was their biggest fear of integration. In an accompanying article in that same issue experts cited a loss of racial purity and a sexual anxiety growing out of the stereotypes of African Americans as oversexed.

Obsessed by race, white communities North and South, rural and urban, sought every means to maintain our own US version of apartheid and keep people of color isolated and separate. One of the most effective strategies to maintain de facto segregation was the use of the ruse of "local option." It manifested itself in the debate over who was "white."

The 1896 Supreme Court *Plessy v. Ferguson* ruling had affirmed legalized segregation. The question, for the next sixty years was, "Who was white?" What about all those people of color who were not Negro? Could white people legally provide separate services to Chinese and Japanese persons as long as those services were "equal?" "Separate but equal" was interpreted in many different ways until the 1927 case of *Gong Lum v. Rice.* Gong Lum was a Chinese immigrant living in Mississippi who sued for the right to send his American-born daughter to the local white school. Gong Lum argued that there was no other school to send her to because no Asian school existed. Both Mississippi and the Supreme Court rejected this argument, saying because she is not white, she must attend the "colored" school. The court also said that because *Plessey v. Ferguson* had established "separate but equal" as constitutional and applicable to all races, state and local authorities had the right to determine who is white and what white meant.

For many areas, determining who was white came down to numbers. California, for example, separated all peoples of color from whites except Mexican Americans who were considered white. In Seattle, both before and after WWII, Japanese Americans attended predominantly white schools. Chinese were few in number in many cities, so they constituted no "threat" and were frequently allowed in the white schools. If the local white populace took a hard line they might require them to attend the colored school. The same held true for Indian children living in urban areas where there was no "Indian school." In Dulac, Louisiana, the Houma people were not recognized by the federal government as a "tribe," yet they were denied admission to the local white schools. The Houma did not attend school until religious groups created "mission schools" especially for them.

Such local option prevailed until the 1954 *Brown* decision reversed *Plessy v. Ferguson,* ruling "separate is inherently unequal." Yet despite that ruling, "local option" remained in place. This right of states and locales to determine who was white served as the cornerstone of Southern white resistance to racial integration for the next twenty years. Less than a decade after the "War to Save Democracy," the white South resisted integration in large measure by stretching out compliance with the law. By forcing the federal government to go to court, district by district, across the South, the Southern strategy was to exhaust the government and the courts. In so doing Southerners hoped that the increased cost of litigation and enforcement would test the nation's resolve and ultimately, its commitment to desegregate.

The 1957 Battle of Little Rock was emblematic of the white resistance that would continue for decades. The Little Rock crisis arose when the federal courts ordered the integration of all-white Central High School. It was the first major test of the federal government's resolve. President Eisenhower was reluctant to get involved. Ike was neither pro-integration nor anti-integration, he said. Regardless of this public fence-sitting, those close to Eisenhower said he did not favor shoving integration down white people's throats. Nonetheless, under pressure to enforce the court's decision, he mobilized the National Guard to ensure that law and order was maintained.

In October 1962, white rioting reached a zenith with James Meredith's entrance into the University of Mississippi. Already, white mob violence was growing. White mobs hit and spit at black children as they enrolled in Little Rock's Central High School in 1957 and in New Orleans public elementary schools in 1961. When James Meredith attempted to register as a student at Ole Miss in 1962, riots broke out on the campus with whites marauding, damaging state and university property with impunity, burning cars and threatening the safety of anyone, white or black, entering the campus. The Governor of Mississippi, Ross Barnett, attempted to block Meredith's entrance, passing a law that "prohibited any person who was convicted of a state crime from admission to a state school." This law was directed at Meredith, who had been convicted of "false voter registration."

To put down the violence, Governor Barnett insisted that the US Army be brought in as a show of overwhelming force. Otherwise, Barnett said to then US Attorney General Robert Kennedy, the white citizenry of the state would feel he had caved in too easily to the federal takeover of the school. Barnett told Kennedy that he could only submit to the overwhelming force and prestige of the US Army. Otherwise, he would be expected to fight on by his white constituents. At one point in the negotiations, Gov. Barnett agreed to James Meredith's registration on the condition that his picture be shown with US Marshalls aiming their guns at him.

In Mississippi, mobilizing the National Guard further enraged the whites who were rioting against James Meredith in the first place. The Mississippi National Guard in 1962 was an all-white defense force, dedicated to the preservation of state-sanctioned white supremacy. When nationalized, some of the same men who had been rioting went home, put on their uniforms and returned to Ole Miss to protect James Meredith. At least that is what one heard.

Even as federal marshals were escorting James Meredith to the registration office at Ole Miss, Mississippi's white supremacist legislature was taking action to preserve its sanctity. On October 3rd, the Mississippi House of Representatives passed Resolution 18, which proclaimed, "Each and every act...of the sovereign state of Mississippi...has been legal," and "Each and every act of the Attorney General and the President of the United States has been illegal."

The riot at Ole Miss was happening at the same time as the tense standoff between President John F. Kennedy and Russian Premier Nikita Khrushchev over nuclear missiles placed in Cuba and aimed at the United States. To most Mississippians at the time, the Siege of Oxford was far more compelling.

The State of Mississippi was still in full revolt after the federal forces made the state temporarily relent. It had lost the "Battle of Oxford" but not before its intransigence and devotion to white supremacy had held off federal efforts to desegregate the university for more than a year. The final battle was one of the bloodiest head-on fights the US Army had encountered since Korea. Although the official death toll was two, including a French photographer, no one really knows how many people were killed and who did the killings. But we do know this: No one was ever tried much less convicted of killing anyone.

Professors and administrators, protesting "intellectual straight-jacketing," left Ole Miss in droves after the "Battle." History professor James Silver, who had coined the term the "closed society," was targeted. Speakers were screened for their views on integration. The campus director of religious life, Will Campbell, was forced to leave. His so-called crime? He played host to a black journalist.[2]

The State had seriously considered closing the school. Statewide opinion polls had indicated overwhelming support for closure. Accrediting agencies considered yanking Ole Miss' accreditation. Only promises to do better to safeguard academic freedoms staved off action. The administration at the university had been stripped of any power or authority during the months prior to Meredith gaining entrance. They were cowed by the some of the most virulent racist demagogues in the nation's history.

Chapter 11

Preparing for the Civil Rights Movement

It was never brought to my attention by any history instructor I encountered, whether in high school or in the university setting, that Reconstruction had to do with fundamental restructuring of the nation. No one brought to my attention that the Thirteenth Amendment did not completely outlaw slavery in the US but allowed it as punishment for a felony conviction by the criminal justice system. In my history books, Reconstruction was treated as an aberration — a revenge strategy taken out on the South by a gloating North.

Reconstruction, as I learned it, was a period in which dignified white Southern leadership was forced to submit to the excesses of the victorious North carried out and exploited by notorious opportunists whom we called "carpetbaggers" together with Southern traitors called "scalawags." This was typical of the type of education I received, especially my history lessons. I know now that my teachers were under severe restraints. They had to be careful in everything they said. A teacher would lose her or his job in a minute if she was perceived as "teaching civil rights."

My history teacher in tenth-grade American history, Harold Porter, had been my sister's high school principal. She knew him as a rather gruff by-the-rules type. By the time I knew him, he was no longer principal, but my American history teacher. He was no longer so gruff and had a sort of avuncular, storyteller persona who taught daily from a text edited by Columbia University historian David S. Muzzey.

"Get your Muzzey out," would greet us third period every day. "What does your Muzzey say?" Mr. Porter would shout. It almost sounded dirty to 1960s teenagers. Mr. Porter had a coconut hanging from the chalk board and students dec-

orated it over time with a beret and a cigarette so the coconut looked like a brown-skinned jazz musician or be-bop artist. The coconut was the closest we got to class-room integration in the years I attended school in Helena.

If you messed up in class or on a test, "Muzzey" would get you. Muzzey is what we called Mr. Porter. Detention was "the meeting of the coconut." Muzzey was great. I loved history class. It was all about white people. Then again, that was all I knew. My world was all about white people. Civil rights was bustin' out all over, but to me, civil rights was a television show. It came on at 6:00 o'clock every night. It was called the evening news. You could shout at it or turn it off. Like Muzzey and the coconut.

Vera Miller was the finest teacher I ever had. She was Jewish. She was strong, outspoken and loud. Nothing about her was demure or genteel in the traditional white Southern manner of doing things. Mrs. Miller was my eleventh grade English teacher, but I had known her only as the mother of a friend with whom I played Babe Ruth League baseball. She would yell from the top of the bleachers cursing at the umpire and imploring me and others on the team to get off our rear ends and make something happen — get a hit or strike out someone. I could not imagine "Sarge," as we called her, teaching English. But she did. Oh, how she did.

Vera Miller knew her constraints. She had to be careful. It was only fifteen years or so from the death camps in Hitler's Europe. Civil rights was similar in ways we did not understand. Civil rights was never spoken of without preceding it with a Goddamn or, maybe if you were real religious, just a damn. She knew. We didn't.

Mrs. Miller was relentless. She did not suffer fools gladly. She had the habit of pushing her long, pointed, well-manicured fingernails into my scalp (and others') saying "THINK. THINK." She would stride into class and without a word write "HATE" on the board. Then she would order us: "WRITE." What did I do? I THOUGHT and I WROTE. Today, I might call 911 on her. I will never forget Vera Miller. Master Teacher.

History in the United States is broken into eras and sometimes a stand-alone decade. This causes a fragmented view of the world and hides the impact of history on our own lives. The Civil Rights Movement was not something that had a beginning and an end to it, yet in the US we confine it to a particular period in the nation's history, approximately 1954 – 1968. One could argue that the freedom movement began when the first African was kidnapped and transported by force to the Americas. Similarly, the resistance of Native Americans also began with the arrival of the first Europeans. The Puerto Rican Independence Movement began in 1898 when Puerto Ricans were traded like baseball cards in the treaty that ended the Spanish-American War. None really began or ended with dates.

The moral fiber of the nation is best understood in the lives of persons called "abolitionist," "runaway," "rebellious slave," "suffragist," "warrior." In the twentieth century they were called "labor organizer," "outside agitator," "feminist," "womanist," "civil rights worker," "liberation theologian," "community organizer." These are the individuals who stood, sometimes unknowingly, against the race construct and for a nation built on equity among peoples and against white supremacy. These are the people who asked, "Why are people poor?" and "Where do we go from here?"

The Civil Rights Movement succeeded because it was a movement steeped in the history of a people — people who had a sense that an historical moment was at hand. Over the years 1954 – 1968, this movement was built by ever-widening constituencies whose sense of possibility spread among peoples and groups like few times in the nation's history.

The Civil Rights Movement rivaled the Revolutionary War and Civil War as an era of profound change in America. The tentative and private opposition to slavery shared by several Founding Fathers such as John Adams, his wife, Abigail and son, John Quincy Adams (who in 1820 wrote in his diary that slavery was "the great and foul stain upon the North American Union") grew into a roar of opposition among abolitionists like William Lloyd Garrison and the South Carolina-born Grimke sisters. Later still, Radical Republicans such as Congressman Thaddeus Stevens added his passionate opposition to slavery to the Movement's rich heritage. President Abraham Lincoln had his moments of fierce resistance to the enslavement of African Americans. He stirred the country's freedom flames with his eloquent Gettysburg Address and later the powerful and liberatory Emancipation Proclamation.

Civil rights leaders took organizing lessons from the abolition movement and certainly from the labor movement. In addition they were inspired by Ida B. Wells' campaign against lynching from the 1890s through the 1920s. Wells' movement gained stature and strength as it was publicized through NAACP editorials in the *Crisis*.

Groups such as the Southern Leadership Council (SLC), the Southern Council on Human Welfare (SCHW), The Women's International League for Peace and Freedom (WILPF), the War Resisters League (WRL), the Southern Conference Educational Fund (SCEF) and the Christian Student Movement (CSM) all preceded the Civil Rights Movement period and gave the movement its roots. The peace organization, Fellowship of Reconciliation (FOR), founded in 1915 in the United States by sixty-eight pacifists, including Norman Thomas, A. J. Muste, and Jane Addams, would in 1941 inspire James Farmer, George Houser and others to organize the Congress of Racial Equality (CORE) to apply FOR principles of nonviolent resistance to Southern Jim Crow. Farmer, Houser and Bayard Rustin were notable figures prior to 1954 and remained so throughout their lives. In fact, Rustin and Houser organized the Journey of Reconciliation in 1947, the first of the Freedom Rides to test the ruling of the Supreme Court of the United States that banned racial discrimination in interstate travel. Farmer would help organize not only CORE, but also the 1964 Freedom Summer. He was the only one among the Freedom Riders to be present at both the FOR/CORE freedom rides in 1948 and the SNCC-led rides of 1962. George Houser, who died in 2015, had been as politically active in his nineties as he had been his entire life. Houser spanned the eras of the social justice struggle in the United States and also world-wide. He was a leading figure in the international efforts to free South African liberator, Nelson Mandela, after 27 years in prison on Robbins Island, just as he has been an active opponent of capital punishment and a war resister in every US military action since the end of WWII.

Like Houser, Dorothy Height moved with great skill through the movements of the twentieth century. For over forty years she was President of the National Council of Negro Women and was on stage and spoke at the March on Washington in 1963. Height was an advisor to Democratic Presidents Roosevelt, Truman, Kennedy, Johnson, Carter and Clinton. She was a confidante of Eleanor Roosevelt and an advocate for the doomed Equal Rights Amendment to the Constitution. She was active in the causes she held dear until her death in 2010. She was ninety-eight years old.

All white-led organizations like the Southern Council on Human Welfare (SCHW) and Southern Conference Educational Fund (SCEF) would be painted with the communist brush and hounded out of existence or find themselves severely compromised by the 1960s. The Women's International League for Peace and Freedom (WILPF) and the War Resisters League (WRL) struggle on, holding strong after almost a century of liberation work. Jim Dombrowski, joined by Carl and Anne Braden in 1956, would lend their organizing genius to the cause as long as they lived. Dombrowski, a Methodist minister, had been active in justice causes since the 1930s. He was a co-founder of SCHW and later the Highlander Folk School along with Myles Horton, his wife Ziphia, and Don West. Because of his activism, he was a primary target of the House Un-American Activities Committee (HUAC) in the South. While his name has not remained as recognizable as some others, the organizations he led made vital contributions to the Civil Rights Movement.

Carl Braden is another name that gets lost. Although he was eclipsed by his wife Anne's fame and longevity (Anne outlived Carl by more than thirty years) Anne always made clear: "We were a team." The Bradens were seen as such by the movement leaders. In 1954 the two were tried for sedition by the State of Kentucky in the aftermath of selling a house to friends of theirs, a black couple named Andrew and Charlotte Wade, just one day after they bought it. The Bradens and the Wades saw this sale as a tactic to circumvent Louisville's segregated housing patterns. What began as a private stance against segregation soon exploded into a local firestorm as whites living in the neighborhood reacted violently. After months of antagonism and vitriol aimed at the Wades, complete with nightly drive-bys and phone threats, the house was dynamited and destroyed beyond immediate repair. The Bradens were similarly threatened and ostracized by the white community. Louisville District Attorney, Scott Hamilton, took the tack that the Bradens were communists and sold the house to the Wades not as a stand against the injustice of segregation, but to foment hostility between the races. This, he claimed, was a well-known strategy of communists. Hamilton charged this constituted an attempt to undermine the laws of the State of Kentucky and thus violated the State Sedition Acts then in force. Carl Braden, a Louisville native and father of three young children, was convicted and sentenced to fifteen years in state prison. The trial lasted almost two weeks. Carl was released on bond after seven months and determined to appeal his conviction, which had become a national cause célèbre among progressives. Anne Braden was also charged but never tried. The United States Supreme Court invalidated state sedition statutes in April 1956. The case was over. The fight against white supremacy continued.

Ella Baker was a key figure who spanned both the pre-war social justice movements of the North and the post-war Civil Rights Movement in the South. Baker impacted the growth of the NAACP as the Director of Field Services from 1940 through 1946. Prior to her work with NAACP, she had been active in New York City black radical movements since the 1930s. Baker personified the relational model of community organizing through her travels, often under cloak of night, to the most remote hamlets of the segregated South, signing up members for the NAACP and preparing local leaders for the upcoming civil rights struggles. Never someone to stand out or require attention, she had a special affinity for young organizers and was one of the few "elders" that the young guns of SNCC and CORE always wanted at the center of their planning strategies. She is today recognized, if somewhat belatedly, as a "Master Teacher" and icon of the freedom struggle. She belongs in a select circle of black liberation leaders in the US that includes nineteenth century visionaries like Turner, Tubman and Douglass; early twentieth century leaders like Garvey, Du Bois, Wells and Bethune; and civil rights giants such as Marshall, Lillian Smith, King, Hamer and Malcolm X.

CHAPTER 12

Civil Rights Organizing North and South

The first time I went north of Memphis, Tennessee was in the spring of 1965. I was nineteen years old. I flew to New York City to be interviewed for a summer internship with Lafayette Avenue Presbyterian Church. The church was in the Fort Greene section of Brooklyn. Again, it was my friend Nibs Stroupe who arranged the interview. I was somewhat nervous, but mostly I was excited about the prospect of living in New York and being a part of this church's outreach program to the youth in Fort Greene. The youth were all black and the church was all white. Segregated churches were nothing new to me, but reaching out to the black community definitely was new. In my experience in the South the races, especially black and white people, rarely mingled, much less worked or played together.

The summer staff at Lafayette Avenue Presbyterian was comprised of at least one young person from each state where possible. Nibs and I were from Arkansas. The other kids were from all over the US. I was intimidated by the prospect of working with young people "from the North." To me, anyone not from the South was from the North. The group was mostly white, but not altogether. Another first for me, working with black people as peers, that is: black people not given to be subservient to whites. I was in another world and I liked it. I was assigned to Fort Greene Park about three blocks from the church. I was given a baseball, a bat, and a glove and told to "go for it" or something like that. Later I would call that experience my first taste of community organizing. I went to the park, sat on a bench with my ball and bat and let young people come to me. They did. For most of the summer, I had fifty or so kids, ages twelve to fifteen and it became not work at all for me, but playing ball just as I did back home. I learned a lot that summer. Some of the older kids would point out youth who were part of gangs and explain to me why this was true. I remember one older girl telling me that gangs were becoming passé. When I asked why, she said "because of continental clothes." They were all the rage and teenagers did not want their clothes "messed up." Who knows if this was true, but I never forgot her telling me this. These kids were not much younger than me. They were, however, much more sophisticated. They were urban where I was from a small town. Many, I learned, had never been outside of Brooklyn. I noticed that I was freer to move around than they were. I was nervous, but never scared or intimidated. I had been taught to be afraid of black people who looked you in the eye and were not subservient to whites. My fears were unfounded and another myth of white supremacy was proved false. My Aunt Peggy called upon a Presbyterian magazine editor with whom she was friendly to write an article about me. She did. For the first time I was recognized and put on the cover. I was named and singled out. The other kids in the park were not. No surprise there, looking back.

I enjoyed tremendously Bible study which happened each morning before we went out to our assignments. I had never heard the Bible taught as the Rev. George Knight taught it. He called it exegesis, a term with which I was not familiar. It had to do with "unpacking" the Christian scriptures and reading them within the cultural context in which they were written. I ate it up. I couldn't wait for Bible study. I don't know if other kids liked it as much as I did, but like it I did and I assumed Nibs did. Bible study is something I grew up with, but I had never heard the Bible taught from a social justice perspective. For me it was always used to justify segregation. I loved this new approach and so I would for the rest of my life. That first summer in Brooklyn was so transforming for me, I went back the summer of 1966. At LAPC, as we called the church, I saw for the first time blacks and whites working together. My outlook on the world was changing. I owed it to Nibs, George Knight and New York City.

The Southern Civil Rights Movement owed much to Northern organizing efforts in cities such as New York City, Washington, DC and Detroit, which went back decades. New York City was not the liberal oasis that many white progressives purported it to be. De facto segregation existed throughout the city's five boroughs and was rigidly enforced. Despite the iconic status of the Harlem Renaissance and the fame of many of its artists, musicians and athletes, New York was unfriendly territory for blacks. Real estate practices pushed most African Americans and Puerto Ricans into wretched living conditions in burgeoning ghettos in Harlem, East New York/Brownsville, the Lower East Side and the section of town that came to be called El Barrio on the East Side of Manhattan. Wall Street did not hire black brokers and Manhattan hotels turned away celebrities such as Duke Ellington and Count Basie. Even Harlem's famed Cotton Club served an all-white clientele.

Civil rights leaders were acutely aware of the emerging radical and pan-African ferment in the North. New York was the base for many such militant groups and organizations. Progressive Labor, the Communist Party, USA and the Socialist Workers Party members mingled with — and struggled with — internationalists representing newly-liberated nations from the Caribbean, Africa, Asia, and the Middle East. Groups like the Black Popular Front brought organizers together in New York representing a wide variety of philosophies and strategies for change, from neighborhood clubs to the Garvey movement to the Nation of Islam. This radical ferment, beckoning people from all over the world to the home of the United Nations, was reported by newspapers and other media and then disseminated widely, including in the southern United States. While Southern civil rights leaders often appeared less willing to directly confront white supremacy, they were acutely aware of their situation and were greatly influenced by liberationist rhetoric.

Washington, DC, a heavily black city with little statutory authority to govern itself was as segregated as any Southern city. Black slave labor largely built the Nation's Capitol. Activist Randall Robinson, visiting the White House in 2000 with his young son, was stunned:

> To erect the building that would house the art that symbolized American democracy, the United States government sent out a request for one hundred slaves....In exchange for the slaves' labor the government agreed to pay their owners five dollars per month per slave...[1]

Since the nation's founding African Americans had flocked to Washington, DC, for nowhere else did the country's promised freedoms shine brighter. After the Civil War, freed blacks by the tens of thousands were drawn to it because it symbolized the ideals of the democracy. But the reality of life there was far different. Blacks in Washington,

DC were pushed to some of the nation's worst slums; jobs were restricted, except for artisans of the building trades, to the most menial and low-paying vocations. The most prestigious jobs for blacks were at the White House where, over time, descendants of the enslaved Africans who served the founders of the republic became the elite of black Washington society. Black residents were reminded daily of America's version of apartheid. Even local ordinances were subject to Congressional approval. Segregation was as severe as it was in Birmingham or Jackson. All the more shameful today, Washington DC retains a mere set-aside status for its black citizens, its sole Representative a non-voting member of Congress. It exists as a promise unfulfilled, a monument to the enduring nature of the race construct.

Detroit was freedom central for many Southern blacks leaving the cotton fields by the millions to work in the nation's fledgling automobile industry from the 1930s through the early 1960s. It was a city of great promise and brutal race relations. Even the United Auto Workers, one of the nation's most progressive unions, could not produce a quality of life free of discrimination and segregation for its black members. As Detroit became home for nearly one million blacks, whites fled the city. What was once the nation's fifth largest city in the 1950s, with a population of 1.8 million, would by the beginning of the twenty-first century have a population half that size.

Because of the strength of the unions in Detroit, wages and benefits for black workers were among the highest in the nation. Within only a few years a thriving black culture began to develop. The music industry rivaled its counterparts in Nashville and New York, but Barry Gordy's musical empire, Motown by name, was more than a genre; it was the soundtrack for the Civil Rights Movement. Artists too numerous to mention would sing the songs that the nation danced to whether black, white or brown. Smokey Robinson and the Miracles, Diana Ross and the Supremes, Marvin Gaye, Lil' Stevie Wonder, the Temptations, Al Green, and Sam Cook, would all record for Motown and Movement victories would be accompanied by a beat and tempo like none before. Motown, along with its southern cousin in Memphis, Stax Records, composed the musical score of the Movement.

But Detroit was also ugly. It was bitterly segregated and most blacks lived under conditions of poverty that rivaled any city in the nation. Black-owned businesses were few. Opportunities outside the automobile industry were limited. The white automobile companies did not hire blacks as executives or even middle management except in rare instances. Even the unions placed blacks in the most dangerous, lowest paying jobs, and only those entry level positions at the lowest rung of the ladder. While blacks would eventually climb that ladder, it was never easy and never facilitated. It was grit and grime for all workers. It was grittier and grimier for blacks. For example,

> At the Dodge assembly plant, black workers constituted an estimated 60 percent of the work force, and virtually all were in low skilled and semi-skilled positions . . . Black workers were almost invariably assigned to the most onerous and lowest paying jobs. Generally, as the proportion of black workers grew in the factory, the working conditions tended to deteriorate. Tasks that had been performed by two white workers were assigned to one black worker. Black workers characterized this as n-----mation.[2]

The white working class of Detroit was less than a generation old. Many white Detroiters migrated north from the Appalachian Mountains and the West Virginia hills. White Detroiters were often formerly poor sharecroppers who had never lived in an urban area, never made wages enough to live on, did not know what a union was or an employee benefit, and, of course, had rarely known black people. As a result of union wages and structural access because of their race, whites in Detroit began to own their own homes for the first time. They were ripe for exploitation bred of race privilege. Neighborhoods built as white working class enclaves were tinder boxes set to explode with even the slightest threat of a black family buying a house on their block. On more than one occasion during the 1930s through the early 1950s, Detroit whites rioted against blacks. For example, Wilkerson describes the riot of June, 1943:

> One of the worst riots ever seen in the United States, an outbreak that would mark a turning point in American race relations. . . This was the first major riot in which blacks fought back as earnestly as the whites and in which black residents, having become established in the city but still relegated to run-down ghettos, began attacking and looting perceived symbols of exploitation, the stores and laundries run by whites and other outsiders that blacks felt were cheating them. It was only after Detroit that riots became known as primarily urban phenomena, ultimately centered on inner-city blacks venting their frustrations on the ghettos that confined them.[3]

Detroit was race. Detroit is race.

Chapter 13

The "Big One": *Brown v. Board*

In McComb and later in Helena we ridiculed everything about blacks. We thought only Negroes put mud flaps on cars and painted them in bold colors even when the cars were old and rundown. Anytime one of us would wear a brightly colored shirt or sweater, inevitably one of my cohorts would ask, as an awkward conversation starter, "What N----- did you steal that shirt from?" "What N----- sold you that suit?" On and on. Black preachers drove old Cadillacs and black women wore outlandish hats. It was N----- this and N----- that and any conversation from the mid-fifties onward that went beyond family and things close to home would get around to the federal government and civil rights and black people in general. "A good white man could whip ten colored men," I would hear from an uncle or my father while watching boxing on television. Even then, as a young one of nine or ten, the declaration seemed ludicrous. Seemed to me, some colored boxer was always kicking some white man's butt. But I stayed silent. By the time I was twelve, I was questioning some things. At least in my mind I was. A lot of these things had to do with religion. I would ask my mother, "How come the Bible says Jesus says we should love our neighbors, but we don't let Negroes come to our church?"

Give my mother credit, she always answered in a sort of abstract manner, employing a Socratic method. "What do you think?" she would ask me. "I think it is wrong," I would say. She would reply, "Well, sometimes people just can't do what Jesus says. They're not ready." She never defended it. Just tried to give some explanation for it, leaving an opening for me to take, if I chose to later. My mother was like a second string quarterback. She did not start the game, but she was on the sideline waiting, teaching me the game, just in case I was chosen to play someday.

I probably would have continued being a stereotypical white Southern boy but for the presence of certain people in my life. Nibs Stroupe was one of them. He was my best friend and although not family, he was a constant presence in my growing-up years in Helena, Arkansas. Nibs and I were the same age and we were in the same class at school. We played Little League and Babe Ruth League baseball together and together we both pledged the same high school fraternity. Both of us went to Arkansas Boys State. He ran with the same crowd as I did. He was a Christian and later went into the ministry, same as I did.

But Nibs was different. His father was not around and I did not understand a mother and son by themselves. He had no sisters or brothers. I did not understand that either. I had three sisters. I thought everybody had brothers and sisters. But, most of all, Nibs was smart. I mean real smart. He was savvy too, about as savvy as one could be from Helena at the time.

Nibs was the first person I knew who liked jazz. I didn't like jazz. It was mysterious to me. I couldn't understand it with everyone playing different things all at once, or so it seemed to me. Besides, I thought jazz had no lyrics. There were no stories being told about breaking up and hard work, hard drinking and going to jail like the stories in the country music that was played in my house. To me, jazz didn't have the same beat as rock and roll. Nibs, without ever saying it, convinced me that sophisticated people liked jazz. I kept that to myself and later I would say I liked jazz when I never really did. Nibs liked Ray Charles. Not just the Ray Charles that sang "Whadda You Say" and "Hit the Road, Jack" but the Ray Charles who sang jazz standards. I remember him showing me the album cover and thinking "Wow, Ray Charles is a jazz player!" The cover shocked me. But, I didn't say anything.

I wanted to be like Nibs. Not as smart because that was impossible, but like him. I wanted to know things like jazz music and later what I came to understand is theology. Nibs and I were both religious. Not like everybody else, but like theologians were religious. We once floated out in a boat at Moon Lake near Helena and became immersed in a discussion of "the messianic consciousness of Christ," attempting to discern the very moment Jesus realized his divinity. My Baptist preacher shooed us away with an admonition to go play outside when we tried to engage him in the discussion. Nibs' Presbyterian preacher was away when we went to his office. It probably was just as well.

Most of all, Nibs was for "civil rights." This was the big "no-no" in my life. I think I knew white people could be for civil rights. I might have understood by the time I was in my early teens that two members of my own family were "for civil rights." But it was never said outright and never discussed. Nibs was different. He spoke about it and into my life came a dawning that would shape me from that moment. I would watch what he read and I would read it. I would listen to what he said and I would say it — only to myself, not aloud. Nibs pointed out to me that our school was segregated, so was Little League baseball, so were our churches. I didn't know it could be any other way.

Nibs said it could be different. That was what being "for civil rights" meant.

The movement that had its roots in the abolitionist period and slave revolts of a century earlier and in the early twentieth century peace and racial justice movements was poised by 1954 to move on the nation's race construct. It required a combined and coordinated effort by ministers, attorneys, congressional officials, the courts, labor leaders, community organizers, students, philanthropists, artists, entertainers, athletes, journalists, and hundreds of thousands of everyday men and women across regional and racial lines. It was the most successful assault on white supremacy since the Civil War.

The National Association for the Advancement of Colored People — the NAACP — under its courageous leaders, W. E. B. Du Bois and Walter White, would take the national lead. Founded in 1909 during a period of government-sanctioned lynching and white racial rioting and lawlessness, this extraordinary organization depended largely on white resources for financial support in its early years. The NAACP gained support from the Howard University School of Law, founded in 1869 to train lawyers committed to helping black Americans secure and protect their newly established rights. Charles Hamilton Houston, Dean of Howard's School of Law, organized the NAACP legal department in the 1930s to challenge Jim Crow. By 1939, the department had been spun-off as the NAACP Legal Defense and Educational Fund, Inc., or simply LDF. LDF produced some of the greatest lawyers in US history, notably Thurgood Marshall, Jack Greenberg, Constance Baker-Motley, Robert Carter and William Hastie. Charles Hamilton

Houston and his cadre of Howard/LDF lawyers played a role in nearly every civil rights case before the Supreme Court between 1930 and *Brown* (1954). Ella Josephine Baker, who joined the NAACP staff in 1938 and served as director of branches from 1943 to 1946, mentored the student movement leaders throughout the 1950s and 1960s.[1]

All of the years of organizing against "separate but equal" and segregation in general foreshadowed "the movement that sprang up overnight." The NAACP Legal Defense Fund had been "whittling away at state-mandated segregation" in schools throughout the '30s and '40s.[2] By 1946, NAACP national membership was over 600,000, with growing numbers of chapters throughout the South despite enormous white resistance. So frightening was an organized black South to the white Southern psyche that several states sought to have the NAACP banned. Patricia Sullivan, in her history of the NAACP, writes:

> Five states required the NAACP to register and provide membership lists. The refusal of the NAACP to abide by a court order to turn over membership lists in Alabama led to the banning of the association from Alabama for nearly a decade...The NAACP was also banned from Arkansas and Texas for a period of time...[3]

It almost didn't happen. Overturning "separate but equal" was a daunting task. It was unexpectedly aided by the newly appointed Supreme Court Chief Justice, Earl Warren. After Chief Justice Vinson died in 1953, President Eisenhower appointed the Republican ex-Governor of California. Warren was viewed both by Eisenhower and political observers as a conservative choice. He was expected by most to vote against *Brown*. Warren's Republican credentials were impeccable. While governor of California, he had taken an active role in formulating the WWII Japanese internment policies. Warren had also been staunchly pro-business and anti-labor unions throughout his early career. As Attorney General of California, he had been considered fair-minded but deeply anti-communist. He had criticized California Governor Culbert Olson for pandering to labor by releasing "politically powerful communist radicals." Olson had supported paroles of labor leaders, including Tom Mooney, an avowed socialist and leader of San Francisco's Local 164 of the International Molders' Union, who had been convicted of a fatal bombing although numerous witnesses placed him and his co-defendant Warren Billings (no kin) miles away from the scene of the crime. Tom Mooney had become a rallying point for labor in the twenty-two years since his conviction. Olson pardoned Mooney in one of his first acts as Governor. Warren was furious. As a member of the Pardon Advisory Board, he refused to grant clemency to Mooney's co-defendant, Billings.

As Chief Justice, however, Warren quickly understood the momentous impact the *Brown* decision would have on the nation's racial construct. He felt strongly that the decision needed to be unanimous so that the court could speak with one voice. He was also considerably persuaded by the NAACP lawyers to the fundamental anti-constitutionality of *Plessy v. Ferguson.* Once seated as Chief Justice, Warren took the position that racial segregation was un-American. In one of the greatest political shifts in American history, Earl Warren presided over a legal decision that transformed American society. For that he became a beloved symbol of racial progress for some and a hated symbol of federal intrusion into the lives of white Americans for others. The social contract was not destroyed, but profoundly damaged. It was the San Andreas fault line for white Southerners. They predicted that the "Big One" was inevitable. It was only a matter of time. The nation had been unalterably changed.

What was the "Big One" exactly? What was feared so by whites and especially those in the South? It was more psychological than anything. The world as they knew it had been turned on its axis by *Brown.* Since the beginning of white supremacist thought and ideology, the "Big One" was interracial sex or, as the late Dr. Welsing hypothesized, "the genetic annihilation" of the white race. Most whites would have not understood what she meant by such a term, but whether it was in a classroom or a swimming pool, race-mixing according to white supremacists was a foregone conclusion once social interaction was permitted. The schools were just the first step. Integration would lead to social contact between the races, and this would lead to interracial dating and inevitably, interracial marriage. It is interesting that after at least three centuries of white racial superiority indoctrination that so many whites feared this. The constant drumbeat that blacks were ugly and unattractive and thus undesirable as sexual partners was, of course, always a lie. White men had sought out black women as they had white and indigenous women, from the very first encounters across race demarcations. Because of the power differentials rape of black women had been commonplace throughout history. Race-mixing or miscegenation, as it was called by whites, masked profound anxieties on the part of white men about their own sexuality. Fear of black men raping white women was a time-honored social control mechanism used by white men to manage white women. But what if it were not rape? This was the "Big One" indeed.

CHAPTER 14

The Black Community Ups the Ante

Blacks and whites occupied two different worlds in both McComb, Mississippi and Helena, Arkansas where I grew up. Black people were ever present but it was as if a different plane of existence had been created for each of us. Except for certain retail exchanges like at a corner grocery on the border between one neighborhood where blacks lived and another where whites lived, the separation was total. Blacks could not walk through a white neighborhood without a purpose such as going to and from work. They could not saunter or wander through neighborhoods. They could not pause or stop to observe the architecture of a particular house. It wasn't just the large institutional barriers such as what school one attended or hospital or where you might rent a house or buy some land, it was the casual nuances of life, like walking in a park or stopping to smell the flowers in someone's garden. Everything was about race and there was no neutral ground.

I remember in 1960, the white high school in Helena had a terrific football team with an amazing group of athletes who also won the State Basketball Championship that same year and in the summer were State Baseball Champions. Coincidently, Eliza Miller High School, the "colored" school in town also had a great team featuring Willie J. Ross who would later star at the University of Nebraska. Three players from Central High, the white school, would sign with the University of Arkansas. Central lost one game that season in an upset to the team from Jonesboro, Arkansas farther upstate. Walking out of the stadium that night I overheard a young boy, probably nine or ten, say "Ya'll need Willie J." He could not have come into the stadium and would not have been sold a ticket. He could hang around outside and share his commentary with us white boys as we exited the playing field. "Ya'll need Willie J." Certainly we did. Not even football and the prospect of winning a state championship could bring the races together.

Another early encounter with "race lines" had to do with the radio. By the 1950s as rock and roll burst onto the scene for white teens and the transistor radio meant you could carry your music anywhere, whites would begin to listen to black radio. This was not always approved of, but it couldn't really be prevented. And besides, couldn't whites go wherever they wanted, do whatever they liked? Black musicians and singers were hot on white mainline stations. Wilson Pickett was one such black rock and roller who in the sixties became known to white teenagers. He had a number of hits including "Mustang Sally" and "Land of a Thousand Dances." A friend of mine, Bill Meyers, and I noticed a poster announcing that Wilson Pickett would be playing at the Eliza Miller Gymnasium Saturday night. Segregation or not, we were going to hear Wilson Pickett.

We got there, probably a bit nervous and anxious. We were not scared. White folks could go where they wanted to go. We could go to the black church every now and then. We could sit in the stands at their football games. We could shop in their section of town and did when we wanted to buy liquor or other contraband items. The reverse was not true, however.

The first signal that something was up was the sparseness of the crowd. About twelve people were in this cavernous gymnasium. There were at least two other white people. When "Little Willie Pickett" was announced we knew we had been had. A boy singer maybe twelve years old bounded out on the stage to, I guess, eight family members and four white kids. It was maybe the first time we were tricked by black folk. It wouldn't be the last.

Helena, Arkansas, a Delta town, was steeped in music, white and black. It was rock and roll and rhythm and blues and it was everywhere. Each day at noon Sonny Boy Williams would play the King Biscuit Hour on the local station KFFA from the Dreamland Café on Yazoo Street, the black shopping strip downtown. I would listen to his blues, off and on, for years and years. It was part of the backdrop of my life. It was much later, long after I left Helena, that I learned he was world renowned. Sonny Boy Williams was a legendary bluesman. I acted like I had always known it, but I didn't. Roosevelt Sykes was from He-

lena. Bobby Blue Bland played the Dreamland regularly as did many other famous bluesmen and women.

There were white musicians, too. Some of them also hit the big time. The first one I remember was Conway Twitty. His sister was in high school with my older sister Bonnye. Conway's real name was Howard Jenkins and he started out as a rock and roller. His first two hits "It's Only Make-Believe" and "Lonely Blue Boy" were high on the national charts and we all watched Conway when he sang on American Bandstand with Dick Clark televised out of Philadelphia. The lesser known, but legendary rocker out of Helena was Ronnie Hawkins. He would dramatically impact the white music scene of the 1960s although he, himself, was not as famous as others of that era. Ronnie Hawkins and the Hawks would be bankrolled early on by Charlie Halbert, the father of one of my classmates. In our eyes the Halberts were rich, but a bit louder rich than other rich folk in Helena. Charlie Halbert backed rock and rollers, owned a motel, had an interest in the ferry that was the only means of transport to Mississippi and a shortcut to Memphis before the Helena Bridge opened in 1960. There was something flashy about Charlie Halbert.

A piano player extraordinaire named Willie "Pop" Jones played the clubs around the Delta. He played the Teen Club, an alcohol-free gathering spot across from our home that sponsored weekend dance parties for white kids in Helena. Willie "Pop" was phenomenal, but he chose to stay behind when in 1960 "Ronnie Hawkins and the Hawks" went north along the Mississippi River, playing the clubs up river, all the way to Canada where Hawkins also became a legend. One young man that did go with him was Levon Helm, a thirteen-year-old high school drop-out from Marvell, Arkansas who played the drums. Not too many years later Levon Helm would be one of the mainstays of the "Band," Bob Dylan's backup band when he went electric, but considered in its own right as one of the greatest groups of the rock and roll era.

I met my first wife at Conway Twitty's Moon Lake Resort. She was from Marvell. She said she was actually from Turkey Scratch outside Marvell and so was Levon Helm.

After 9:00 p.m. in the evenings the only radio stations you could get were from the big cities. We could get three stations out of Memphis, all rock and roll; we also got WDIA out of Memphis where one DJ was B. B. King and another *was Rufus Thomas who had big hits with "Walkin' the Dog" and "Do the Dog," a rather salacious dance number that was all the rage for a while. Out of Chicago and WLS, you could get the Dick Biondi Show which was white rock and roll. I would learn a lot about Chicago's high schools and neighborhoods listening to Biondi night after night. Late at night you could get from Nashville, Randy's Record Shop with John R and the Hoss Man, who played black music. It was from WLAC. "Tell 'em the Hoss Man sent ya." On WLAC you could hear Barrett Strong and Little Willie John and "Big Mama" Thornton. These were black musicians who didn't get air time on the white stations, but if you were white and in the Delta, you grew up listening to them. John R would sell you "Five Hundred Baby Chicks" mail order, for $13.95 plus shipping and handling. The Wolfman from Del Rio, Texas would sell you a prayer rug complete with a picture of Jesus for $13.95 also. It was said that the Wolfman broadcast over a 150,000 watt channel whose transmitter was in Mexico. Some said you could pick him up over barbed wire.*

When Earl Warren's Supreme Court voted in favor of the plaintiffs in the historic *Brown* decision, he earned the undying enmity of every segregationist in the US. "IMPEACH EARL WARREN!" stickers, placards and billboards became as much a part of the Southern highway landscape as SEE ROCK CITY on barn roofs and BURMA SHAVE on sign posts. The "Warren Court" became a euphemism for liberalism and judicial activism in the United States. But it had not been all Earl Warren's doings. Nor the decades of legal groundwork laid by the NAACP.

In every Southern town there were organizations, private for the most part, that readied the black community for the freedom struggle. Sometimes these were social and pleasure clubs. Often Prince Hall masons played a critical role in developing a community's leadership. The African American church and its Women's Clubs served as leadership development academies as did the historically black colleges and universities or HBCUs, for the generation of organizers and activists that led the assault on institutionalized white supremacy. Ironically, segregation had given black people cover. There were numerous places and settings in the black community where white people just did not go and more often than not did not know existed. Racial segregation in America rendered black people invisible in the larger public sphere controlled and run by white people. This same invisibility worked to their benefit when they began organizing a movement. These "safe places" might be a funeral parlor whose main room could seat seventy-five to a hundred people; a "colored" school basement or auditorium; a record shop; a barber shop, or the Alhambra or Phythian ballrooms which catered to black high society. Even the pep rallies at the local "colored" high school might be a site where information on upcoming activities would be shared with students and teachers as part of the grapevine used to get the word out. Each of the hundreds of leaders in the years to come had a teacher or preacher, aunt or uncle who inspired their future, stiffened their backs and steeled their resolve sufficient to withstand what was about to happen. There was a spiritual dimension as well. Voices from the cargo ships hollered from their sea coffins; spirits of nameless folk hung by their necks and tossed into remote swamps or tributaries cheered the marchers and helped frontliners survive the police batons, fire hoses and cattle prods that were poised to do their damage.

Civil disobedience strategies tried in prior years would serve as models for later boycotts and freedom rides. The Rev T. J. Jemison in Baton Rouge, Louisiana attempted a local bus boycott by black people in 1953, as did C. K. Steele in Tallahassee, Florida. In both cities, there were still sufficient numbers of poor white people who depended on public transportation to keep the transit system afloat. But their efforts planted the seed for a strategy that called for a similar bus boycott used successfully in 1955 by the Montgomery County Improvement Association which, along with the *Brown* decision, birthed the modern Civil Rights Movement. Even in Montgomery, there were strategic decisions. There were other "birthings." Again, some say the decision by Mamie Mobley Till, Emmett Till's mother, to bring her dead son's battered and bruised corpse back to Chicago and allow *Jet* magazine and the *Chicago Defender* to print his visage to the world was the galvanizing force for millions.

Every community had its own beginning moment. In New Orleans the vicious threats rained down upon the four little black girls walking to two separate schools, innocent in their new white dresses. Captured on canvas and the cover of *Look* magazine by Norman Rockwell, this iconic painting is now displayed just outside the Oval Office of the White House, thanks to President Obama.

Similar moments were captured on film and photos in cities and towns across the South. In New Orleans, the Rev. Avery Alexander being dragged by his heels upstairs from the basement cafeteria at City Hall. In Greensboro, North Carolina, black students sitting quietly at the Woolworth counter while whites poured catsup on their heads and ground cigarettes out on their shoulders. In Birmingham there were many starting points from the 16th Street church bombing to the bombing of Rev. Fred Shuttlesworth's home to Selma and the killing of Jimmie Lee Jackson. In a small town like McComb, Mississippi, Brenda Travis and other high school students were jailed when they marched in support of Freedom Riders, adding to the momentum. These were not founding moments of the Movement, but they were galvanizing moments that shocked a people to action.

CHAPTER 15

Civil Rights Movement Strategy

The first time I became aware that there was something afoot having to do with race was in Helena, Arkansas at the town's centennial celebration in 1957. I would have been eleven years old. There was a big banner across Cherry Street which was Helena's main street and primary shopping district. Blacks could shop on Cherry Street but not too many at once. They were required to do their business and move on. They were not allowed to congregate and certainly not "loiter." The black main street was Yazoo Street, one block behind Cherry Street. If there was any "loitering" to be done it had to be on Yazoo and not Cherry.

This banner stretched tight across Cherry Street was one that asked you to vote for Orville Faubus for governor. I had never heard of Orville Faubus, nor was I in any way concerned about who was Governor of Arkansas. It was what was beneath the Faubus for Governor that caught my attention. It said "STOP DAISY BATES" and "Tell Ike We Say No." I did not know who Daisy Bates was at that time. I knew, of course, who "Ike" was. He was the President of the United States and one of the white men who had won World War II. Still, that was of passing interest until the crowd started chanting "Two, Four, Six, Eight, We Don't Want To Integrate," and then "Eight, Six, Four, Two, Ike Says We Have To." "Integrate" was a new word for me then. I think I knew it had to do with race. And maybe I knew it had to do with Negroes and whites going to school together. Maybe not. Daisy Bates was the first organizer I ever heard about. She was not called an organizer, but that is what she was doing. Arkansas white people in 1957 hated her for it. Mrs. Bates was the outspoken critic of the all-white Central High

School in Little Rock, the state capitol of Arkansas. In the wake of Brown v. Board, *she was spearheading the black community's fight to integrate the public schools. Daisy Bates was vilified in the white community. She was called every name imaginable. Every N-word epithet that could be conceived and there were many.*

Later, much later, I would come to understand that there was a Daisy Bates in every small town and big city in the South. In the North too, for that matter. It was years before I saw a newspaper photo of Daisy Bates. I thought she would be nine feet tall. She was normal enough in stature, but women like Daisy Bates were more than nine feet tall in courage and resolve. The psychological warfare waged on civil rights workers like her taxes the imagination. The daily fear and knowledge that this could be the day you get killed by a stick of dynamite from a carload of white toughs thrown through your living room window as you sleep. The sense of psychic agony experienced around the very real possibility that your actions might cause your family members to get killed. It was war in the South and it lasted longer than most international wars did. Countless civil rights warriors often adopted a non-violent posture in the wake of the overwhelming state-sanctioned violent response to their organizing efforts, but the white South was fully mobilized. The white populace constituted a voluntary citizen militia, protected by the state, and made up of local police forces and sheriff departments. When you consider then the impact of local judiciary, court-appointed councils and segregated juries impaneled to uphold white supremacy, the courage and fortitude of Daisy Bates and others like her strains credulity.

What do the heroic examples of people like Daisy Bates mean for the psyche of white people? For many whites, the examples of Daisy Bates and Rosa Parks sparked our commitment to civil rights. While these commitments might take years to nourish, it is possible for some of us to look back and point to an incident or a learning and say, "That's when I began to get involved." For many others of us, however, we never saw the heroism and courage implicit in the actions of those black people who became known for their involvement with civil rights. Mrs. Bates was not heroic in the white community of Helena, Arkansas. She was cursed and ridiculed at every turn; she had to force Little Rock authorities to offer her police protection. This is another irony because again the police force was all white and seemingly dedicated to keeping blacks in their place. Even as some whites began to take their own stands against segregation and risk all they had in opposition to the hate and violence happening around them, the situation also reinforced white supremacy. One might have been "for civil rights" as a white person, but the dominance of white people in every phase of life was so evident that the normality of it had to be internalized. One might view the unfairness of it all, but that view was from a standpoint in which white supremacy remained normal.

I entered Ole Miss in September of 1964. James Meredith had left the school a year before in August of 1963. Ole Miss in the sixties was a surreal experience. Race hung over the campus like a dense fog. Cleveland McDowell replaced Meredith on campus. He was in the law school and the lawyers hired to keep Ole Miss white were doing all they could to force him out. But, Ole Miss had been changed. It would never be the same again even as the atmosphere of white supremacy remained for many years after these brave deeds took place. By the time I arrived, the first black women students were on campus, including Constance Slaughter who would be the first African American woman to graduate from Ole Miss law school and a major civil rights attorney. We had a rare snowfall that year. I stood by as white students pummeled these young black women with snowballs, really ice cubes wrapped in snow, and some were knocked to the ground. I remember watching with horror, but still just watching. I assume their names were lost to history. Just white students being white, I guess. Some of us threw the snowballs. Some of us watched them being thrown. Same difference. Like the professors and administrators who had earlier remained silent as violence reigned, I had not stood up yet either.

Looking back, what I didn't know amazes me. I knew there had been a riot, but I had no idea of its particular viciousness. I knew a "colored man" had enrolled at Ole Miss, but I had no idea of what he endured to do so and what he survived to stay there. Surely, the story of James Meredith, had he fit the profile of civil rights hero, would be right there with Rosa Parks and maybe a notch or two below Dr. King in the pantheon of black heroes we revere today. But Meredith did not invite such adulation. He was stubborn and iconoclastic. He was as likely to criticize fellow blacks as white supremacists. He hated living with federal marshals even as they prevented him from being murdered. There is no doubt that he would have been. Not to me. Some coward would have shot him, hiding, lurking in the dark.

Four years later, James Meredith, in 1966, led a march from Memphis to Jackson against the advice of the civil rights leadership who viewed it as suicidal and non-strategic. After he was shot by an assailant hiding in the bushes off High-

way 51, others had to rush in to take his place in one of the riskiest circumstances in movement history.

I had come a long way or so it seemed to me and others whom I met. My father thought so, too, but not in the way I might have hoped he would. He felt I was duped. Taken advantage of by certain teachers and preachers, Rev. Knight in particular. He was worried about how this transformation, as it were, would affect my career chances and choices, but to me, I was on my way. Being liberal, as it was called, back then and even today, was my way out. To where, exactly? For me it was always to New York City and other points north. I wanted to attend graduate school at Yale or Columbia. There was a certain inferiority complex I was trying to overcome. I thought people and places in the North were better than the South. I was both embarrassed being from the South and intimidated by the thought of having to compete with those more "advanced" than I was or thought I was anyway. Alas, it was not to be. I did study in the North and worked there at different times, but I never outran my raising. I never moved away from my family. Regardless of what else I might have accomplished, I was still very much Southern and very much a white Southerner. I had to reconcile with that if I wanted to find my place in the world.

In the spring of 1968, after the assassination of Dr. Martin Luther King Jr., black students at Ole Miss took over the YMCA building on campus. I was right there with them. I can't remember why they chose the YMCA. Most students were taking over administration buildings around the country. Maybe we were lost, who knows? The word got out quickly and in a moment the building was encircled by howling white students chanting "N-----s Get Out! Burn It Down!" (Didn't anyone go to class at Ole Miss?)

The police came and demanded we exit the building. The black students resisted. All of us were scared, but defiant. The year 1968 was not too many years distant from the cross-burnings, church bombings and armed police who were members of white race groups. Someone suggested that I had to go. No whites in the building. It was just me anyway. A debate ensued: Should I stay or leave. I had supporters. I had detractors, but in hindsight the detractors were right. If I were allowed to stay, the story tomorrow would be about me. They knew that and I didn't. Yeah, but that mob outside was not thinking about such fine distinctions. I would be crucified unless the Lord intervened. He did, or some other representative of the divine. The Chancellor shut the school down. A four-day weekend! Black radicals and white supremacists alike split in an instant. The revolution at Ole Miss could wait. We would take it up later. Fighting racism. Down South, in 1968.

Major victories were won in 1954 and 1955, capping a struggle that had been waged for years to bring down the structures of systemic racism in the country. While none of these structures actually came down, the *Brown* decision and the Montgomery Bus Boycott spawned actions that resulted in civil rights acts passed by Congress in 1958, 1964, 1965 and 1968. Each of these acts widened the cracks into the construct of race in the United States.

While the earlier civil rights bills were weak compared to those that followed, each signaled the greater change to come. By 1958, a decade had passed since Truman had integrated the Armed Forces and set up the federal Economic Opportunity Commission. Even though the nation as a whole was still inching forward at its best "with all deliberate speed," it was time for the generations of those defined by the "anti-social contract" to take the lead.

When do protests and demonstrations become a "movement"? When do efforts to improve "race relations," often carried out by ministers and town officials intent on bringing white people of moderate views on race together with "responsible Negro leadership" become an all-out mobilization against structures of oppression? This was not a linear process. In small towns and larger cities in every area of the nation, organizing strategies, protests, demonstrations linked to efforts to foster greater dialogue and understanding among the races would happen (it seemed to many white people) "all at once." Black people wanted change, Now! They had so for many years, centuries even. White people cautioned moderation and against "going too fast." It was like a courtship with the forces of change wanting to consummate the relationship immediately as proof of sincerity; those not sure what change would entail stressing the need to wait.

Since its founding in 1909, the NAACP had been the unquestioned national leader when it came to the race question. It was not the only organization working for the rights of Negro citizens, but it was national in scope and had tremendous name recognition. The NAACP was seen as radical by the politically conservative and such established forces as state and city governments, school systems and the mainstream white press. It was seen as moderate, slow-moving and accommodationist-to-a-fault by radical and liberal strategists on the left. Still, the NAACP was everywhere after the *Brown* decision and its identity was synonymous with civil rights for black Americans. Chief Legal Advocate, Thurgood Marshall, became the NAACP's leading light especially after the Legal Defense Fund was separated from the primary day-to-day operations of the organization in 1939. Marshall had argued *Brown* before the US Supreme Court and was destined to become the Court's first African American justice in 1966, appointed by President Lyndon B. Johnson.

After many years serving under Walter White as editor of the NAACP's the *Crisis,* Roy Wilkins became executive secretary of the organization in 1955, and executive director in 1964. Wilkins played a key role in the unfolding strategies of the Movement as it took on more of a national posture after the early Southern campaigns.

Wilkins was eclipsed by the charismatic Martin Luther King, Jr. in national exposure and name recognition. King's soaring rhetoric and front-of-the-line presence since the successful Montgomery Bus Boycott had made him the undisputed champion of the Civil Rights Movement. Dr. King had helped found the Southern Christian Leadership Conference (SCLC) in New Orleans in 1957, a coalition of black church leadership largely in the South. SCLC now constituted King's organizational base.

In these early years after the Supreme Court's *Brown* decision, civil rights campaigns followed a certain pattern in communities across the South. SCLC always worked with local black ministerial associations to coordinate actions which usually focused on voter education and registration and sometimes tested public accommodations. Not all black ministers were supportive of Dr. King and SCLC and a few actively opposed the confrontational methods employed in the Civil Rights Movement. Rev. Joseph Jackson's National Baptist Convention (NBC) was the largest association among black Baptists. Rev. Jackson was a rival of sorts of Martin Luther King, Jr. Dr. Jackson was not in agreement with the strategy of confrontation exemplified by Dr. King. Nor was he in favor of the Black Church alliances with radical movements, some of which were suspected of being communist. The National Baptist Convention member churches, however, were key to local civil rights organizing regardless of Dr. Jackson's reservations. Martin Luther King knew this and attempted to walk a tightrope between himself as a loyal member of the National Baptist Convention and his growing militancy as the movement grew. The constraints NBC membership placed on him, however, were added pressure on Dr. King to form his own Progressive National Baptist Convention in 1961. PNBC was a national extension of the Southern-based SCLC and was for King a distancing by him from the National Baptist Convention.

Non-violent resistance to racial injustice was a major principle of Dr. King's strategy. Dr. King was a disciple of Mahatma Gandhi. So was the Reverend James Lawson, a United Methodist minister at Fisk University and later at Vanderbilt, both in Nashville, Tennessee. Both ministers invoked the principle of "moral suasion" against their opponents. James Lawson, in fact, was a major influence on the movement with his non-violence ethic. He taught many movement activists how to react to the violence perpetrated by white groups without giving in to violence itself. Rev. Lawson was influential particularly with students in and around Nashville, Tennessee and the Southeast at schools like Shaw and Morehouse. Diane Nash, a student at Fisk University in Nashville was a disciple of the methods Lawson taught and in 1960 she would emerge as a founding member and leader of the Student Non-Violent Coordinating Committee (SNCC). Nash coordinated the Freedom Rides in 1961 – 62 when the level of violent resistance by whites threatened to stop them altogether.

Few of the black student leaders were in favor of "turning the other cheek." Rev. Lawson had to be convincing with his principled Gandhian stance. He knew if black students fought white police in the South many of them would suffer grievous injury, even death. They would also be blamed for instigating the violence. This was standard operating procedure. James Lawson's name has not continued to be known as widely as the years have passed outside the core of those involved in the movement and those within the United Methodist Church. But his legacy remains strong among those who were there.

Gandhi had used the principle of non-violent resistance to build a movement designed to undermine the moral legitimacy of the all-powerful British Empire. Dr. King, Rev. Lawson, and later Cesar Chavez, used it to challenge entrenched white supremacist power structures whether these were major corporate interests, state legislative bodies or the US Congress. The three of them believed in the inherent "goodness of man." This was a belief sorely tested by the ever-escalating violence civil rights workers faced. All three were influenced by theologians such as A. J. Muste, Reinhold Niebuhr, Howard Thurman and

George Houser. Non-violence was a strategy designed to shame a nation rooted in white supremacy. It worked and then again, it didn't. They practiced it. Southern police forces — most police — and the Klan did not. Not everyone agreed with this non-violent mentality. Certainly, many did not share the belief in the "inherent goodness" of people whose national empires had been built on the backs of people of color and to whom a belief in the superiority of the white race was fundamental.

Woven throughout even these "non-violent" early civil rights years were individuals, groups and communities determined to protect this freedom movement, by any means necessary. Particularly in the South, where guns were a way of life, defensive — often quiet — actions like standing guard when the Klan was on the move, saved untold lives. In Jonesboro and Bogalusa, Louisiana, the Deacons for Defense and Justice organized based on this recognition that some people would only respond to determined and armed defenders. As civil rights journalist Charles Cobb argues in his 2014 book that catalogues armed defensive activities in the Civil Rights Movement, "this non-violent stuff'll get you killed!"[1]

One criterion for SCLC intervention in a local community was the degree of resistance likely to be encountered by the mobilized black masses under SCLC and SNCC leadership. The greater the resistance, the more national publicity the campaign would engender and more sharply would the moral battlegrounds around segregation be drawn. This tactic was one reason whites would often charge Dr. King with fomenting trouble or "stirring things up." But it was a necessary and effective tactic that King and SCLC/SNCC used to great advantage.

Whites did not always use violent tactics of resistance. In Albany, Georgia, Sheriff Laurie Pritchett countered SCLC's strategy by refusing to directly confront the civil rights legions. His arrests did not employ brutality, but he followed the arrests by dispersing those arrested to different jails around the county. This served to deflect the mass impact of the protests. Pritchett welcomed Martin Luther King, Jr., promising to arrest him and house him in his new jail. Some thought King would be lost and possibly even die in Pritchett's jail. While Sheriff Pritchett, in many ways, fit the classic stereotype of the ultra-resistant Southern law officer, his counter strategy foiled Dr. King's and SCLC's plans, forcing a retreat after King was released from jail. Albany was an example of a campaign which at first seemed to fail. It proved to be a serious challenge for civil rights forces. Charlie Sherrod, with his wife Shirley, was the lead organizer for the Albany campaign; he remained in Albany and is still an organizer there. Eventually segregation was broken in Albany, but the first campaign provided hard lessons for the movement.

Saint Augustine, Florida, presented the opposite scenario. The lead SCLC organizers, Rev. C. T. Vivian and Rev. Wyatt T. Walker, were met with an enraged and mobilized white citizenry. It would severely test the staying power of King's people in the face of unrestrained police violence coupled with unchecked white mob actions. Civil rights organizers in St. Augustine were pummeled by white youth, rocked and beaten by women and men alike, threatened with lynching, murder by drive-by shooters and house bombings of any locals tempted to harbor the organizers. Civil rights workers were followed in and out of town. Motels, even in the black community, dared not rent the civil rights workers rooms and preachers whose churches provided them meeting space lived in second-by-second fear that their sanctuaries would go up in flames.

The Student Non-Violent Coordinating Committee (SNCC) came out of a conference held at Shaw University in Raleigh, North Carolina in 1960 with master teacher and organizer Ella Baker playing a crucial role. Between 1961 and 1967, SNCC would organize throughout the South and would become a national symbol for youth organizing that would impact not only civil rights strategy, but campus-based opposition to the Vietnam War, the draft, and US imperialism. In addition to Diane Nash, other organizers with SNCC included activists such as Stokely Carmichael (later Kwame Touré), Bob Moses, John Lewis, Bob and Dottie Zellner, Tom Hayden, Mary King and Casey Reagan to name but a few. Free Southern Theater grew out of SNCC and was directed by SNCC organizer John O'Neal. The SNCC Freedom Singers featured Bernice Reagon later of Sweet Honey in the Rock fame. O'Neal would assume coordinating responsibilities for the Mississippi Summer Freedom Schools after the departure of Staughton Lynd in 1965. Lynd was a white activist professor from Yale who laid some of the theoretical groundwork for the Mississippi strategy. He was one of the nation's most influential historians and social critics.

SNCC complemented, confronted, and cooperated with SCLC and other civil rights groups. Seen as more direct and confrontational than SCLC by some, SNCC needs to be viewed in the context of the

Movement's overall purpose and goals. In fact, most white people saw little difference between any of the different civil rights organizations or approaches. To the white South, they were all under Dr. King's control and their mission to destroy "the Southern way of life" was the same. Few admitted to any differences between the acronyms nor could they tell them apart. This was true regardless of intra-movement conflicts and competitions. For most whites, it would have been difficult to name a civil rights leader other than Martin Luther King, Jr., except for the local minister "causing all the trouble." In a still larger context, Dr. King, himself, was seen by the same Southerners as under the control of either Northern liberals or New York Jews or still even more sinister, "the communists."

Sixty years later, some white Southerners would continue to denigrate Dr. King. Former Mississippi Governor Haley Barbour stirred up a tempest in 2010 when he spoke of his growing up in Yazoo City. "I just don't remember it as being that bad," he said. "I remember Martin Luther King came to town, in '62. He spoke out at the old fairground and it was full of people, black and white." When asked what King had said that day, he replied: "I don't really remember. The truth is, we couldn't hear very well. We were sort of out there on the periphery. We just sat on our cars, watching the girls, talking, doing what boys do. We paid more attention to the girls than to King…"[2]

Civil Rights Movement strategy attempted coordination of efforts whenever possible. In 1960, SNCC leaders, inspired by successful sit-ins two years earlier led by NAACP youth at drug stores in Wichita, Kansas and Oklahoma City, organized students from the Agricultural and Technical College of North Carolina to sit in at the downtown Woolworth's lunch counter in Greensboro, North Carolina. The tactic blazed across the South and other parts of the country, aided by its impact on a growing national television audience. Those who "sat-in" suffered tremendous abuse and harassment from whites who doused the protesters with catsup, syrup and concoctions too complex to name, and burned them with cigarettes as they persisted in sitting quietly at the counters. The lunch counters and cafeterias eventually had to submit to serving the young black customers, although some held out for months and others closed for good.

In New Orleans, the sit-ins at Woolworth's on Canal Street were the first civil disobedience experience for future CORE (Congress of Racial Equality) organizers Jerome Smith, Dodie Simmons, Oretha

Castle, Richard Haley and Ike Reynolds, several of whom were then students at Southern University in New Orleans. These early organizers would comprise the vanguard of "Freedom Riders" the following summer.

Leaders of the non-violent Nashville movement would join with students from other historically black colleges and some white schools in the North, in organizing the "Freedom Rides." These would be modeled after the CORE/FOR 1948 Journey for Reconciliation that had been thwarted by mechanical problems and never made it into the Deep South. The 1961 non-violent activists experienced some of the greatest white violence of the movement, including beatings in Birmingham and a bus bombing in Aniston, Alabama. Despite these threats to their lives that caused many civil rights leaders to call for a halt to the rides, SNCC organizers took up the Freedom Riders' challenge, carrying forward with a series of "rides" from different starting points throughout the South. "Freedom Riders" persevered over a two-year period, facing more violence and beatings in bus terminals at Rock Hill, South Carolina and again in Birmingham. When one group was finally escorted into Jackson, Mississippi, under police protection, it was the beginning of the end of legalized segregation in interstate travel in the South. These student-led coalitions brought new words into America's vernacular like "sit-ins" and "freedom riders" and "outside agitator."

Chapter 16

Civil Rights Leaders — Exiled, Murdered, Jailed

My classmates stood and cheered when President Kennedy's assassination was announced over the school's intercom. I was in the eleventh grade in Helena, Arkansas in 1963. Even then, the cheers seemed rehearsed. How could teenagers express such rank emotion from something so vile and tragic? Was this something they had heard at home — "someone should shoot the son-of-a-bitch"? Just the year before, we had cheered the President for standing up to the Soviet Union in the Cuban missile crisis. The crisis was the threatening prospect of Soviet nuclear missiles ninety miles from the US shoreline. Kennedy had backed down the Russian premier, Nikita Khrushchev. Who knows what really happened? Now, we welcomed his brain being splintered by a rifle bullet next to his wife. A lone gunman did it.

The Kennedys were for "civil rights." This is the reason we cheered. Anyone "for civil rights" should have his head blown off. No one expressly said it, but I knew it. There were only two things for which we cheered so raucously back then: either a victory by the Arkansas Razorbacks (or, in my case, the Ole Miss Rebels) in a football game, or the defeat — in this case the murder — of a suspected civil rights leader. No international intrigue like missiles in a communist Cuba would have done it. Civil Rights. That was the reason. Later, we would say the same when John Kennedy's brother, Robert, was killed. The Kennedys were for civil rights. That's what got them killed.

Five years after John Kennedy's assassination, in April 1968, the news of the assassination of Dr. Martin Luther King Jr. reached us in Oxford, Mississippi, where I was a senior at the University of Mississippi. There was a similar uproarious reaction among whites. What made us react this way? Of course Dr. King had it coming big time. He was *civil rights.*

What would haunt me over the years was the radio broadcast from one of the Memphis stations. Dr. King had been shot. The Memphis police were pursuing the assailant down Lamar Avenue, Highway 78, toward the Mississippi state line. He was driving a white Ford Mustang. They had him in their sights. He crossed into Mississippi, the Highway Patrol had him. They missed him. He got away. I remember thinking, "Really, now."

James Earl Ray, the infamous killer of Martin Luther King, Jr., poor white, vagabond, drifter holed up in a black section of Memphis in a rooming house. Not an object of police suspicion. Tension was at a boiling point. The strike by sanitation workers had garbage piled high in the streets. Rats were everywhere. Dr. King was warned to not come back. He knew it. "I have been to the mountaintop," he had declared to those assembled the night before in Claiborne Temple AME Church. "I might not get there with you." Go figure. Wait! They caught him! James Earl Ray was apprehended in London, having traveled to England via Toronto with money in his pocket? No way. No credit cards. Another lone gunman.

One year later I was teaching high school in Byhalia, Mississippi, about thirty to forty miles from where I was living in Memphis. A friend of mine was teaching there and said they needed another white teacher in this all-black school. I jumped at the chance, being unemployed at the moment. On the anniversary of Dr. King's murder, I asked the principal if I could take the kids in my class to the One Year Anniversary March in Memphis. Originally he was against the idea, fearing something might happen. I assured him nothing would. Well, something did happen. Halfway through the march a mob of toughs rushed the crowd from an alleyway and caused havoc. The police responded with tear gas and billyclubs. It was all over TV and beamed to the homes of families in Byhalia. Upon our return we were met by a band of parents worried about their children and by the way, who was this white teacher who felt this was a good idea. The principal said nothing and let me take my lumps. My students loved the whole trip, tear gas and all.

Assassinations, murders, kidnapping and exile confronted black liberationists throughout the country during the 1950s, '60s and '70s. In the South, ordinary citizens were subject to brutal beatings at the hands of white race-gangs, police officials and regular white citizens. While Southern white supremacists knew they had lost the fight for their hallowed "way of life," they would continue to struggle mightily — and violently — before they would wave the white flag. Meanwhile, they still waved the bloody shirt of resistance. Lynchings had abated after more than a century of unrelenting white mob violence, but they did not stop completely. Mack Charles Parker was one of the last "state-sanctioned" hangings. In 1959 Parker was taken out of a Poplarville, Mississippi jail cell whose door was left unlocked. Accused of raping and kidnapping a white woman and her son, Parker was mob-rushed, taken from the jail house, beaten and hung. His dead body was thrown into the Pearl River. There was no doubt that local law enforcement officials were involved in the crime. After a FBI investigation, nine people were arrested and turned over to the grand jury. No one was ever indicted for the lynching of Mack Charles Parker.

Liberty, Mississippi farmer Herbert Lee was killed in his truck as he was bringing cotton to town to be ginned on September 25, 1961. His murderer was a white elected official, Representative E. H. Hurst, who shot him in broad daylight in front of several witnesses. Just one day before Lee's murder, Bob Moses had invited John Doar of the US Department of Justice to McComb to hear directly from blacks being threatened for their involvement in the movement. To no avail. No charges were ever brought against Hurst. One witness to the Lee murder, Lewis Allen, later admitted he lied to protect himself and his family. A little more than two years later, after repeated harassment by local police officials since Lee's killing, Allen was murdered in his own driveway, one day before he was to move north.

Not just in Mississippi. Robert F. X. Williams was run out of North Carolina, in 1961, after he had encouraged black citizens of Monroe, North Carolina to defend themselves by taking up arms against repeated police violence. He fled the state and later the country and lived in exile, first in Cuba and then China. Williams returned to the United States in 1969. The State of North Carolina finally dropped all charges against him in 1975. Williams worked at the University of Michigan's Center for Chinese Studies until his death in 1996.

In 1963, as murders, bombings, and arson in the South were becoming more and more commonplace, Dr. King and SCLC called for a March on Washington to pressure President John F. Kennedy and the Congress to intervene and stop the unchecked violence being perpetrated by whites on black people involved in any sort of "civil rights" activities. Some of the worst violence lay ahead and Klan-led raids and assassinations were picking up steam. The March on Washington is now a part of American folklore. Every year during Black History Month, Dr. King's "I Have a Dream" speech is played over and over with often the not too subliminal message that Dr. King's Dream has come true. A black man is President, after all.

Much like the Million Man March a generation later, however, it was different back then. The nation was on fire and Martin Luther King's assassination was rightly feared as a possibility. A pantheon of civil rights veterans and social justice advocates, labor organizers and black celebrities were on the stage. Mahalia Jackson sang the national anthem. John Lewis, already the victim of police beatings and jail sentences, spoke about the role of youth in the people's struggle and religious leaders from all faiths were there. Dorothy Height, even then a civil rights veteran dating back to the 1930s, was on the podium and would speak to the multitudes. She had forty more years to go.

It was the largest gathering of its kind in the nation's history up until that date. The crowd was estimated at 250,000, but some said there were many more, at least a half million or so. The movement was on the move. Nothing could stop it, but in the next five years Martin Luther King, Jr., John Kennedy, Medgar Evers, Jimmy Lee Jackson, James Reeb, James Chaney, Michael Schwerner, Andrew Goodman, Viola Luizzo, Malcolm X, and Robert Kennedy to name only the most famous would be dead. Every one of them shot by "unknown assailants" and every one, except Malcolm X, by white gunmen working anonymously. But, with violence everywhere, something was conspiring and these were just the famous ones.

For white people, regular white people, not the ones who spoke or who were in attendance, but the ones who were afraid of where this was heading, it was not a celebratory occasion. Whites were beginning to organize their own movement.

Birmingham and Selma constituted major victories for the civil rights forces. Southern sheriffs played right into the hands of movement strategists. In Birmingham, Eugene "Bull" Conner had been Director of Public Safety since the late 1930s. He swore that as long as he was sheriff, "blacks and whites would never segregate together [*sic*]." Conner anticipated the wave of civil rights forces with a well-armed and militant white police force primed to defend white Birmingham at all costs. The city was no stranger to confrontations between white and black. Rev. Fred Shuttlesworth was the leader of the local black ministerial alliance in Birmingham. Shuttlesworth was fiery, outspoken and absolutely fearless, some would even say reckless. His home had been fire-bombed three times with himself and his family inside. Miraculously, no one had been hurt. Shuttlesworth was defiant, unbent and possibly more than any other movement activist with the exception of John Lewis, unbowed in the face of enormous threat to life and limb. How Rev. Shuttlesworth survived to live more than forty years until his death in 2011 is a remarkable story.

Birmingham was controlled by the Ku Klux Klan. Bull Conner both protected and used them. Many of his officers were members of the Klan including, it is said, Conner himself. The weapon of choice in Birmingham was the fire bomb. Striking usually at night and under the protective cover of both the dark and the police, KKK nightriders created a climate of fear that struck horror in the city's black community. "Bombingham" was no misnomer.

Together with Rev. Shuttlesworth, Wyatt Tee Walker, one of the SCLC founders and its executive director from 1960 – 1964, planned the tactics of the direct action protests. The Birmingham campaign lasted throughout 1963 – 1964. In September, 1963, Klansman Robert "Dynamite Bob" Chambliss blew up the Sixteenth Street Baptist Church killing Addie Mae Collins, Denise McNair, Carole Robertson and Cynthia Wesley, all between eleven and fourteen years of age. Another twenty people were injured. Chambliss was not arrested until almost fifteen years later in 1977. For those fifteen years he roamed free even as law enforcement including the FBI knew he had done the bombing. He died in prison in 1985.

After the 16th Street bombing, SCLC organized a "Children's Crusade" to shore up the civil rights ranks that had begun to decline as violence against protesters escalated and murders and fire-bombings went unchecked. Teenagers joined the fray, leaving school during school hours to march on downtown businesses and stores. Conner met them with unbridled fury. For the first time, the violence was captured on television. The nation was shocked by the images of young people fire hosed with such ferocity that they were blown up against brick walls and wooden storefronts with police dogs snarling and biting them unrestrained by their police handlers. Southern defenders of segregation were exposed and accused of condoning the madness. The White Citizens Councils attempted to blame Dr. King, as always, for instigating the mayhem. When he was arrested and jailed, Dr. King wrote his famous "Letter from a Birmingham Jail" castigating his fellow white clergymen for remaining silent in the face of such immorality and injustice. Diane McWhorter, a white Birmingham native, has chronicled these cataclysmic days in her 2001 Pulitzer prize-winning book, *Carry Me Home: Birmingham, Alabama, the Climactic Battle of the Civil Rights Revolution.*[1]

The Birmingham triumph — the desegregation of its businesses — inspired similar campaigns. In a ten-week period, records show, at least 758 demonstrations in 186 cities sparked 14,733 arrests.[2] President Kennedy, who had called for civil rights legislation in May, 1963 brought Congressional leaders to the White House in October 1963 to press for the bill's passage. He was assassinated a month later.

Violence continued to escalate throughout the South. Medgar Evers, State Director of the NAACP in Mississippi was ambushed and killed by white supremacist and Klan member, Byron de la Beckwith, outside his home in Jackson, Mississippi in June, 1963. De La Beckwith remained free until 1975, when he was finally convicted of conspiracy to commit murder. He was paroled in 1980, though another trial in 1994 ended with his being convicted of first-degree murder for killing Evers. In a sign of changing times, Mississippi's Supreme Court upheld the conviction in 1997. De La Beckwith died on January 21, 2001.

Even as violence spread throughout the summer of 1963, civil rights organizers in Mississippi initiated a bold strategy: a Freedom Vote Campaign. By August, 27,000 unregistered black men and women had cast protest ballots in polling places set up in black churches and businesses. Building on the success of this initial "freedom vote," COFO, the Council of Federated Organizations, was a vehicle used to coordinate an overall state strategy. COFO recruited SNCC and NAACP activists from across the South, plus seventy young men from Yale and Stanford Universities, to organize a statewide "Freedom Vote Campaign." Despite harassment and intimidation, more than 83,000 blacks and a few whites cast ballots for NAACP president Aaron Henry for governor in November. As CORE organizer David Dennis said, this mock election "did much more for the movement, toward uniting Mississippi, than anything else we have done."[3] Within weeks of the Freedom Vote Campaign, SNCC and CORE began to plan for what would be called Mississippi Freedom Summer of 1964. SNCC organizer Bob Moses and others had decided that the terrorizing of black people in the South would end only when the movement reached across all sectors of society. Bob Moses, the architect of the project, was most concerned about the sense of entitlement that white students who made up the large majority of the volunteers from the North might have and the impunity they might feel regarding Southern customs and culture. His concern was as much about how they might offend Southern blacks with whom most of them would be living as it was about how they would interact with Southern whites whom he knew they would offend. He warned them that this was not an exotic excursion to some out-of-the-way place. He said some might be killed. He was right.

The very day in 1964 that Mississippi Freedom Summer started, the names of Andrew Goodman, Michael Schwerner and James Chaney became nationally-recognized names following their brutal martyrdom at the hands of Klansmen. Andrew Goodman, twenty years of age from New York City had just days before joined the summer volunteer contingent; Michael Schwerner, a New York activist along with his wife, Rita, had been in Mississippi since January of '64. They recently had joined with the other mostly white college kids in Oxford, Ohio to be prepared by SNCC veterans for what lay in wait for them in Mississippi. James Chaney was only twenty-one years old, but already a seasoned black activist from Meridian, Mississippi. Chaney had just met Goodman and had known the Schwerners only a few months. Sheriff Lawrence Rainey and Deputy Cecil Price were key plotters among the Ku Kluxers responsible for their abductions and murders. The three men's bodies were found six weeks later in a gravel pit outside Philadelphia, Mississippi. The murders shocked the nation.

Freedom Summer, in 1964, brought around 450 white people, mostly young and mostly students, to Mississippi. Everybody in Mississippi knew the civil rights volunteers worked solely in the black community, registering blacks to vote; holding freedom schools to teach not only basic civil rights, but black history classes and organizing principles and strategies as well. Bob Moses and other SNCC leaders were right to be concerned about how the volunteers, especially the white ones and chief among them, the white women, would be perceived in both the white and black communities. There were no white homes for white freedom summer workers to live. Any white person who offered any assistance at all was risking his or her life and livelihood. Some reached out nonetheless. It had to be done with the utmost care and secrecy. Most white volunteers stayed in black homes which did not mean that blacks were not risking their lives. Everything about civil rights risked black lives.

The Freedom Schools have become legendary. The first ones were in the Delta and in eastern Mississippi around Meridian. The schools were in mid-size towns like Greenville and Greenwood; likewise in smaller Mississippi towns like Indianola and Clarksdale; later in Philadelphia and many rural hamlets. There were some who felt the Delta was less risky than other parts of the state because the population was so heavily black. No one who lived there thought that way. There was no place in Mississippi where one could be assured of his or her safety if one was involved in civil rights organizing. Organizer, actor, and SNCC activist John O'Neal had state wide responsibility for coordination of the Freedom Schools. In the summer of 1964, O'Neal moved to McComb, Mississippi to work with those organizing Freedom House in the "colored" section of town. These locals included SNCC (later COFO) organizers Curtis Hayes (Muhammad), Hollis Watkins, as well as white SNCC activist Dennis Sweeney, and a host of local black teenagers who assisted in voter registration and community events.[4]

McComb was possibly the most violent venue in the South for civil rights organizing. The Klan controlled McComb and bombings and arson were so common that federal authorities considered declaring martial law and bringing in federal troops to maintain order. In 1961 students at Burglund High School in McComb walked out in support of voter registration, integration of public buildings and facilities, and overall support for the aims of the movement. Brenda Travis, Jacqueline Byrd (Martin), Joe Martin, Bobby Talbert, Joe Lewis and many others were expelled and refused their high school diplomas. It was not until 2006 that the McComb Public School System, in celebrating the introduction of a civil rights history course into the high school curriculum, recognized and honored those who walked out for their sacrifice and contributions those locals had made. While the students who led the walkout were never allowed to graduate from Burglund High School, all graduated from other high schools around the nation and all are now receiving their just recognition and honor.

By the time Freedom Summer had ended, organizing in Mississippi was occurring in every part of the state, yet the threat of firebombs, arson and assassination had not abated. Violence would continue until 1968. In the midst of these organizing efforts, Mississippians founded the Mississippi Freedom Democratic Party (MFDP) in 1964 in a challenge to the regular, all white Mississippi Democratic convention delegation in Atlantic City, New Jersey. This was a shock to the national Democratic Party leadership and especially to the head of the Party, President Lyndon Johnson. The MFDP's aim was to unseat and delegitimize those delegates elected in all-white Democratic primaries. The ruckus was played out on national television and captured the imagination and attention of the nation. The country had rarely seen anything like it. Such intraparty fisticuffs were supposed to take place behind closed doors. Not this time. The country was introduced for the first time to the spell-binding testimony of Mrs. Fannie Lou Hamer. Mrs. Hamer was a Mississippi woman who sharecropped on Senator Eastland's plantation and who had little formal education, and yet who organized across the South once exposed to the movement by SNCC organizers in 1962. She and other colleagues were beaten severely by police in Winona, Mississippi, as they returned from a strategy session in Alabama just months prior to the convention. Her account of this near-death experience before a national audience gripped everyone who heard her. It was not the last time she would confront and shame the powerful defenders of white supremacy. Not just in Mississippi either. As a result of this national calling-out, the Democratic convention leaders offered a sop to the MFDP. Fannie Lou Hamer and Rev. Ed King, the white chaplain at Tougaloo College and a long time civil rights organizer in Mississippi, were asked to accept "honorary" status as delegates to the convention, but were not allowed voting privileges. They refused. The convention was taken by storm. The MFDP commanded media attention beyond the Mississippi freedom organizers' most fervent expectations, but ultimately the national leaders of the party chose entrenched power and process over moral conscience and moved to expel the MFDP from their ranks.

The regular Democrats, who had since the Reconstruction era promoted and enforced white supremacy in Mississippi, carried the day. It was a shocking rebuff to those African Americans and their white supporters who believed, erroneously as it turned out, that white liberal Democrats like Hubert Humphrey, Walter Reuther, Sargent Shriver, and even Lyndon Johnson, would match their civil rights rhetoric with decisive action. As some put it, the hypocrisy of the Democratic liberal establishment demonstrated beyond any doubt that systemic authority and priorities would hold sway over any justice efforts or moral claims that lacked such systemic power and access. As FDR had a generation earlier in passing New Deal laws, President Johnson needed the old line Southern Democratic support. In the end, Senators Stennis and Eastland proved more indispensable than either Mrs. Hamer or Rev. Ed King. One could only wonder what impact the seating of the Freedom Democrats might have had on the Civil Rights Movement over the next four years had political and social morality won out in Atlantic City. Instead, violence and suppression continued unabated against any effort to make racial equity real in Mississippi. The worst was still to come. The 1964 Democratic Convention and the rebuff handed to the MFDP was a turning point for many civil rights veterans who as a result lost all hope in white America. Bob Moses would soon move to Tanzania to study under Kwame Nkrumah; Stokely Carmichael, soon to become Kwame Touré, would move away from Dr. King and other civil rights leaders and become one of the primary exponents of what would be termed "Black Power."

President Johnson won re-election by a huge majority. His victory was so substantial and overwhelming that some Republicans mourned the death of their party. But Mississippi was in the forefront of what a generation later would manifest itself as a tidal wave of conservative resurgence. Eighty-seven percent of the white Mississippi vote went to the Republican Party candidate, Sen. Barry Goldwater of Arizona. Over the next forty years, Republicans would become a surrogate for a white people's party. The leopard can change his spots. The party of Lincoln became home to the still-entrenched old guard of Southern segregationists. White Mississippians saw it coming before the rest of the nation.

SCLC decided to organize a march from Selma to Montgomery in January 1965, to dramatize white resistance to voting rights for all Americans, a fundamental right in a democracy. Again, resistance was strong and again whites would depend on the local police and state highway patrol to stand-in for them. The first march at the Edmund Pettis Bridge in Selma ended in a bloodbath and police riot. Once again it was caught on tape and sent out to the nation. Police brutality and a complete disdain for the civil rights marchers' purpose dramatized the inevitable results of segregation. Violence had occurred a day before the march when Jimmie Lee Jackson, a local man in his early twenties, was killed, allegedly by an Alabama state trooper. Jackson's murder was not given much attention in the white press. But the reaction in the black community was profound. For the first time many local residents began to see themselves in the racial politics that heretofore had been waged by forces outside their immediate domain. The killing of Jimmie Lee Jackson brought many into the Movement for the first time.

The first Selma march also resulted in the murder of Rev. James Reeb, a Unitarian minister from Boston, who was in Selma representing the American Friends Service Committee (AFSC). Chased down an alley, Rev. Reeb was clubbed to death by police. This murder of a white clergyman caught the attention of the nation.

Outside of Detroit, Michigan, Viola Luizzo was living in a suburb. After learning about the violence of the first Selma march, she decided to go south and involve herself in "the Movement" in the spring of 1965. Throwing herself into the task immediately upon arrival, she was at the wheel of a car with four black men as passengers, returning from a voter education rally in the town of Marion, Alabama. The car was ambushed by night riders who were said to be members of the Ku Klux Klan. Luizzo was killed instantly. Her companions were not killed, but were immediately arrested. Viola Luizzo had been in the South less than forty-eight hours. It is said the FBI undercover agent, Gary Thomas Rowe, who also witnessed the bombing of the Sixteenth Street Baptist Church in Birmingham, which killed four young girls preparing for their Sunday School class, was in the car with the Klan members. Mrs. Luizzo was one of the earliest white martyrs of the Civil Rights Era. Her funeral was held in Detroit, attended by many prominent members of the Civil Rights Movement including Dr. King, Roy Wilkins, and James Farmer. Michigan Lieutenant Governor William G. Milliken, Teamsters President Jimmy Hoffa, and United Auto Workers President Walter Reuther were also among those in attendance.

Less than two weeks after her death, a charred cross was found in front of four Detroit homes, including the Luizzo residence.

Luizzo's murder is a case study in the annals of civil rights. Viola Luizzo did not fit the profile. She was not an idealistic white Northern college student with time on her hands. Viola Luizzo was a wife and mother who left her husband and children back home in Detroit to join the movement for civil rights. She was older than the typical volunteer.

She was married. She was not working outside the home. Within the movement, she was heralded. Outside the movement, and especially in the South, she was vilified as a home-wrecker and a mother that did not care about or for her children. She was called a whore and was routinely said to have been having sex with black men. The fact that she had not been in the South long enough to shake hands with anyone, black or white, must have been lost in translation. Nonetheless, Viola Luizzo has never acquired the iconic status of so many other civil rights martyrs. The besmirching of her name and the sullying of her character seemed to have worked.

Luizzo's name was inscribed on a civil rights memorial in the Michigan State Capitol. But only in 1991 was Liuzzo honored by the Women of the Southern Christian Leadership Conference with a marker on the highway (Highway 80) where she was murdered in the Ku Klux Klan attack in 1965.

After Luizzo's murder, Dr. King called for a national response to the Selma police violence. He called for representatives of all major mainstream church denominations to join him at Selma for a second march the next weekend. Selma broke the back momentarily of the overt police violence against civil rights protesters. It led immediately to President Johnson going on national television to deplore the murderous events of Selma and to demand that Congress pass the Voting Rights Act of 1965, which guaranteed the right to vote for all citizens regardless of race.

Over fifty years later, the nation looked back and celebrated the 1961 Freedom Rides, the 1963 March on Washington and the 1964 Freedom Summer. Movement leaders were lionized across the nation from Mississippi to the Nation's Capitol. Yet most white people seemed to be indifferent spectators to what is now called "black people's history."

Chapter 17

Ongoing Resistance to Civil Rights

Immediately outside the city limits of Oxford, Mississippi in 1964 was a billboard with its message, "MARTIN LUTHER KING AT COMMUNIST TRAINING SCHOOL," with an arrow pointing to the young Rev. King. I had a curious reaction to it given the times and my upbringing. I assumed it was true even though I had no idea what a communist training school was or where one might be. I guess I thought it was either in the Soviet Union or somewhere up North. But I also didn't care. I knew I had some type of admiration for Dr. King even if I would have had a hard time articulating what the admiration was. Part of it was cheering for the underdog which was a private conversation I would have with myself for years where racial mores in the South were concerned. Another aspect of it was that Martin Luther King, Jr. seemed to be living out the Christian teachings I was getting in church on Sundays. In my surroundings the mere mention of Dr. King would cause a torrent of racial epithets from any white people around. He was called Martin Luther Koon, a fraud, a communist, a n----- preacher who someone should shut up. Dr. King would be vilified as to his "real" intentions and said to be a dupe of foreign agents. I would hear people say that he was no Christian because the Bible doesn't believe in race-mixing. Otherwise God would not have made some of us white and others of us colored. I heard that Dr. King (never spoken of with this amount of respect) was supported by New York liberals and Jews and that he should be ashamed of himself for causing so much violence. This was a recurring theme in my growing-up days: It was the Negroes who were causing the violence. However brutal the white attackers of black people were, it was the fault of black people. Negroes provoked white people into violence with "all this civil rights nonsense." "Things were just fine before civil rights" was a common refrain, as was "Negroes down here are happy and like things the way they are."

Interestingly, I didn't hear this at home. My father was very conservative on all issues and especially on race. You knew he was against "all that's going on," but he was a gentleman and did not use profane language and did not denigrate other people. It was clear where he stood, but he did not sit us down like some fathers did and instruct us on the fine points of white supremacy or in attacking persons like Dr. King. Looking back, I found this compelling.

I started reading "good books" when I was a junior in high school. One of the first ones I read (probably at the suggestion of my friend, Nibs Stroupe) was James Baldwin's Another Country. *I wrote my reflections on what I had read on the front inside cover. In fact, I got in a habit of doing this; then I would put the book with its marginalia away on my book shelf. A few years later, when I was in college at Ole Miss and a budding liberal on the race issue and civil rights in particular, I happened to pull* Another Country *from the shelf and noticed my father had written a response to my reflections. What I have never forgotten about this is that he never mentioned it to me. His response was reasoned and muted and offered a critique of what I had said, but there was no reprimand or scolding in his words. In retrospect, I realized I was being allowed to develop on my own even as the context in which this was taking place was one of violence, murder and bloodshed. This combination of active reading of the civil rights literature, my growing involvement in whatever actions were taking place in Mississippi and Memphis, and the continuing effort on my part to acquaint myself with graduate schools in the North where my interests in history could best be met were transforming me and creating in me a new persona — one based on my actions and not just intellectual pursuits.*

Both before and after the Selma marches, voting rights campaigns continued to be waged in towns all over the South. The right to vote along with access to public accommodations like hotels, restaurants, and public transportation were the presenting issues in most local campaigns. Change did not occur quickly. Groups like SNCC and CORE and in Mississippi, COFO, could not be everywhere at once. Still, significant integration did not occur until the late 1970s in many places. There were several reasons for this. Resistance to the Civil Rights

Movement was often a small town affair. Towns like Albany, Georgia; Selma, Alabama; Bogalusa, Louisiana and McComb, Mississippi were battleground sites with civil rights armies pitted against small town police by day and Klan terrorists at night.

Business establishments that were locally-owned offered more resistance over time than did emerging national chain stores and retailers. Locally-owned restaurants, motels, apparel shops, jewelry stores, even banks and insurance companies could refuse to do business with blacks. Because the reach of white supremacy was so long, insinuating itself into every facet of both white and black life, testing the boundaries of race had severe repercussions.

Often whites would refuse to eat in an integrated restaurant or even spend the night at a hotel known to allow blacks and other "undesirables" as guests. One could feel the "chill" when someone entered an establishment who did not "belong" there. The tension that arose and the potential for a "scene" to occur were palpable. This was not just a Southern phenomenon. It happened in all-night truck stops, movie theaters, drive-in burger joints, and anywhere white kids "hung-out" across the country.

Most main streets in the South and Southwest depended on black and Mexican American shoppers. This was certainly true on the weekends. But within the stores themselves, racial mores persisted. Usually blacks, "Mexicans" and Indians could not handle merchandise that might be bought by white shoppers. They could not try clothes on in the dressing rooms. These were reserved for whites. "Coloreds" could not use the store's bathroom. Patterns of segregation existed everywhere. Inside or out it was the same. One was raised breathing the air of racial social decorum.

Boycotts of these locally-owned businesses were a tactic consistently employed in parts of the South. In northern Mississippi boycotts were waged in Clarksdale, Mississippi as early as 1961 and throughout the decades of the 1960s and 1970s boycotts were waged all over the South in large cities like Houston and small towns like Grenada and Holly Springs, Mississippi. In Bogalusa, Louisiana, a boycott led by the Bogalusa Voters League lasted more than a year. Writer Peter Honigsberg, who was assigned to the Bogalusa movement while he was a student at the New York University School of Law and interning with the New Orleans-based Lawyers Constitutional Defense Committee, recalls in his memoir Crossing Border Street:

> The pickets in Bogalusa had continued nearly every day for more than a year, and the white-owned businesses were suffering. During the previous Christmas season, they had been so frustrated at the success of the boycott that they called in the local Klan to break up the demonstrations.[1]

Economic boycotts hurt quasi-segregated white-owned businesses because these businesses were economically dependent on black patronage in the South and Mexican Americans in the Southwest to survive. Boycotters were vilified by the white community. It was one thing to shout "Equality Now!" while on the march but it was another thing to cut off white people's livelihood. Not many white people appreciated the irony of a boycott. It was the flip side of what whites had done for two centuries to blacks: cut off the money supply. Boycotts were successful if they could be sustained. This wasn't easy. It took real commitment and real staying power to boycott because blacks and Mexican Americans shopped on main street, too. So boycotts entailed sacrifice by those parts of the community instigating the boycotts. The greater good had to prevail for them to work.

It was different, in some ways, for businesses such as restaurants which were national franchises like Howard Johnson's or Holiday Inn. Often located directly adjacent to interstate highway exits, such businesses were more susceptible to federal law than small-town mom and pop operations. Name brands with national clientele and a public persona could not afford to be less than welcoming to any of their customers. Some, like Shoney's and later Denny's, attempted to follow local custom when it came to discrimination against blacks, but lawsuits eventually broke their will as well as their bank. Nonetheless, ending Whites Only policies that had been in place for years took time. Old customs died hard. The interstate highway system itself played a role in efforts to end segregation in public accommodations. Not only did it give travelers access to nearby national retailers, it began to break the extreme isolation of small towns across the South. This was true across the country, throughout Midwestern and certain Far West states where strangers were often suspect. Strangers who were "colored" were all the more so.

Because whites in Mississippi, Arkansas, and other Southern states had more mobility than did blacks and Mexican Americans, they were not as dependent on local businesses outside of grocery stores, gas stations and pharmacies. Whites had to be courted, even placated, to remain loyal to local businesses. Most whites ignored the downtown white merchants even though they detested the boycotts. In northern Mississippi, whites would travel to Memphis to shop; in the southern part of the state, New Orleans was a favorite destination. In Texas there was Dallas and Houston. When whites and blacks had to intermix downtown, there were often unwritten codes as to when and where blacks could shop. The same was true of Texas towns that depended on Mexican Americans' business. There was an appearance of openness that belied ways of doing things that kept white supremacy firmly in place and in charge.

Most whites in the South felt segregation would last forever. There was a wall of silence in the white schools and churches about the challenges being mounted to end segregation. White supremacy itself was under attack. Still, it was impossible to be oblivious to what was happening. One knew about "civil rights" but was assured by white leaders that nothing would change. If you were an "average white citizen" or a white child growing up in any of the Southern states, it could all seem far away. Denial was profound among whites, but at the same time there was a certain schizophrenia at work. On the one hand reactions to the *Brown* decision were virulent and bombastic. Among those most opposed to integration and to any interference on the federal government's part with the so-called "Southern way of life," there was both deep resentment and even hatred about what was at stake. On the other hand, white people denied anything was happening.

White Citizens Councils sprung up across the southern United States by the hundreds. It was a rare small town that didn't have one. At first they were put forth as a "gentleman's" or a "businessman's alternative" to the rowdiness and violent image of the Ku Klux Klan. The White Citizen's Council purported to oppose integration and federal government interference in local Southern affairs by legal means. Even in 2010, former Mississippi Governor Haley Barbour could fall back on that myth. Asked why Yazoo City's public school integration avoided the violence seen in other towns, Barbour said:

> Because the business community wouldn't stand for it...You heard of the Citizens Councils? Up north they think it was like the KKK. Where I come from it was an organization of town leaders. In Yazoo City they passed a resolution that said anybody who started a chapter of the Klan would get their ass run out of town. If you had a job, you'd lose it. If you had a store, they'd see

> nobody shopped there. We didn't have a problem with the Klan in Yazoo City.[2]

Yet the alliance between "good government forces" and the "race mobs" of the Klan was both presumed and readily remarked upon. No one kidded themselves. The white South was rock-solid. No variance from the segregationist line was tolerated. From classroom to living room the message was the same: Challenge it and there was a price to pay.

The idea of a White Citizen's Council came from a small town dentist named Dr. Thomas Brady of Indianola, Mississippi. White Citizen's Council members wore white shirts rather than white sheets. The White Citizen's Council was an organizing tactic. It depended on the network of white institutions that linked together pastors of local churches, school boards, white women's clubs and white-owned small businesses. A businessman, however, was likely to be a trustee of a local Methodist, Presbyterian or downtown Southern Baptist church. During his career he might sit on the local school board, be a member of the Kiwanis or Lions Club, or the local medical society.

The KKK did their business in the dark and while masked. Groups like the White Citizen Councils or Downtown Business Associations were strictly nine to five. After five, however, the conversation might move to the country club, the local bar association or even the church supper. Until the late 1960s, the Klan had the tacit support of "respectable" white people. Many whites who themselves would never join a mob, rationalized the violence as "the Negroes' fault." They focused their ire especially on Dr. King whom they saw as continually creating situations that led to violence. "It was not our doing, but we understand why it was done," was the mantra. This was true even in the North. In a Chicago suburb where white mobs in 1966 nearly killed Dr. King as he led a march for fair housing and open accommodations, white critics of Dr. King claimed that he should have known better, that he had brought the violence upon himself. The antagonism was directed toward "outside agitators," a staple fed to white people by parents, ministers, teachers, and white elected officials.

The South was solid. Segregation would be defended with the same dedication and ferocity that characterized the early Civil War years. The idea of secession, however, which many whites would still have preferred, was no longer a realistic option. Even so, whites would use every means at their disposal, legal and otherwise, to fight what most whites still viewed — one hundred years after the Civil War — as an example of federal infringement upon constitutionally-embedded states' rights and an individual's personal choice. This had not changed.

Chapter 18

White "Race Traitors" in the Civil Rights Movement

Later, much later, I would learn that many whites were, in fact, grappling with this system of white supremacy. I just was never told about them. People like Lillian Smith with her seminal book, Killers of the Dream, *and Jessie Daniel Ames and her work against lynching were unknown to me. In McComb, over time I would learn of the stands some white residents took against the violence sweeping the city and others who were welcoming to civil rights workers. Many years after the events, my sister, Patti, would tell me about the Heffner family who had to flee McComb under death threats because they played host to "civil rights workers" during the summer of '64. This was true even though one of their daughters had recently been selected as runner-up to Miss Mississippi and competed as an alternate in the Miss America Pageant. The Heffner's actions were seen as a serious, even traitorous, breach of Southern racial etiquette. White Mississippians were proud of our beauty queens.*

In my own family, there were those who opposed segregation and worked to bring about civil rights. It was a subject never discussed, though sometimes hinted at. My Uncle Bob and my Aunt Peggy in their work with the Methodist church were serious opponents of the racial status quo. Uncle Bob moved to Memphis after the war and for the next forty years worked to inch his local church forward on issues of race, gender, and sexuality. In Memphis, Bob partnered with more famous civil rights activists such as the Reverend James Lawson.

My Uncle Bob knew and admired Rev. Lawson, who was a future Bishop of the United Methodist Church and a confidant of Dr. Martin Luther King, Jr. Rev. Lawson was a lead organizer and supporter of the garbage workers strike in Memphis in 1968 and his presence in Memphis was one reason Dr. King agreed to get involved.

Uncle Bob began a coffee house ministry in midtown Memphis in 1967 and "Common Ground" became a gathering place for interracial strategy sessions and celebrations around campaigns like the garbage strike in 1968 and others that followed. Uncle Bob stood with tenants in Sugar Ditch, Mississippi, twenty miles down Highway 61 from Memphis in the early '70s. He was a part of the first integrated citywide church choir in Memphis in 1978. Uncle Bob was one of those quiet white civil rights proponents who graced the South throughout the Civil Rights Movement. It was risky business. He had to be careful what he said and to whom he said it. He could not be too public without risking exposure that could bring opprobrium on himself, his family and his fellow associates. This was the South's own "silent minority." They were all over. But caution was the word and it had nothing to do with aversion to risk. It was risky in those years to be even a cautious civil rights worker regardless of race.

Likewise, my Uncle Cliff lent his name to a McComb newspaper advertisement taken out by certain white citizens calling for an end to the racial violence that was paralyzing life in McComb in the early sixties. It was a courageous act in 1965. I wish I had known he did this. I would have been so proud of him, but I now understand why he had to be prudent. Putting your name on a civil rights petition as a white person in McComb could get you killed. I was almost sixty years old before I learned that Uncle Cliff had signed that public petition to end violence in McComb. I was probably more proud of him at sixty than I would have been at twenty. But, I would have been proud at any age. Still am.

The one person I knew who was a "civil rights worker" in the family was Peggy, my aunt, and the youngest of the nine Billings children. Although I cannot remember this being discussed openly, I knew from a young age that Peggy was doing work that had to do with "Negro rights." I knew that much. It was whispered. It was never discussed when I was around. Peggy was always described as "living in New York" and "a missionary to Korea." But one knew growing up that Uncle Bob and Aunt Peggy were different. It was just never explained what that difference was, exactly. They were different in numerous ways. But both had an unyielding and consistent bent toward justice.

Peggy Billings, working out of her New York office located at 475 Riverside Drive, was Secretary for Racial Justice in the Women's Division of the United Methodist Church. The Women's Division was the most outspoken and involved of all sections of the UMC during the civil rights years. Peggy, mentored by one of the most stalwart social justice organizers in the nation, the legendary Thelma Stevens (also a Mississippi native), succeeded Stevens in 1968. Peggy Billings maintained Stevens' commitment to equal rights and humane treatment under the law for all people. For the next thirty years, Peggy Billings brought her sense of justice to every major human rights struggle in the United States and around the world. From civil rights to women's rights and from the Law of the Sea to the rights of lesbian and gays within the church, she was either in the forefront or right behind the scenes. Her influence and impact on literally hundreds of United Methodists over her years of leadership in the church was formidable. One of those was me.

Peggy's work with the Women's Division spanned the globe, but she never lost sight of the civil rights movement in the South. Following the path made possible by such giants as Mary McCloud Bethune, Ida B. Wells, Jesse Daniel Ames, Eleanor Roosevelt, Dorothy Height and Thelma Stevens, Peggy Billings and Arkansas-born Theressa Hoover, General Secretary of the Women's Division, used their offices to finance, publish, and publicize human rights campaigns happening around the world. Jesse Daniel Ames, Thelma Stevens, Peggy Billings and Theressa Hoover were all Southern women in the struggle for civil rights and social justice and there were many more.

What I heard growing up about Peggy was limited to a story here and a rumor there. It was rumored that Peggy was photographed with Dr. King and the photo was making the rounds in Mississippi. It was rumored that she had been told not to enter Mississippi because the authorities "were afraid for her safety." My favorite "rumor" was no rumor at all. In the heat of the battles being waged in McComb by the early sixties, the pastor of the local Methodist church, where a number of members of the family attended, paid a visit to Uncle Cliff suggesting to him that Peggy would be "more comfortable" if her name was removed from the membership roll of the church. Uncle Cliff is said to have replied: "I am sure she would be. And while you do that, remove the rest of us, too."

Bogey-men have always haunted the South when it came to its cherished white way of life. A century before the Civil Rights Movement, it was the Abolitionist and the rebellious black male slave. In 1960, it was the outside agitator and the civil rights worker. Held in particular disgust, however, was the native Southerner who came to be viewed as a racial turncoat. For those white Southerners deemed in support of efforts to tear down white supremacist institutions and who favored the end of segregation, there was reserved a special hostility. Throughout US history, white people who broke racial ranks and attempted to forge perceived common interests with those of "colored" people paid a price. For most of our nation's history, coming together across racial lines cost white people home, hearth, and income.

A sort of mind control flourished in the Deep South, a way of seeing the world that had been ingrained in white Southerners for generations. To buck it made life unbearable. For white men to be against segregation or "for civil rights" meant that you would be fired or boycotted, forced to leave town to get your haircut, car fixed, or house repaired. For a white woman to support civil rights against her husband might lead to divorce. To join her husband in any actions against segregation meant being cut off from social functions or prestigious volunteer positions and receiving constant telephone calls threatening to blow up your house, even kill your children. For white children if their parents became known as being "for civil rights," it meant being beat up on the playground, attacked while going to and from school, being "blackballed" from sororities and fraternities, and finding it impossible to get a date to the prom. This "way of life" was undergirded and supported by church, home and school. The Bible was taught and interpreted with an eye on segregation. Any pastor preaching to the contrary was quickly reprimanded and usually transferred or fired. Any teacher bringing civil rights into the classroom or who seemed sympathetic to the plight of "Negroes" was not rehired.

Those few who dared to test the boundaries of psychological and societal segregation were shunned, ostracized, threatened and boycotted. It is almost beyond imagining to think that any white Southerner would speak out and challenge the racial status quo. Yet some did. In every Southern town there were those who, however cautiously and within certain well-defined parameters, supported the efforts of "colored" people to achieve equal rights. This, too, had its limits. Among whites, it was assumed that moderates would not "act" on such beliefs.

If one was a professor or a writer and to some extent even a minister, especially if one was Episcopalian, such beliefs would even be tolerated. That is, if one did not attempt "to stir things up." But white Southerners who did act were seen as race traitors. They were most often held in deep contempt by other Southern whites.

White ministers in the South involved themselves in civil rights activities at their own peril and at great risk to their careers, livelihoods, and even their lives. Many worked behind the scenes, and those who did speak out or join marches were often moved or were forced to hand in their orders. More than a few were fired and others had to leave town. But even in the Delta region of Mississippi, home to some of the bitterest racial antagonism in the state, thirteen white clergy signed a Declaration of Conscience in 1965[1]. The Declaration decried the violence that was raging across the state and implored white Christians to live up to the teachings of Jesus. There were certainly some clergy who made courageous, death-defying stands against the evils of segregation and supported the civil rights workers. The Reverend Duncan Gray, an Episcopal priest whose son would one day be Bishop of the Mississippi Episcopal Diocese, did more than speak out. He acted on his beliefs. In so doing, he could have easily been killed during the riot at Ole Miss. Duncan Gray would be steadfast in his commitment to justice. So would other Ole Miss campus ministers like Jimmy Jones and before him the Rev. Will D. Campbell.[2]

Black ministers had their churches bombed, burned to the ground and trashed as a result of harboring civil rights workers or allowing their sanctuaries to be used for meetings and strategy sessions. At least a dozen black churches were bombed in McComb alone during June of 1964.

White campus ministers probably had the most freedom to support the Movement among white clergy. Rev. Will D. Campbell, a campus minister at Ole Miss from 1958 –1960, used his position to bring speakers to campus who spoke out in defiance of Mississippi racial norms and behaviors. Campbell was not fired, but enthusiastically encouraged to leave by university officials and white Baptist denominational leaders. He went on to work for the National Council of Churches Racial Justice Office throughout the 1960s and mentored a generation of younger white clergy, some of whom are still active today. Campbell's ability to relate to poor Southern white supremacists, including Klan members, was a rare gift among white clergy. The Rev.

Ed King is a Methodist minister and native Mississippian who was unquestionably the most visible white civil rights activist in the state from 1963 to 1968. He continues his work in Mississippi today. King was Chaplain at Tougaloo College, a HBCU in Jackson and one of the key players in the founding of the Mississippi Freedom Democratic Party.

White Southerner Bob Zellner was almost a martyr on many different occasions. Said to be the first white person on the Student Non-Violent Coordinating Committee (SNCC) staff, Zellner was the prototype of the Southern white "race traitor." Like Lillian Smith, Anne Braden and Thelma Stevens a generation before, Zellner was not an "outsider." He was from Alabama, the son of a Methodist minister, and a college student at Spring Hill College in Mobile when he became active with SNCC. Zellner's courage and fearlessness are the things of legend among white Southerners who followed in his footsteps a generation later. Bob, as a white Southerner, brought down a particular wrath from defenders of white supremacy reserved for such Southerners. Zellner was stomped on the steps of McComb, Mississippi's City Hall in broad daylight in 1960. It is said that members of SNCC cried when they decided that whites should no longer be SNCC organizers but needed to find ways to organize in the white community. Bob and his wife, Dorothy Miller (Zellner), continue to this day to organize, teach and lecture for social justice across the United States. Bob's role in the civil rights movement gave him a place in history, although dominant culture historians largely ignore his role and downplay the violent reprisals on white people like him. This became the norm in writing about the civil rights period. Whites were often not identified either in photos or history books. To the white child — indeed for all children — the impression was given that no whites were in the Movement.

Even moderate, behind-the-scenes, modest actions led to serious repercussions. Consider the Heffner family I first heard about from my sister Patti. Hodding Carter, a Mississippi newspaper publisher of the *Delta-Democrat Times,* in his book *So The Heffners Left McComb,* tells how this middle class white Episcopalian family, whose daughter was runner-up to Miss Mississippi in 1963, was forced to leave their home because of threats and harassment following a gathering at their McComb house where "civil rights workers" were present. The fact that these "civil rights workers" were all white and members of a church mission project from "up North" was of no moment. Appearances of sympathy were proof enough. The Heffners' behavior went far beyond established white norms of conduct. They entertained the volunteers in their home and invited others to hear their story. Red and Malva Heffner became active in Mississippi civil rights work, attending conferences, meeting with SNCC and CORE leadership, and going public with their support by writing letters to the editor of the two largest Mississippi daily papers. The Heffners were forced to leave McComb within weeks of their defiance of white Southern customs. They moved to Jackson, Mississippi, but met a similar reception there. Finally they moved to a suburb near Washington, DC where they continued their work in support of civil rights.[3]

In some ways, white Southerners were more honest than those in the North where race was concerned. The North protected whites and white supremacy in ways the South did not. De facto social segregation was as pronounced in most Northern cities as anywhere in the South. Small towns in the North were much more likely to be "all white" than in the South. While the history of segregation was different in the North, the reality of white systemic control was the same everywhere in the United States. There was no social equity regardless of which section of the country one was in. There was no legal or financial sector in the US where wealth or jobs or educational opportunities were equally distributed among whites and people of color. Housing was always segregated except for the poorest of whites and newly-arrived European immigrants. Wherever whites lived, if economics began to dictate racially-integrated housing patterns, whites, however poor, attempted to leave. As George Lipsitz notes,

> The suburbs helped turn Euro-Americans into "whites" who could live near each other and intermarry with relatively little difficulty. But this "white" unity rested on residential segregation, on shared access to housing and life chances largely unavailable to communities of color.[4]

Moving into an all-white neighborhood or suburb was a major milestone on the road to success in America. It was the American Dream.

It took almost two decades for most Southern cities to even begin to comply with the 1954 *Brown* Supreme Court ruling. Yet in 1966, when Dr. King moved with his family into a Chicago ghetto to begin his Chicago Freedom Movement, his reception was just as mean and violent as it was in the South. In August, when marching through

Chicago's all-white Southwest Side, angry crowds of whites threw rocks — hitting Dr. King in the head — and shouted threats so vile and immediate that the police refused to allow a similarly planned march in neighboring Cicero, claiming they could not guarantee Dr. King's safety. Ironically, it was the marchers who were blamed for the hostilities. It was an article of faith among whites that violence was not their fault. The civil rights workers, especially Dr. King, had brought the reaction upon themselves.

Northern school segregation was rarely challenged because it was largely due to extreme housing segregation. De facto segregation was not against the law. Earlier Supreme Court school desegregation decisions had outlawed only the *de jure* segregation prevalent in Southern schools. The decisions did not condemn *de facto* segregation that existed in Boston and other Northern cities. Indeed, in the Supreme Court's unanimous opinion in *Brown,* Chief Justice Warren stated, "Segregation in Boston public schools was eliminated in 1855." It was segregation all the same.

When, in 1971, the Supreme Court ruled in *Swann v. Charlotte-Mecklenburg* that utilization of measures which were "administratively awkward, inconvenient, and even bizarre" to achieve integration was legal, parents in cities like Boston were appalled. Boston was certainly segregated. So as the Supreme Court began to turn its attention away from schools in the South to focus on those in the North, the justices soon discovered that achieving desegregation in Northern schools would require different tactics. The strategy of assigning students to schools closest to their homes, the solution for Southern desegregated schools, did not work in the North because of segregated housing patterns.

The very idea of busing white students to former "colored" schools was met with fury on the part of white parents. Throughout the 1970s, white "ethnics" (as the blue-collar opponents of busing were frequently called) defended their turf. In 1972, for example, whites in Pontiac, Michigan, a blue-collar city near Detroit, held violent anti-desegregation demonstrations and destroyed several school buses. Violent opposition occurred in parts of Cleveland, Newark and Yonkers, N.Y.

But it was Boston, a bastion, it was thought, of social liberalism, which proved to be profoundly obstinate where race and integration were concerned. White, working class Bostonians, often called "Southies" because of their concentration in the neighborhoods of

South Boston, were on the front line of resistance. In the fall of 1974, their inchoate rage and the violent attacks on black students being bussed to attend formerly all-white schools exposed the nation to virulent racism, Northern style.

White violence in Boston, rivaling anything in the Southern US, demonstrated how difficult compliance with the Supreme Court's order was going to be across the nation. The anti-busing crusade foretold racism's future manifestation: Race would not be mentioned. Opposition to busing would not mean opposing the ideals of integrated education. It would just mean that, because of racialized housing patterns, integration would be impossible.

Nothing in the violence caused most of us as whites to take a look at ourselves and personally confront the demons that possessed us. Even when four young girls were murdered at the 16th Street Baptist Church in Birmingham in 1963, or when teenagers were knocked down by blasts from fire hoses with German shepherds snapping at them, or when shards of glass from shattered school bus windows bloodied children's faces, most whites held fast to our innocence. We blamed the "Negroes" for putting their own children at risk, exposing them to police counter attacks as a mere tactic in the race wars. This still goes on today. Whites will usually deny any racial intent on their part in any situation or controversy that occurs. It will be blacks who are blamed for bringing up race. "Playing the race card" is a way for whites to claim that blacks are merely whining or making race an excuse for their own failures to take personal responsibility. This deflection, or transference, as mental health therapists call it, maintains white supremacy while absolving whites of any role in its continuation.

Integration was merely a phase in many cities and towns across the nation. Whites in cities — North and South — moved as quickly as possible to the suburbs; whites in the small-town South created private segregation academies. By 1990 racial segregation for all intents and purposes had returned throughout the nation.

Chapter 19

Radicalization of the Civil Rights Movement

I have always assumed my politics were those of the left, as they say, but it has been an uneasy relationship. I have seen the world from the vantage point of one rejecting the extreme conservatism in which I was raised, but never fully embracing or feeling fully embraced by those whose politics I supported. It has been a lifetime of contradictions, ricocheting between the "down home" cultural roots of my white Southern upbringing yet striving for recognition by those looked upon as radicals or leftists. I finally wound up calling myself "anti-racist."

Race has been my fixation, even obsession. I have engaged the world around race because race has been the one constant in my political life. Not class, not gender, not sexuality, but always race. I did not look for intersections. Does this mean I have been passed by those whose understandings now encompass all of the oppressions? Not at all. For me, it has been crucial to stay focused on race. If not, I will surely escape my accountability to people of color. I must stay focused so I can understand how white supremacy interferes with a class or gender analysis. At least it does for me. I must confront all oppressions as a white person, and more specifically, a white male with an anti-racist foundation. Otherwise, I uphold white supremacy even as one on the left.

I always come back home. We were not self-identified by class or even by gender. My people were resistant to class identification and try, as the left often did, to bring us together across race lines, race was what divided us. Our lives were lived with a certain, often unspoken, allegiance to the nation's race construct. I have been in many a meeting or organizing campaign where the calls were for a united class-based approach to whatever issue was before us that moment or that day. Only rarely, and even then destined to quickly flame-out, have I seen class supersede race. It could never hold. At these sessions I heard people speak of organizing "working people" or "poor people," but in my head I wondered who they were talking to. Not my people. It was the same with gender-based organizing. It was not going to work with the women I had grown up with, lived among, who made up my family circle. But race could do it every time. When white advantage seemed at risk, even if race was never mentioned, we knew what it was and we fought back with every cliché-ridden phrase provided us. "Why can't we just put it behind us?" "Why must everything be about race?" "What is it that makes blacks so angry?" "We earned what we have." "No one handed it to us." "They need to take personal responsibility for their situation." "It is certainly not my fault." Appeals to class solidarity or gender equity were just ignored — sometimes even mocked.

Fact is, I have an inferiority complex when it comes to those called left wing or progressive. I never felt accepted. I was never truly one of them. Maybe I am not angry enough. Maybe I did not want to ultimately displease my parents or my sisters or my cousins. I just couldn't throw it away. I couldn't cut the bonds. Not that anyone on the left ever asked me to do this. This has been an internal discussion between me and myself all my life long.

Dr. Michael Washington, at one of the People's Institute national trainings in the mid-80s, asked me once: "Are you going to visit your parents after this? Don't they live near here?" We were in Waveland, Mississippi at the very spot where SNCC asked its white members to leave and go organize in their own communities. I certainly did plan to go home. As soon as the gathering was over, I was out of there. But that is not what I said. I hemmed and hawed and said something to the effect that I was unsure if I was or wasn't going to visit them. He must have read my thoughts and said to me: "Let me get this straight. You can love our parents, but you can't love your own. You can love black people, but not your own white people? Get your ass home. Tell 'em you love them. Then, maybe we will allow you to continue to work with us in the black community." MAYBE.

My awkward dance with the left did not stop me from currying favor with those whose critique of the dominant American culture was that it needed funda-

mental transformation, even if it took taking actions outside the parameters of the law. I was drawn to this analysis, even as I was afraid of it. In 1965, while still at Ole Miss, I met the Rev. Jimmy Jones who was the United Methodist campus minister. Jones had followed in the footsteps of Rev. Will Campbell and Rev. Duncan Gray and was the fourth white person whose politics shaped my view of the world. Jimmy Jones was founder of a coffee house just off the campus in Oxford. He was joined by a Presbyterian minister and an Episcopal priest. The "Earth," as it was called, was a sanctuary for me. The persons who passed through were often well-known. Peter Yarrow of Peter, Paul, and Mary fame sang there. Staughton Lynd and Allard Lowenstein spoke there. So did Marian Wright (later Edelman), the first black woman to be admitted to the Mississippi Bar. Entertainers like Mississippi Fred McDowell performed at The Earth.

Most of all, it was where I would spend hours with Jimmy Jones talking about race and Mississippi politics and the Vietnam War. The Earth was one of the very few places in Mississippi where blacks and whites came together to meet, socialize, and sometimes even date one another. This was risky business. Interracial romance was still taboo in Mississippi and would remain so for many more years. Still it happened. The atmosphere created by Jimmy Jones and his co-workers was rare indeed. Jones was cool. The first time I met him in his office on the campus, he was wearing a tight black tee shirt with his sleeves rolled up, his cigarettes stashed inside the cuff. He had wavy black hair and sideburns. To me, he was daring and ultra hip. He was also one that pushed back against the white supremacy world of Ole Miss which was still reeling with the aftershocks of James Meredith's forceful integration of the state's most segregated institution. I witnessed him split apart a crowd of angry and obnoxious white students who had encircled the few black students, trapping them in Oxford's town square, and lead them to safety. It was a courageous act. I think it averted an ugly scene where racial violence was about to boil over. He might have saved someone's life.

Jimmy Jones took an active part in the Mississippi Freedom Democratic Party. I wanted to be like him. Someone told me he was a dangerous white man. I was not sure why they said it, but I do know it was said. I had not yet met the Rev. Ed King, the Chaplain at Tougaloo College, who was often called "the most courageous white man in Mississippi." Dangerous was a serious charge back then. It meant a willingness to engage in violence to topple white supremacy. I had only known of those willing to engage in violence, if necessary, to preserve white supremacy. I never heard Jimmy Jones utter a word about violence. Quite the contrary, in fact. Was violence justified to overthrow the system? This question would remain with me.

Over the years I had many mentors whose politics were radical, even revolutionary. Farnsworth Lobenstein in New York City, one of the organizers of People Against Racism (PAR), was an outspoken revolutionary. I was drawn to Lobenstein and to PAR, but they were ultimately too scary for me. I was not ready for what they talked about. I hung around the edges, but never ventured into the inner circle. This would become a pattern with me. There were highly-principled people who felt that the US would never voluntarily relinquish white supremacy. It had to be destroyed. Taken down. Some were killed in shoot-outs with police; others went to prison and spent most of their lives there. Some are still in prison and will die there. I couldn't do it. I don't feel my stance was as principled as theirs. I think I was just scared.

The Civil Rights Movement had become in every way, by early 1968, a worldwide human rights movement. People across the globe, from Jackson, Mississippi to the new African nations were rising up in great numbers to throw off the yoke of colonialism and white supremacy and to demand justice and equal rights. Worldwide revolutionary movements fueled hopes of the freedom movement of the black South and vice-versa. African peoples long-colonized by various European nations began to shake off European colonialism and to organize a pan-African revolt against imperialism. Similar movements were growing in Asia and in the Middle East. In the Americas a revolutionary movement was victorious in Cuba and growing in other Latin countries. Students were in rebellion on every continent. In South Africa, for example, student leader Stephen Biko, who helped found the Black Consciousness Movement ("black is beautiful") became a martyr of the anti-apartheid movement in 1977. He died "under suspicious circumstances" while in South African police custody.

The Black Liberation movement had always understood and been undergirded by the following premise: Collective redress of grievances, organized and accountable to a grassroots black constituency, and rooted in the historical memory of liberation struggles across the globe, had brought down Jim Crow. It was this collective organizing strategy that fueled THE DREAM.

Malcolm X did not enter mainstream white consciousness until well over a decade after he had become a major national leader in the Nation of Islam. His debut came about during a question and answer session following a major speech in midtown Manhattan on December 1, 1963, when Malcolm X spoke about John Kennedy's assassination as an instance of "the chickens coming home to roost." To black liberationists like those in the Nation of Islam, America had fomented violence, so it was not a surprise that the president had become a victim.

Malcolm X struck fear in most white people. His out-sized rhetorical denunciations of racism in US society were unsparing. He did not offer the olive branch of racial reconciliation as did Dr. King. His vision in his early years did not include the "beloved community" nor was his "dream" articulated in ways similar to King's. He was fearsome, unapologetic and terrifying to whites. Many who claim to be adherents of Malcolm's philosophy today might not have been so adamant in their support in the early 1960s.

In fact, MLK, Jr. and Malcolm X were both heroic in their own right. While today progressive whites often contrast and critique strategies utilized by Malcolm X and Dr. King, only those who lived with the constant threat of death to themselves and their families — leaders like Rev. Fred Shuttlesworth, John Lewis, and Paul Robeson — have the right to criticize. It is said that the FBI wanted King dead. After Malcolm X's break with the Honorable Elijah Muhammad in 1964, it was said that the Nation of Islam wanted him dead too. The stories vary, though one thing is certain: They're both dead — assassinated. In 1970, Black Panthers Fred Hampton and Mark Clark would be hunted down and shot by the FBI while sleeping in their Chicago apartment. Like Malcolm X, they were guilty of rhetorical excess.

There has always existed a radical black critique of white supremacy in the United States. From the slave ships leaving the West African coast to the present, there have been those who said white supremacy would never voluntarily renounce itself. Frederick Douglass is often quoted in this context: "Power concedes nothing without a demand. It never did and it never will." What differentiated the more radical approach from those who were dedicated to bringing white people along with them was the threat of violence on the part of the subjugated black masses. Revolt has always been white people's biggest fear. If black people rise up and defend themselves then no white person is safe. Retribution has been the psychological threat. "If blacks gain power they will do to us what we did to them" is the litany one hears in white circles.

Yet history debunks this fear. Attacks on whites by blacks have been rare. Yes, there have been some going as far back as Toussaint L'Overture's 1802 rout of Napoleon's army in Haiti, liberating Haiti from France's control. This was warfare, however. Toussaint did not advance on the French who were not part of the military. A decade later, Charles Deslondes, an African enslaved outside New Orleans in St. Charles Parish, Louisiana, led a revolt and vowed to march on New Orleans and kill white people. Deslondes's 1811 rebellion against slavery was the largest in the history of the US. Deslondes didn't make it to New Orleans. Troops were mustered and he was killed along with several of his co-conspirators. All were beheaded with their severed heads placed on fence posts at the entrance to the city as a stark reminder to others who might harbor such rebellious notions. Still another decade later, in 1822, Denmark Vesey in South Carolina attempted to organize a revolt among enslaved and free blacks, but was found out, arrested and hung. White officials kept the plot and the conviction secret for fear other blacks would get the same idea. In 1831, Nat Turner in Virginia broke free of his enslavement and successfully eluded capture, only to return thirty days later determined to organize blacks to join a rebellion and to kill white people. Turner was also found out, arrested, tried, hung and then skinned. Throughout the history of the United States taking up arms against white people has been met with unflinching reaction and force by state-sponsored police action, sometimes even the military.

What is instructive in these and other rebellions is that whites were protected by the power of the state, its police and even the military when needed. This is implicit in Kly's social contract. Rebellious Indians or slaves represented the anti-social contract. No quarter was given, none taken. Yet the internalizing of white supremacy renders most whites incapable of understanding the desire by black peoples to live self-determined lives without white guidance and control. Over generations, and particularly since white supremacy is no longer legal, whites have absorbed the curious and ahistorical message that US systems and institutions are not based on race. Defying common sense and amid overwhelming evidence to the contrary, whites are taught the state is neutral, that its institutions act independently of each other and are accessible to anyone willing to work hard and stay out of trouble. As systems are increasingly divorced in the public eye from their racial intent, whites cannot understand people of color's desire for their own institutions. Whites are socialized to view institutions as benign and possessing no ill effect. Therefore there is no legitimate reason for Black Nationalism. Yet, no people of color have the resources to build institutions outside white control in our race-constructed nation. Self-determination is more complicated than meeting and strategizing with no white people around. Eventually, the race construct meets you head on.

Ironically, segregation came closest to making black self-determination possible. Self-contained communities like pre-1960s Harlem made radical black thought possible in cities and towns across the nation. The Garvey movement would not have happened in an integrated society based on white supremacy. Neither would the Nation of Islam, the Black Workers Congress or even the Black Panthers. These movements for black liberation required the cultural protection of blackness where there are no white people around to listen, debate, or report back. This is the history of radical approaches to black liberation or nationalism. The race-based social contract demands it. No Harlems? Nowhere to go.

White supremacy presents itself in many different ways. In the classrooms of the nation, especially in higher education, white voices predominate. This means not only that white students speak more often or are more out-spoken in their views than others in the classroom, but that the institution itself speaks with "white voice" through the curriculum, the standards imposed to graduate, even the pictures of past presidents that adorn the walls. Whiteness is everywhere. People of color can't get away from it while whites are trained not to see it at all. Even black revolutionary theorists have to submit to white appraisal: in faculty meetings, student evaluations, and tenure hearings. If a black scholar doesn't "fit-in," she or he doesn't obtain tenure. Black educators have to live a lie in post segregation America.

Toni Morrison says in *Race-ing Justice, En-Gendering Power:*

> Minus one's own idiom it is possible to cry and decry victimization, loathing it when it appears in the discourses of one's own people, but summoning it up for one's expediently de-racialized self. It becomes easy to confuse the metaphors embedded in the blood language of one's own culture with the objects they stand for and to call patronizing, coddling, undemanding, rescuing, complicitous white racists a lynch mob. Under such circumstances it

> is not just easy to speak the master's language, it is necessary. One is obliged to cooperate in the misuse of figurative language, in the reinforcement of cliché, the erasure of difference, the jargon of justice, the evasion of logic, the denial of history, the crowning of patriarchy, the inscription of hegemony; to be complicit in the vandalizing, sentimentalizing, and trivialization of the torture black people have suffered. Such rhetorical strategies become necessary because, without one's own idiom, there is no other language to speak.[1]

As long as such free thought remains in the classroom or on the street corner, it poses no threat to the racial arrangement. Only when radical black ideologies attempt to go public, by organizing or even force of arms, do the race-constructed systems legitimized by state power take them down.

CHAPTER 20

Lessons of the Civil Rights Movement

By 1965, I had joined the Movement. I don't know who knew that besides me, but I was on board. I had just enrolled at Ole Miss and while I still followed its sports teams, I was very aware that James Meredith had just left. His presence was felt everywhere, as though he were still on campus, which felt like it could explode at any moment. I heard outrageous stories about how the Army personnel assigned to protect him were treated. Students, as they went in and out of any building, were subject to search especially in the dormitories near Baxter Hall where Meredith, himself, lived alone. Pillow cases stuffed with razor blades and feces and soaked with all manner of things exploded on the walls of his dorm; cherry bombs were tossed on Baxter Hall's roof at all hours of the night; unrelenting racist cat-calls threatened his life. I was told this was mild compared to what he had endured his first months on campus.

I was aware that Medgar Evers, the charismatic head of the NAACP Mississippi office, who was often compared to Dr. King, had been ambushed and killed in 1963 by a Klansman named Byron de la Beckwith. Even though Beckwith's high-powered weapon was left at the scene, equipped with a telescopic lens and with his thumbprint on it, and even though others testified that Beckwith boasted about shooting Evers, Beckwith was nonetheless not convicted of the shooting. That was nothing new. No white man had ever been convicted of killing a black man in Mississippi. It would be thirty years before Beckwith was convicted of killing Medgar Evers.

Now, in January 1968, his brother, Charles, was running for Congress. Most people in Mississippi, white and black, thought his campaign was a suicide mission.

Given the number of Mississippi murders of civil rights workers in just the three years prior to Evers' announcement of his candidacy, there was ample reason to believe it true.

This was my chance to get my feet wet, as they say. I could become a volunteer for the Evers campaign and get my first taste of the "Movement." I could become a civil rights worker. I was twenty-three years old and I was ready. I don't know what I expected this experience to be. I think I envisioned it as some type of pep rally, like before football games. My friend and classmate David Molpus had told me about Evers and what his election would mean to Mississippi. Molpus was from the Delta as I was. His father was a minister in Belzoni, Mississippi and one of the pastors who signed the 1965 Declaration of Conscience calling for an end to hatred and violence. He was forced to resign his pastorate as a result. But, back to me. I certainly did not expect to be assigned to the white section of town. My job was to go door to door and pass out "Charles Evers for Congress" leaflets and engage those whites who so chose to be in a conversation about Evers' platform. None chose to.

This was democracy in its rawest form, I was spat upon and chased away by someone who told me to wait while he went and got his shotgun; dogs were loosed upon me. An elderly lady who reminded me of my grandmother and who, I am sure, given the times and the place, was a Christian, cursed me as if cursing were an art form. I had doors slammed in my face and my parentage called into question. It was the longest hour thus far in my young life. It also helped me when later in life I would be challenged to address hostile white folks in Undoing Racism® workshops. I would tell myself when confronted with such anger and rage, "It can't be worse than the Evers campaign."

Speaking to other white people about race and racism is the most difficult task one can take on as a white, anti-racist organizer. There are many reasons for this. The sense of individuality among whites makes it easy for us to deny anything that might otherwise incriminate us when it comes to race. Another challenge is our definition of racism is usually confined to individual acts of meanness or overt prejudice. Most of us whites have not been exposed to understandings of the institutional and systemic nature of racism. We are stuck in the individual dynamics of racism. In fact, no small number of us feel black people are not only racist toward white people, but enjoy privileges and access to power that whites no longer have. Also, whites have learned not to talk about race and racism but to use coded language em-

ploying stereotypes to apply to all people of color and especially to blacks. My style has changed over the years moving from stridency and accusation to a more listening and supportive posture. At least I hope so. Not everyone would agree with me on this, I suspect.

For many of us of a certain age — both people of color and whites — to say "I grew up in the sixties" is a statement that needs no explanation. The term means many things. Many, who in their teens and early twenties were shaped by civil rights and the Great Society and anti-war efforts, might never have actually participated in a rally or a strategy session. Yet we identified with the movement through certain songs and anthems that were like sacred hymns. For us, regardless of what we are doing now, the fact that we grew up in the sixties conjures memories of challenging the status quo, marching for "Negro rights," and protesting the draft and the war that made the draft necessary. Even among those who never marched and never raised our voices in protest there is a persistent sense of pride of accomplishment.

The Civil Rights Movement was steeped in music, dance, art. "Culture is the lifeblood of a people — a way of life; without culture the people die," asserts Ron Chisom, co-founder and 35-year director of the People's Institute. He explains, "Without a sense of culture, organizing efforts often fail to take hold of a community's spirit." Jim Dunn, co-founder with Ron of the People's Institute, was a poet and singer. Building on his experiences with civil rights artists, Jim invited such luminaries as Odetta, Holly Near, Pete Seeger, and the Rev. Frederick Douglass Kirkpatrick to bring their musical messages of liberation to every event. In New Orleans, similar gatherings would take on a local flavor with Mardi Gras Indians, Second Lines and demonstrations of "the hambone," a tradition rooted in Africa's "Gumbo Dance." From these experiences came wisdom: When the poets rhyme, musicians put a beat to it, and muralists paint it on the wall, you have a movement.

The degrees of participation in "Movement culture" spanned the spectrum of politics and ideology. There were those who on an individual level just wanted the signs taken down and an end to overt bigotry and hatred. There were others who wanted strict enforcement to end discrimination in employment, education, and housing. Many were gradualists who would claim support for "civil rights" but who were concerned that change not be too fast or too demanding. Still others criticized the "Movement's" leadership and tactics as too accommodating and compromising in the face of the racial status quo. Some saw civil rights as a beginning step in a radical deconstruction of the capitalist system, a sharp break with established power arrangements and even the ideological basis upon which the government rests.

In the People's Institute, we saw civil rights as a means by which the nation could begin to live up to its most fundamental ideals enshrined in the Declaration of Independence and embodied in the Bill of Rights, extended now to all Americans. Jim Dunn would quote from the Preamble to the Constitution and ask, "What does it mean to have a 'more perfect Union'?" To him "more perfect" had to mean undoing racism.

One could argue that the 1950s were the real civil rights years. Most white people joined up in the 1960s. In the '60s the pro-civil rights legions won the moral battle for the soul of the nation.

Systems change when there is collective outcry demanding such change. Systems change or alter their course when they must — when they have no choice. Organizing in the future may be different than it was in the past. Maybe mass street action will not be the only or even primary strategy to challenge the inequities of our race-constructed society. But collective action is essential whether on the street or through the internet. This is as true for forces on the political right as it is for those on the left. As Francis Fox Piven and Richard A. Cloward asserted in their classic 1979 study, *Poor People's Movements: Why They Succeed, How They Fail,* "Whatever influence lower-class groups occasionally exert in American politics does not result from organization, but from mass protest and the disruptive consequences of protest."[1] The movement that had emerged from grassroots organizing efforts in the 1950s had roots hundreds of years old — since enslaved Africans revolted from the day of their arrival in this country. This was a movement that, by the late 1940s, had witnessed the organizing prowess of giants like Marcus Garvey, A. Phillip Randolph, Dorothy Height and Ida B. Wells. It was a movement that would shake the very foundations of the nation's racial caste system. The victories — from voting rights to public accommodations, from university admissions to fair and open housing — would be achieved in less than two decades between 1954 and 1968. No community in the United States was untouched by this ferment. No movement in United States history, with the possible exception of the emancipation era victories themselves, made a greater impact on the nation's social order. By 1968, millions of people around the world looked to the black community of the United States as the moral exemplar for their own liberation struggles.

How then to guarantee and extend the victories of the Civil Rights Movement? For organizations like the People's Institute this meant that our analyses and strategies had to be rooted in a sense of history. For history would demonstrate that the Movement was led by black people who were largely invisible in the leadership ranks of other progressive movements like the labor and women's rights movements of the nineteenth and twentieth centuries. The Civil Rights Movement had been able to unite under its "big tent" the many disparate struggles dedicated to achieving justice and human rights for people marginalized by the dominant culture standard-bearers. This sense of belonging to something bigger than each person or group permeated all those working for justice and equal rights. Groups inspired each other and came together when the moment called for solidarity beyond issues and tactics. Latinos of many stripes joined, including Cesar Chavez and Dolores Huerta's United Farm Workers Association in the West, Baldemar Velasquez' Farm Labor Organizing Committee (FLOC) in the Midwest, La Raza in the Southwest, Young Lords on the East Coast and Roberto Maestes' El Centro in Seattle. The American Indian Movement joined with the white-led anti-war movement. The re-invigorated student movement, moribund since its heyday in the 1930s, together with the modern feminist and gay rights movements all were inspired by the Civil Rights Movement led by African Americans. This was its unique character.

Even as the Movement took on different issues and presented different faces depending upon what part of the country one was in, its sense of connection could be traced to the leadership of people of color. These leaders were not hesitant to discuss racism. They understood the value of their leadership in a nation seeking to break the shackles of white supremacy. They understood that white people were still too tied psychologically to the ideology of white supremacy to offer effective guidance to the liberation of people oppressed by racism for many centuries.

The Civil Rights Movement created a profound shift in consciousness among its rank and file participants. It impacted people's identity and sense of self. It became, for many, a point of personal departure — a turning point in their lives. Those who witnessed this brief moment felt that, finally, this nation was about to banish racism and inequity from the national landscape. The words of Dr. King resounded around the nation. Many even dared to believe that the words of the nation's creed, "all people are created equal," might finally mean something to its black citizenry, to Puerto Ricans, Afro-Caribbeans, Mexican Americans, Asian-Pacific Islanders and Native Americans.

Parts of civil rights history are now woven into American folklore. The history books in public schools now teach about its most famous heroines and heroes like Mrs. Rosa Parks and the Rev. Dr. Martin Luther King, Jr. Malcolm X is touched upon in some high school textbooks that also reference Harriet Tubman and the Underground Railroad she helped to create. Blacks are portrayed as worthy and uplifting. Whites, both those most resistant to the movement and those most connected to it, are rarely personalized or recognized. Whites in the civil rights period are usually Presidents or would-be Presidents — the Kennedy brothers, Lyndon Johnson, maybe Chief Justice Warren. Blockbuster films such as *Mississippi Burning* erroneously create white FBI heroes.

The reality of the Civil Rights Movement was this: Mexican Americans, Puerto Ricans and blacks came together, joined by the American Indian Movement and other justice-seeking church, student and labor groups to build a multi-colored movement led by people of color that stoked the imagination and created a sense of possibility like no other movement in the nation's history. This mosaic was made visible to the entire country through televised reports, urban organizing efforts, and national calls for a united front against everything from the Vietnam War to table grapes. The sight of Cesar Chavez and the UFWA heading down Pennsylvania Avenue in solidarity with Martin Luther King Jr.'s civil rights masses, joined by the American Indian Movement with its message of survival, resilience and self-determination, plus white people from every corner of the country, fueled the sense of possibility that together we would alter the course of the nation's woeful racial history. This coming together was in part what led Dr. King to announce his plans for a Poor People's March on Washington slated for the late spring or early summer of 1968, plans so tragically interrupted by his assassination in Memphis on April 4th. In calling for the Poor People's Campaign, King was attempting what many had historically hoped for yet never obtained — a movement that would unite working and poor people across lines of race and class.

This, alas, would not happen in 1968 either. It was not for want of trying. Rev. Ralph Abernathy and other SCLC stalwarts would soldier on and build an encampment, Resurrection City, on the National Mall near the Nation's Capitol. But the campaign was beset by problems from the outset. The country was still in mourning and try as he might, Rev. Abernathy was not Martin Luther King, Jr. The country was emotionally spent. The black community was increasingly angry. Dr. King was the apostle of non-violence, but many questioned where it had gotten them. Just another killing from a "lone, white gunman" like the one who had shot Medgar Evers, the Kennedy brothers, James Meredith, and now MLK.

Smoke could still be seen wafting from the burned out sections of DC's black neighborhoods from uprisings that engulfed it and other communities across the US in response to Dr. King's assassination. Resurrection City was drenched by huge downpours turning it into a mud bath. The media coverage was constant, though not always flattering. Devoid of its spiritual leader, it was easier to criticize both its purpose and its timing. This tent city was portrayed as a failure although more than fifty thousand people participated in the march and braved the many obstacles for more than six weeks during which time Robert Kennedy was also killed. Participants in Resurrection City were deeply disheartened. It was the last great rally of the Civil Rights Movement. Echoes of this era would be heard again in 1995 with the Million Man March for "atonement, reconciliation and responsibility" called by Minister Louis Farrakhan and attended by black men from every walk of life and economic strata. That was the largest march in US history, but receives scant mention today. Fifteen years later, the Occupy Wall Street movement spread to over fifty cities in the US in protest of the ever-growing income disparities in the United States between the top 1% of the richest Americans and the other 99%. In the 2010s, Black Lives Matter and the Dreamers spark even broader justice movement-building.

The Movement did not reach everyone. For those white people who did not go to college, it was not a decade of rebellion and protest. White working class kids and even many young people of color went to work or to Vietnam. They answered the call to war as they had always done and they worked for a living in-between. War not only provided jobs, possible access to college, and on-the-job-training, but it offered an opportunity to serve your country. Blacks, Latinos, Native Americans, Asian Americans and working class whites joined up to go to Vietnam where, ironically, the battlefield was called "Indian Country."

Lessons of the Civil Rights Movement are many. At the turn of the twenty-first century, Anne Braden, life-long anti-racist organizer and activist, gave these insights when asked what current day organizers should learn from the history of the Civil Rights Movement:

(1) The issue is racism because racism destroys democracy.

(2) We must build a multiracial movement bringing all segments of the society together.

(3) When African Americans organize, the nation moves.

(4) Organizing for social change must be from the bottom-up.

(5) We must re-capture the audacity of the 1960s.

Organizing was key to the victories of the "Movement." There was no arena nor neighborhood where the impact of organizing was not felt. The Civil Rights Movement was characterized by important departures from previous social change efforts in the United States. Organized people of color had rebelled frequently and even, as Indian nations, waged war. Black-led revolts and indigenous-led warfare against European and later United States invasions span the first one hundred and fifty years of the nation's existence. But the Civil Rights Movement was waged within the system. It was a struggle for the nation's soul, one that challenged the very tenets upon which the country was founded. Whites made crucial contributions to the Movement and in some instances paid with their lives. But the Civil Rights Movement is unique. In the black communities of the US, in the barrios of the Southwest and Northeast, and on the reservations that dot the western plains and northern extremities of the nation, people of color's efforts to dismantle white supremacy — or at least to mitigate its most discriminatory impacts — are the real story. For the first time, whites took a backseat to the incredible mobilized strength of people who, from the founding of the nation, had been marginalized and prevented from participating in its social contract. Communities across the spectrum of color organized around their own historical grievances, doing so in ways that allowed all to come together on a national level under the big tent strategy of the Civil Rights Movement's leadership. This story has been well-chronicled, but it deserves a re-telling. The public face of the movement was "of color." This was new. In all the great movements in the United States up until this time, from the movement to abolish the enslavement of African Americans to the great labor and suffragist movements of the late nineteenth and early twentieth centuries, people of color had been relegated to the background. Their voices in decision-making circles had rarely been heard and even less recognized. Certainly there was the courageous work of Harriet Tubman, Sojourner Truth and Frederick Douglass in the period before and after the Civil War. But even they had to confront the assumptions that, despite black leaders' courage and brilliance, white people were more capable of leadership. These were false assumptions internalized through generations by white and black and brown people alike: White people are superior; people of color are inferior.

The movement for civil rights was different. From the lettuce fields picketed by the United Farm Workers to the black church fully-mobilized and activated, buttressed by the great moral symbolism of the American Indian Movement, this was a movement national in scope and both local and international in impact. It constituted the biggest challenge to the racial status quo since the Civil War.

CHAPTER 21

Growing up Preaching in the Land of "Dog Whistle Politics"

As a boy, I enjoyed the preaching at church every Sunday. Not everyone did, not even some of the adults, but I did. I owe my mother credit for this. She would talk to me throughout her life about preachers who came to her hometown of Leakesville, Mississippi, and made such an impact on the people there. They were like movie stars to us, she would say. They might stay a week and always with a church family. It was an honor to be asked to host an evangelist. There were no hotels and few reputable restaurants back then and it was the Great Depression on top of it all. She especially liked the "traveling preachers."

Later, I looked up to and admired those preachers and seminary professors who could pull from the Christian scriptures messages applicable to the present day which, back then, meant the 1950s and '60s. But, they had to be careful. They had to be sure they weren't perceived as being "soft on civil rights." I don't think any of the preachers I listened to at church could have been accused of that heresy. Few seminary professors either.

My Christian faith has always been important to me and has usually served me well. Before the church (the white church in my case) was taken over by its most conservative elements and before a literal interpretation of the Bible became de rigueur *in some circles, the mainline churches set the bar for Christian orthodoxy; their basic liberal theology held sway over its national reputation and agenda. This would change over the years until today the church is seen as basically a re-*

actionary and even exploitative force, more associated with anti-abortion than civil rights.

I am a Biblically-based preacher and a Christian anti-racist social activist and organizer. Except I don't preach much anymore. The MAAFA was an exception. Still my identity is tied to being a minister and a preacher who believes the church's presence in the world must come from an anti-racist understanding. This, of course, is much different than the church I grew up in. There, white supremacy was a given. In more liberal environs one did good works and helped people in need, but the fact that white people were superior in every way to people of color, especially black people, was never questioned. Jesus was portrayed as white and someone like me never considered anything else. Of course Jesus was white and all the Biblical hero stories like Moses parting the Red Sea, Daniel in the lion's den, Samson and Delilah, were all about white people. Even as my consciousness about the world began to expand, I didn't challenge white dominance and white prerogatives. It was what being white meant and it had always been this way. I never thought about it. Until I did.

In 1962, when I was sixteen years old, I was asked to preach the Youth Day sermon. This was at the First Baptist Church in West Helena, Arkansas. With little but youthful exuberance I preached on the sin of segregation and why Jesus saw all people as equal. It was the first time I saw people sitting on their hands. It was a first for me, but it would not be the last. A similar reception awaited me nearly forty years later, while I was speaking at a Mennonite statewide conference in South Carolina. I asked my friend Tobin Miller-Shearer what the assembled audience had to say. He said one-third of them really liked you, one-third said they really disliked you, and one-third said they had heard you before. Tough talk from the Mennonites.

The Undoing Racism® workshops have often proved a barometer of my faith. To people of color, my avowed Christian faith seems to make it easier for us to connect. For whites it can be a turn-off. Not always mind you, but often. It's interesting to me that so many whites are secular, professing their distance from, if not disdain for "organized religion." This despite often working in or studying people of color and their communities or culture. Where is our accountability for our actions?

I have some thoughts about this. It seems to me when systems and institutions work for white people in the race-constructed society, and as a result of this, we internalize our superiority, then maybe we have no need for God or Jesus or other manifestation of the sacred. On the other hand, if the systems have not worked for you and the institutions are experienced as oppressive, you reach out for a lifeline. Maybe that's just me. While some white people affirm their spirituality, I think this bears close watching. After all, individualism and cultural appropriation play right into white supremacy.

One of the primary casualties of the Civil Rights Movement was the loss of the white working class from the progressive coalition that had prevailed for most of the twentieth century. Many white progressives have tried to forge an alliance with working class whites; except in isolated incidents such efforts have been impossible to sustain. Race and the declining influence of unions in the United States have pushed working class whites further and further to the right. By 2015, after seven years of a black President, the GOP's hard-right rhetoric dominated the party and the number of poor and working class white people with less than a college education who identified with the Republican Party continued to grow. This is an irony that can only be explained through understanding the social contract and the inherent promises to white people embedded in it. A web of self-interests among the economic elite, the academy and media, sanctioned and legitimized by the power of the state, sustains white privilege. This unspoken preference for white is what has held poor and working class whites in support of an arrangement that does not serve their best interests — except the self-interest of being white in a race-constructed nation. This social contract has worked since the founding of the republic.

As the Civil Rights Movement began to threaten the racial status quo, white leadership in this country developed a new mantra: black advancement would be attainable only at white expense. While white Southern demagogues had used this tactic since the onset of African enslavement, primarily in the South, by 1960 whites throughout the industrial heartland and manufacturing centers of the nation were being convinced of its truth. George Wallace, possibly the most outspoken segregationist of his time, was elected governor of Alabama four times between 1962 and 1987. In the 1964 Democratic presidential primary in Wisconsin and Indiana, Wallace received 30% of the vote. In Maryland, he got 43% and might have won outright but for a high black voter turnout. This shocked both pundits and politicians and the lesson was not lost on them. Wallace, known for his rabid racism and frequent use of the N-word, cleaned up his speech in Wisconsin and began to speak of threats to the American way of life by "pointy-headed" East Coast professors, Ivy League intellectuals and bureaucrats in the federal government in Washington, DC. Wallace's rhetoric resonated with his white audiences who began to see him as a spokesman who would protect their interests. Wallace convinced white people that blacks were the recipients of federal benefits they had neither worked for nor earned. He ridiculed "lazy" women on welfare and black men who no longer needed to work, but who could live off the public dole at taxpayers' expense. "Taxpayers" would become a euphemism for white people in the 1970s. Wallace touched a nerve long suppressed among the white working classes of the nation. It was no longer just a Southern phenomenon, but a message that worked in the North and even the Western United States. As a result of Wallace's success, and others who imitated his approach, whites who felt threatened by civil rights and later chants of "Black Power" learned that their interests could be protected from blacks, other people of color, feminists, and radicals without ever mentioning the word race. Ian Haney-Lopez would term this "dog whistle politics" — inaudible and unspoken, but heard by white people.[1] In the 2016 presidential election campaign, Donald Trump channeled Wallace, using the language of purity, rage and resentment to build and hold his front-runner status.

The effectiveness of "dog whistle politics" shows up today in the People's Institute Undoing Racism® workshops, where one of the questions participants are asked early in the process is "Why are people poor?" The responses invariably include stereotypes such as "lazy," "welfare cheats," "on drugs," "too many babies," "using my tax dollars," that show just how deeply stereotypes of black and Latino people have been internalized in American society. Rarely does anyone answer the question with deeper, structural answers such as "loss of land," "housing discrimination," or other evidence of institutional bias.

Richard Nixon, disgraced after his defeat in the presidential election of 1960 and his even more embarrassing 1964 loss of the governor's election in California, was elected President of the United States in 1968 on a law and order campaign. The law had been settled by the civil rights acts of the '60s. But social order depended on the race construct that privileged whites over blacks. Consequently, for forty years, beginning with the 1975 Supreme Court ruling in the *Bakke* case, whites have challenged the use of race to preference blacks and others. Ten years after the most dramatic victories over white supremacy in the nation's history, whites had become the victim. Politicians could run against "welfare moms," "federal bureaucrats," and "government regulations" — and win. Whites could deny race had anything to do with it. The nation could continue to function as it was constructed to do.

An organized black community has always been feared in the United States. From the brutal terror of the slave ships to the numbing oppression of the plantation, white supremacists had gone to great lengths to keep down revolt. They understood that people who don't speak the same language nor come from the same cultures find it harder to organize. Nonetheless, there were many revolts and there were many ways to communicate without speaking the same language. One of the reasons that black organizing was so feared was that whites believed blacks were inherently violence-prone and that organizing would fuel black rage.

Whites have always feared retribution from blacks. This is the profound fear, that given the opportunity, blacks will certainly turn the tables on white people. This fear, that black power will come at the expense of white privilege, continues to have currency today. A curious contradiction of internalized white superiority is denial on the one hand that racism even exists, yet, on the other, a fearful belief that because of how they have been treated by whites, blacks will surely repay whites in kind and with vengeance.

To empahsize again: This has rarely been the case. When Nelson Mandela, for example, was freed from Robben Island after twenty-seven years of imprisonment there, he immediately called for the construction of a new nation where racism would not only be outlawed, but one that would invite his former oppressors to stay and help build the new nation. Martin Luther King, Jr. painted a similar vision for the United States. Even when anguished by the 2015 murders of nine fellow parishioners, members of Charleston's Emanuel African Methodist Episcopal Church refused to demand vengeance.

White fear of actualized black power was evident as the Civil Rights Movement moved into a more radical phase in the late 1960s. The now-famous demand by the Student Non-Violent Coordinating Committee to those white people who had been a part of SNCC and other civil rights groups to leave and organize in their own white communities had predictable outcomes. Some whites took the demand to mean organize in your organizations or church denominations or even among the colleges and universities where they were employed. Many whites doubled their commitments to anti-war work and draft protests. Others became immersed in "identity politics," organizing among women, gays and lesbians, environmentalists. Still others became advocates, consultants, urban ministers, teachers, social workers, therapists. Few progressives took SNCC's demand to mean organizing against racism in the white community where they were raised, among their own families and friends. That was too daunting a task. They assumed raising issues of racism would be fruitless, even politically suicidal. There was no money in it; rarely would it have involved career advancement or prestige. Progressives felt confused about what "community" meant: Where did one go to find it? Ron Chisom called them runaway children. They would rather go to jail than confront their parents or kinfolk about their racism. Those rare whites who did were often called "race traitors," "n----- lovers," even "mentally ill."

Because whites are the only group in this race-constructed society allowed to function as individuals, we have internalized our freedom to define ourselves and the community from which we come and thus to which we might return. We also muddy the concept of accountability. To whom are we accountable in our work? Our profession? The agencies who paid us? Those with similar identities? All too often, white progressives aren't accountable to anyone. More often, we are "conditionally accountable" — to those we approve or with whom we agree. Rarely are we part of a profession or identity group or job that prioritizes working against racism. Whites, regardless of our politics or profession, are rarely accountable to organized people of color.

In the aftermath of the social and political revolutions of the '60s, white people on the political right fought to stay relevant. Conservatives who questioned the effectiveness of the Civil Rights Movement were discounted, even ignored, by the progressive elements in the nation. It was not cool to be a political conservative. The right moved about the political edges. Watergate and President Nixon's subsequent resignation had embarrassed conservatives; the wider culture ignored them as hopelessly out of date and on the wrong side of history; the sexual transformation had eluded them.

But they had little to fear: The country was, in fact, moving to the right. Wallace had known it. Nixon knew it; he was just clumsy and given to getting in his own way. An entire generation of people — some called it the Silent Majority — was being challenged by key conservative leaders to wrest control from the hippies and the blacks and a society blinded by libertines, pinkos and Warren-court permissiveness. While the left rested on its laurels, the right prepared to act.

CHAPTER 22

Federal Response to the Movement: The Great Society

I moved to New Orleans in late 1971 with Meredith McElroy who became my second wife and in the spring of 1972 got a job at St. Mark's Community Center which was located at the nexus of the historic African American neighborhood called Tremé and the better known French Quarter. At first, it was just a job that allowed me to work in the community. That's how I saw it. By this time, St. Mark's had been at this particular location for nearly sixty years; but it had recently fallen on hard times. My duties were to assist the bookkeeper, but shortly after I arrived, the bookkeeper up and quit. This worried me at first because I had fudged a bit at my job interview and indicated I knew more about bookkeeping than I actually did. Not to worry. How hard can it be, I thought, and this turned out to be true. I was able to manage the center's books because there was not much to keep track of in the way of the program's finances. I learned by doing and I had quite a bit of time on my hands. Soon I was taking long walks in the French Quarter during the work day and learning quite a bit about its history and relationship to the adjoining Tremé community. New Orleans was, by 1972, officially integrated. Jim Crow days were gone. Separate but equal was over. That was, at least, the city's official position. But in reality, New Orleans was still very segregated as well as still separated.

I would look out my third floor window at St. Mark's Community Center in New Orleans in the early 1970s and notice this older man painting in pastels across the street. I would never seek to meet him and I never inquired of anyone who might have known who he was. After all, he was old and I was a brash twenty-six-year-old wanting to be a part of social change politics and fight injustice. How could meeting him help my cause? He was probably against what we were doing with the black kids in Tremé anyway.

I guess my ageism kept me from meeting Jim Dombrowski, one of the twentieth century's foremost organizers: white resister to Senator McCarthy and the FBI Red Squad, whose case against the House Un-American Activities Committee (HUAC) would make famous the term "chilling effect." Dombrowski, along with lawyers Benjamin Smith and Bruce Waltzer had been arrested in 1963 as subversives by state authorities for their life-long devotion to equal rights, civil rights, and labor organizing. In two famous legal cases of that era, Dombrowski v. Eastland *and* Dombrowski v. Pfister, *the US Supreme Court ultimately decided that raids carried out by both state and federal government officials under the anti-subversive laws violated Dombrowski's First Amendment rights.*

Later I would learn that Dombrowski had helped found the Highlander Folk School in New Market, Tennessee, as well as the Southern Conference Educational Fund (SCEF) and the Southern Conference for Human Welfare (SCHW); and that he was a conscientious objector in WWII. A Methodist minister and graduate of Union Theological Seminary in NYC, Jim Dombrowski fought the notion that radical social justice organizing was somehow un-American and in the South a sure sign that one was either a communist or a communist sympathizer. I missed my chance.

St. Mark's had integrated its recreation program in 1966, but by 1971 all the white kids had stopped coming and the black kids from Tremé had no particular feel for the place. They came either to play basketball or in the summer to swim at one of the few swimming pools in the city open to the black community. That was pretty much it. The staff had dwindled to just a handful of people and the director was very much out of place and out of step with the times. By the end of 1972, she was also gone. That left four of us. In early 1974, I became Executive Director of St. Mark's with no experience and no training or preparation. Certainly, looking back, either one of my colleagues, Nelson Herbert or Margaret Carmbs, was more qualified than I for the job. The big difference was that I was white and they were not, though I did not really see it that way at the time.

Over time I became well-versed — tutored by my remaining fellow staff members — on how the community felt about St. Mark's and how racist it was still perceived as being. During the early years of my time there, I worked and lived as though I was in graduate school. Slowly and at times reluctantly, various community activists began to school me in the basic tenets of community organizing and local community control over program initiatives that impacted their lives. I was a willing pupil and amid many false steps and wrong-headed assumptions, I became somewhat trusted by those in neighborhood leadership positions.

St. Mark's became a lab school for community organizing. This was not only my doing, but I was a willing participant and an eager learner. I approached the job initially with one thing in mind — how to use the vast expanse of the center for purposes that facilitated the Tremé neighborhood's agenda. Whether the issue was a place to meet for mass efforts against rampant police abuse in the city or as a site for a community health center, St. Mark's was there, open, and free.

Yet our only source of funds were church-related and there was precious little of it. If we were to keep the building open, we'd need funding. It was in the search for financial support that I first noticed the designation "501(c)(3)." I didn't know what that meant, but I quickly learned that it was the only way to get funds. In early 1974 the National Division of the UMC wrote and told us to obtain a 501(c)(3). I was very happy. The designation led to grant possibilities and we began to apply for various sources of support to run youth-related programs. We moved quickly to becoming a multi-service provider with an ever-increasing budget and a larger and larger staff. But we were no longer as involved in the politics of the community. Our emphasis had changed from our very nascent organizing efforts to direct services. Unbeknownst to us, we had become part of a national effort to de-politicize community efforts at self-determination. We — both the national UMC and local community centers like St. Mark's — began to move away from community-based organizing. We were so busy with our programs! We transformed ourselves from community organizers who fought for decent housing and education, who demanded community accountability boards to oversee police, into managers of afterschool recreational programs. We claimed we had no time for organizing nor funding to do it. After all, we were doing good work for needy children.

Our story repeated itself all over the country.

The federal government, with Lyndon Johnson's leadership, responded to the Civil Rights Movement by rolling out plans for a Great Society. Johnson's vision for America eclipsed any President's since Abraham Lincoln with respect to racial equality. As someone who had lived in abject poverty as a young person, Johnson recognized the truth in Michael Harrington's 1962 *The Other America:* "Today's poor, in short, missed the political and social gains of the thirties. They are... the first minority poor in history, the first poor not to be seen, the first poor whom the politicians could leave alone."[1]

President Johnson vowed, in his 1965 commencement address at Howard University that the nation was capable of becoming a country where poverty was eliminated for all its citizens. The Great Society, as he called it, would not only end poverty but would bring those historically excluded by the nation's social contract into the mainstream of American life. It would take "affirmative action" to ensure that historically marginalized people of color would have an equal chance for success. Possibly no president other than Johnson could have made it happen. Without Adam Clayton Powell, Jr. in the House and Hubert Humphrey in the Senate, maybe he could not have either. Johnson knew how to get legislation through the Congress. Under the tutelage of fellow Texan and Speaker of the House, Sam Rayburn, and later when he himself was Senate Majority Leader, Johnson knew what buttons to push.

With Dr. King and the civil rights activists in the street, Powell and other liberals in Congress, Bull Conner's attack dogs televised to a horrified nation and the specter of a Kennedy assassination still fresh in the nation's psyche, Johnson, a Southerner, was uniquely positioned to get the job done. The Great Society was powered by an army of government-sponsored efforts designed to end the scourge of poverty, alienation, and legal barriers that had barred blacks and other so-called national "minorities" from societal legitimacy. Johnson believed this could be done. To him, it was a matter of collective will. In quicksilver fashion, the Office of Economic Opportunity (OEO) was created, and assigned primary responsibility to develop and fund programs to implement the Great Society. Such liberal luminaries as John Kenneth Galbraith, the Harvard economist, Sargent Shriver, and Joseph Califano, all Kennedy people, were compelled not to resign but to carry the Kennedy legacy forward. Johnson used the growing Kennedy mythology to his advantage. Although Johnson had from his bully pulpit at the Oval Office carried civil rights much further than the Kennedy administration had been prepared to do, he knew he had none of Kennedy's good looks, media persona or Camelot lifestyle. Johnson spoke with a Texan twang; Kennedy spoke Boston. Kennedy graduated from Harvard Law School; Johnson from San Marcos State College. Kennedy was married to the aristocratic Jacqueline Bouvier; Johnson to Lady Bird Taylor from Karnack, Texas. He needed the Kennedy people and he needed Dr. Martin Luther King, Jr.

The Great Society represented the heyday of government-led intervention in the lives of poor people in the United States. When it came to race, the Great Society of the 1960s surpassed FDR's efforts. Roosevelt had not been able to pass race specific legislation; indeed, he demonstrated no particular urge to do so. The Social Security Act of 1935 excluded workers in agricultural industries and domestic service. This exclusion in effect added to the impoverishment of black women and men, Mexican Americans and other Latinos, Filipinos, and Japanese who were disproportionately represented in these vocations. Had the Roosevelt administration pushed for their inclusion, Social Security might not have passed. Yet thirty years later, the War on Poverty attempted to improve the lot of migratory labor. Emphasizing job training skills, small business development and basic needs like child care and old age services, the federal government added to the more controversial efforts of Cesar Chavez, Dolores Huerta, and the Alinsky-founded Industrial Areas Foundation.

The rhetoric of the Great Society reached its zenith in the 1964 Economic Opportunity Act mandating its Community Action Agencies to act "with the maximum feasible participation of the poor." Successful program applicants would be judged on their ability to involve poor people. Almost overnight, community-based programs designed to alleviate poverty sprang up across the country. Serving infants in day care to senior citizens, programs became like flower gardens, blooming everywhere in the cracked concrete of the nation's most embattled urban areas. Small towns and hill country hamlets likewise grew programs for poor people. In big cities and rural outposts, community-based organizations began to organize with poor people themselves on staff and on boards. Nothing like it had ever been attempted. Big Government provided the funds, but did not operate the programs which, at least in theory, were to be administered by local, community-controlled groups. Cash flowed to groups that six months before might not have existed. This was brand new. Before the Great Society and its declaration of war on poverty, government funding for such initiatives did not exist.

A major contribution of the Great Society era was the idea of the inclusion of "grass-roots" leadership, well described by Lena Bae in an April 2011 *Harvard Political Review* article:

> What was innovative about Community Action was the idea, revolutionary at the time, that the act of participation itself could be transformative; what the poor needed was not the dole, but the opportunity to test their self-assurance to lift themselves out of poverty, and the means to develop and access capacity- and skill-building programs to corroborate that self-determination.[2]

Community leaders emerged in unprecedented fashion during the War on Poverty years. Bypassing traditional means by which one became recognized as an "official" leader, the late '60s and early '70s saw organizers develop who weren't required to meet the university criteria or those of church denominations or even of city hall. Operating often with a mentality that had been forged in the struggles of the Civil Rights Movement, many Office of Economic Opportunity (OEO) leaders were former SNCC organizers such as Marion Barry in Washington, DC, Charlie Sherrod in Albany, Georgia or CORE people like Richard and Oretha Castle Haley in New Orleans.

Despite the excitement generated among grassroots leaders for their voices being heard, fundamental disagreements about sharing power with poor people persisted. In New Orleans, for example, a 1970 survey of board members of the OEO organization, Total Community Action, by sociologist Mary Capps found "...the dominant opinion of TCA board members supports the control of decision-making by the establishment...This leaves numerical dominance and effective control of the board to the establishment, i.e., the non-poor and, especially, the white 'high' class."[3] As one white member said, "Participation by the poor and by minority group members in coalitions of decision-making may be desirable for some purposes, but it will not seriously alter the status quo."[4]

Numerous OEO programs continue to function today. Head Start, Legal Aid Societies, Volunteers in Service to America (VISTA), the Jobs Corps, the Fund for Corporate Broadcasting, the National Endowment for the Arts, and the National Endowment for the Humanities all had their beginnings during the Great Society. There is a tendency to mock LBJ, largely because of how the Vietnam war tarnished his image. Yet under his leadership, the first underpinnings of an inclusive social contract were put in place.

This organizing principle, to act "with the maximum feasible participation of the poor," goes for the most part unrecognized today. It is often lauded, but rarely implemented or made real in efforts to deal with structural problems of poverty and race in the US since these early OEO years. Today, constituents are rarely consulted on programs designed to meet perceived needs of a given community. Layers of intermediaries stand between people impacted by programs and those who provide or establish these services. The principle of "maximum, feasible participation of the poor" is considered an anachronism. Large social service organizations with budgets fueled by grants have never heard of such a principle. It is difficult for them to imagine a time when such a goal would have been a part of federal guidelines. Yet, as the People's Institute teaches, without community participation and accountability there will be no significant change in the lives of people.

Organizing has been relegated to something in the past; it is no longer encouraged, sometimes not even allowed. The non-profit sector, deputized by their 501(c)(3) tax exempt status, replaced community organizing in the 1970s as the means by which poverty and exclusion would be addressed. Community organizing by 1980 would not only be seen as an outdated approach to addressing social ills but one that would not be funded. Schools of social work de-emphasized organizing, selecting instead to stress clinical practice over movement building.

Rose Garrity, an organizer in Binghamton, New York, reflecting on programs designed by survivors of sexual violence and abuse says, "Our movement was begun in our kitchens by women who had been beaten and abused." Today, Garrity notes, the women who founded the work would not be "qualified" to work in the domestic violence arena.[5] Today, programs funded by government or foundations vet those who work in them with requirements and credentials that render only "professionals" qualified. This vetting process takes place today among non-profits and publicly-funded institutions in every program arena in every part of the nation. Movement building is difficult — though not impossible — in such a milieu.

Street organizing, thought to be a strategy that worked only in the past, has been galvanized anew by the ongoing, yet always shocking number of police killings of unarmed black men across the country. After the shooting death of African American teen Trayvon Martin in 2013, #BlackLivesMatter emerged as an "ideological and political intervention," founded by Patrisse Cullors, Opal Tometi, and Alicia Garza, to build connections and lead protests against anti-black racism. Spontaneous uprisings among those most often left out are growing, with increasing clarity of intent, by those willing to "connect the dots." Black Lives Matter, like the Dreamers, is no longer a moment but a movement.

CHAPTER 23

De-Politicizing the Civil Rights Movement: Reasserting the Race Construct

In the summer of 1974 one of the worst tragedies in the long history of gay America had occurred when twenty-seven people were burned to death in what is now called the Upstairs Lounge fire. It was deliberate and deadly. The Upstairs Lounge was one of numerous gay bars in the French Quarter hidden away in the upper Quarter. The fire was an inferno (in 2014 a documentary by the same name won awards around the world). The tragedy was compounded and made more horrible by the refusal of any church in the city to allow a memorial service. Except, as it turned out, St. Mark's United Methodist Church. As director of the community center next door and an ordained minister, I was reached by Bishop Finis Crutchfield (the regular St. Mark's minister was out of town) and told to hold the memorial service at the church. It was a somber honor.

In the spring of 1976, I was asked by the Bishop of Louisiana to assume the pastorate of St. Mark's United Methodist Church in addition to directing the community center. Over the next ten years, St.Mark's became one of the few Protestant churches in the nation with an open and affirmative outreach to the gay community. By 1977, St. Mark's had voted to become a "reconciling congregation," inclusive of all peoples. My ministry also led me, albeit without official church sanction, to perform gay marriages. We were one of the earliest churches to do so in the US.

St. Mark's began to organize with gay community leadership to abolish the repressive "sodomy" laws still on the books in New Orleans. We lobbied city hall to stop the police harassment of businesses that catered to gays and the rampant police violence against gay men in the city. St. Mark's to this day is a church well-known for its ministry to all people. I left St. Mark's in 1981.

During these same years, my organizing priorities took a deeper and more profound direction in other ways. Nelson Herbert introduced me to Jim Hayes and Ron Chisom of the Tremé Community Improvement Association, an act that continues to influence me to this day. Chisom and Hayes were both organizers and culturalists steeped in the rhythms of the city and especially Tremé. I soaked it up. They taught me in ways that were both direct and yet subtle. Chisom and Hayes also introduced me to Barbara Major, then with the Louisiana Hunger Coalition and possibly the most direct and forceful speaker I have ever met. My relationships with all these activists had peaks and valleys. They still do. St. Mark's set the stage for the rest of my life.

I was invited by Ron Chisom and Jim Hayes to join them at regional meetings of the National Tenants Organization (NTO) representing Tremé Community Improvement Association. NTO was led by the Harlem charismatic organizer, Jesse Gray whom Ron Chisom saw as a mentor to him. That same year I began to attend meetings of the Southern Organizing Committee (SOC) where I would meet and get to know organizing legends like Anne Braden out of Louisville, Rev. Fred Shuttlesworth of Birmingham fame, Septima Clarke from South Carolina and Connie Tucker from Tallahassee as well as the Rev. C. T. Vivian, a close confidant of Martin Luther King, Jr. It was an organizers Hall of Fame. SOC believed "as the South goes, so goes the nation." Again, I was privileged to learn from some of the best organizers in the nation just by being in the same room with them. Jim and Diana Dunn were active in SOC and it would be at Rev. Vivian's home in Atlanta with Anne Braden and Ron Chisom where the idea to create the People's Institute for Survival and Beyond would be born. For me, my inclusion in all of this would happen because of Jim Dunn and Ron Chisom and many more organizers from both New Orleans and around the South.

What tied this all together for me was the emphasis we placed on racism and its impact on all oppressed communities. The work with the gay community in New Orleans, for example, had to include an understanding of racism and how it divides and threatens work among otherwise potential allies. Regardless of what form of oppression we were organizing around, racism existed both internally and externally to our efforts. When racism was not understood or even acknowledged, whites would naturally lead and blacks would be expected to follow and racism would be ignored. This happened in all movements whether they were meant to address gender, class, or militarism. It was the setup in the race-constructed nation.

Ironically, the victories of the Civil Rights Movement held the seeds of its demise. By demanding their rightful inclusion in mainstream social and political systems, black and brown communities, especially black leaders, were forced to sacrifice their vision of genuine equity for immediate political and civic gains. The hens, so to speak, were let into the fox's lair. Black leaders became ensnared in a labyrinth of social controls that comprised the dominant culture's institutional life. The very strategies that had gained them access to such institutions in the first place had to be put aside. If black people were to remain inside the halls of systemic power, they had to conform to its rules and ways of being.

The crucial role played by the organized black masses, from store clerks to beauty salon operators, was relegated by the 1980s to "Movement history." Black people were given provisional and conditional entrance into dominant cultural systems — the very structures whose exclusionary policies had fueled the freedom struggle for close to one hundred years! But there was a caveat: They would be allowed in only if they stopped organizing the black community and accepted that racism is just one of many "isms."

This constituted a brilliant strategy on the part of conservative forces! White supremacy and Internalized Racial Superiority meant white people, particularly white progressives, could focus on class, gender, and sexuality. Racism would conveniently fall to the end of the list even though, in a race-constructed society, addressing racism was key to overcoming other important social inequities.

As the mass movement for racial equity began to be dismantled, the People's Institute continued to insist that social justice required a focus on racism and not on other "isms." Some criticized the Institute for being "stuck on racism." But the Institute insisted: If white progressives are given the option to focus on an array of "isms," the discussion will move away from race to other forms of oppression. Whites' discomfort in not being able to be the experts in a movement to end racism — another manifestation of Internalized Racial Superiority — impels them to change the topic.

Yes, the "Movement" could be celebrated on its High Holy Days — the anniversary of Rosa Parks' refusal to go to the back of the bus; Dr. King's "I Have a Dream" speech; the Selma march that confronted the Alabama State police at the Edmund Pettis Bridge; the birthday of Dr. Martin Luther King, Jr. and the anniversary of his assassination. Malcolm X, now safely passed and entombed, would be mentioned in sophisticated urban centers such as New York City. His biography would be widely read and caps marked with an "X" would be worn by white kids with a "Che" t-shirt. But that would be it. February could continue to be called Black History Month and *Eyes on the Prize* would be shown each year on PBS. But to remain in institutional positions, blacks had to acknowledge militant mobilizations as something whose time had passed. To continue showing impatience and anger at continued racial inequities was to risk hard-won gains. The Movement that had changed history would lose its vibrancy before it achieved its vision.

Communities of color were no longer seen as the great moral voice speaking out against white supremacy or the effects of racism and unjust laws. The media and white cultural institutions began to focus on the negative aspects of communities of color. To associate blacks with crime, welfare abuse and violence became commonplace. The drumbeat of these stereotypes greatly impacted how white people saw black and brown communities. The fear factor, always prevalent among whites in the US since the earliest years of European presence in the Americas, was heightened, even encouraged, among the white populace and their institutions. Fears, often unfounded, about black crime and violence continue to stoke the fires of race bias in the US.

Black, brown and red communities were balkanized, split up and fragmented into service areas described by their various pathologies instead of their common racial oppression. Community voices, which had been so strong and compelling in the Civil Rights Era, were replaced by a largely-invisible non-profit social service industry designed not to lift historical oppression but to provide "direct services" to meet community "needs." People living in poor communities — especially communities of color — were moved from the front of the movement lines to the back of the lines at various "social service stations." Welfare lines replaced picket lines. Poor people had to get in line instead of breaking down the lines that were barriers meant to keep them out. One no longer walked the line but had to be kept in line. It was a move from community leadership to community receivership. It was a move away from the goal of enabling people to gain a sense of their own power to a system that fostered dependency not just on government, but on government's not-for-profit gatekeepers. The movement had been severely wounded. Some say fatally.

The rollback of the gains won by the Civil Rights Movement forces began to gain momentum. Leaders who had been part of the movement were now being paid not to organize. Organizations like the NAACP, which had been crucial to Movement successes, would be said by the 1970s to be out-of-step with the times and would be shunned by funders and professional criteria-setters because they provided no direct services. Progressive foundations found the NAACP too conservative in its approach; some younger organizers declared it old fashioned and part of a former generation whose time had passed. These new professionals accomplished what Southern segregationists had been unable to do: marginalize the NAACP and attempt to render it irrelevant.

Some movement veterans made a living by retelling the Civil Rights Movement glory days at conferences and workshops; others would study for the PhD and become part of post-modern academia, publishing their understandings of the nature of oppression in the society and race's role in it. Organizing was in decline; it was no longer funded or recognized as essential to society's continued progress toward justice. That day was done. The veterans were pushed to the side, relegated to a role that was past. Professionals who could operate the new programs now ruled the roost.

The period of the federal government's Great Society programs was relatively short-lived. By 1975, Government funding was ended for organizations who spoke in terms of movement building and collective redress of grievances. Individual, case-based, therapeutic models replaced more politicized, collective approaches to poor people. Schools of social work, in all but a few schools, marginalized organizing and activism and replaced it with an emphasis on clinical practice. Organizing was not stressed as a viable career model. "No money in it." And little prestige.

The Civil Rights Movement was intentionally depoliticized. Issues that arose out of racial oppression were redefined by dominant cultural institutions. They stemmed no longer from this nation's construct of race, but were pathologies inherent in black people themselves and in the communities that produced them. THE DREAM was scaled down, not in the hearts and minds of the people but in the plans and initiatives of institutions external to the community.

De-politicizing work in racially oppressed communities was no accident. It didn't just happen. People did not just move on. Organizing for social justice was pushed to the margins by powerful social control mechanisms — the professionalizing of social services and the funding of what became a nationwide human and social services industry. Servicing the poor became a growth industry, providing careers and professional status for thousands of college graduates each year. "Needs" fueled the social service system and fed the social service agencies' appetite for ever more programs and activities designed to meet those "needs." "Needs assessment" replaced consciousness-raising and political analysis. Social service became a career with advancement opportunities for many highly-dedicated and sincere individuals. It became the mission of literally thousands of organizations. It became the mechanism for channeling millions of dollars each year to institutions that studied and served the poor. Social service agency salaries, though comparatively low, were considerably higher than those of the people they served. Poor people found themselves locked out of decision-making. Even as newly-minted professionals paid homage to those who "kicked the doors of segregation down and made possible our careers and programs," poor people, increasingly of color, were left out. No longer were they the backbone of a struggle for justice whose presence in the streets was crucial to movement victories. Now their names had numbers: They had become "units of service," "minorities," "target populations."

Creating large multi-service programs replaced Movement building. The neighborhood replaced the nation as the context for work. As groups vied for pieces of the government pie, the vision of a national movement was likewise split into pieces.

The transition away from community-based leadership was fueled by resources directed to "intermediaries" who spoke for the community but with limited accountability to them. The primary instrument the government used to reestablish social control was the 501(c)(3) tax-exempt non-profit status for organizations, forbidding them from using gifts and grants for political organizing. This government-induced registration program was unknown to many community-based groups. It had not been extensively used as a social control mechanism until the success of community organizing by the Civil Rights Movement in the

1950s and '60s challenged the US race construct. Like the 1939 Hatch Act (officially known as An Act to Prevent Pernicious Political Activities) that was amended in 1940 to prohibit federal employees, and anyone working for an organization receiving federal monies, from "any active part" in political campaigns, the 501(c)(3) non-profit status was lethal to groups that wanted to organize to make the country's social contract more inclusive.

Organizing around historical redress of grievances was no longer seen as a strategy to confront structural power arrangements. This strategy, which had largely made the movement possible and galvanized so many community level participants, was in the process by the early 1970s of being replaced by a professionalized, highly-specialized, fragmented approach to those historically marginalized communities. It was the anti-social contract renewed.

Today, black and brown communities have become targets of a multi-billion dollar enterprise. Rarely do these institutions approach their work with a political or historical consciousness. Even more rarely do they organize across institutional lines to challenge race-constructed social inequities. Institutions take a "silo" approach to how they address social "needs." As a result, each system gives a different name to racial disparities: "Achievement gap" in education, "disparate outcomes" in health care, "over-representation" in criminal justice, "disproportionality" in human services. Since the word "race" is eliminated from these descriptors, institutions do not have to account for the racial inequities basic to them all. Institutions are no longer accountable to those communities whose residents once marched, picketed, and risked fire hoses and police batons. Accountability in the social service industry is now to those who license, those who determine priorities, and those who fund. Black and brown grassroots leaders, who for years organized their communities to speak "truth to power," now found themselves employed as outreach workers, intake counselors, and case managers, beholden to organizations often headquartered far from their constituents. Service providers were divorced from community, no longer organizing people to speak and act on their own behalf. Service delivery upheld the status quo of white supremacy.

Power — who has it and who doesn't — lies at the root of this systemic reality. In its "Undoing Racism®/Community Organizing" workshop, the People's Institute analyzes how power was taken away from poor communities and resides now with institutions "serving" poor people. This "power analysis" begins with a visual depiction of a contemporary poor community, especially one of color: its boarded up buildings, vacant houses, dilapidated schools, "payday loan" businesses that prey on poor people; police presence — or absence. Poor communities look virtually the same throughout the country, rural, urban, North, South. It is what Madhi Davenport, a People's Institute trainer, calls a "poverty franchise" where billions of dollars are made. Poor communities today are ringed by institutions and larger systems external to themselves that benefit from their continued existence. This network of systems located around and within poor communities act as "feet of oppression" on the people who live there.

Organizing for change was no longer central for these "helping" professions. Organizing for equity was anathema to systems like education, social work, health care. Indeed, organizing was frequently mocked, dismissed as a naive or outdated tactic by academics and policymakers and by those who fund the academy and policy-making. Black leaders who had inspired the Civil Rights Movement and determined its strategy had to modify and professionalize their voices in this rapidly-changing "colorblind" post-civil rights America.

The 1950s is the decade in which the modern Civil Rights Era organizing began, yet it is the 1960s which gets all the credit. Similarly, one could argue, the 1970s were in every way a more radicalized and politically volatile decade than the '60s. But, once again, the '60s gets all the credit. Whatever beginning date is used, the Civil Rights Era had passed and was declared to be over with the end of the Vietnam War in 1975. By then, the country was reeling from a generation of constant shocks to its system. Millions of Americans were sick of it. They had watched ever-escalating body counts for over a decade. They had seen one strategy after another fail to defeat what appeared to be, by all estimates, a vastly inferior military force, possessing neither modern weapons nor the latest reconnaissance technology. This ragtag army defeated the most powerful armed forces in the world! The last televised image of this ignoble affair was of American embassy employees clinging to the running blades of the military helicopters sent to rescue them. Some would say the United States "cut and ran." Blame would be passed around from various occupants of the Oval Office to members of Congress from both parties to military strategists who were said to have fought a conventional war with an unconventional foe. Americans have blamed each other ever since.

Americans were also tired of assassinations and nightly news of crime and cities up in flames. They were weary of those who called for "changing the system" and others who appeared to be "spoiled children" with too much education and too few manners. A steady stream of television shows and movies depicted black men as "get-over artists" and "wife beaters" who did not take their societal responsibilities seriously. The dignity of men long oppressed, captured by the documentary *Eyes on the Prize* and by the 1968 march of sanitation workers in Memphis with black men holding placards that read "I AM A MAN," was replaced by depictions of black men as either fools or gangsters who respected no one, not even their own.

Discreditation turned out to be more powerful than assassination. The "New Jim Crow" would begin as the Civil Rights Movement was called off.

CHAPTER 24

Conservative Counter Strategy to the Civil Rights Movement

In 1969, I was arrested in Oxford, Mississippi, along with two African American friends, for "consorting." At least that is the way the Sheriff in Lafayette County put it. I don't know what the official charge against us was, but as late as 1969 blacks and whites were not to "consort" with each other. Consorting was less a crime than "plotting against the government," meaning the one in Jackson, not Washington, DC, of course. "Consorting" had a more social emphasis, although that could change quickly. And in our cases, it did. What began as a charge of simple theft ended with three of us pleading guilty to charges of felonious grand larceny that might have led to a few years in the notorious Parchman State Prison. Parchman was historically a plantation where enslaved Africans worked for nothing. When it became a prison the terms were the same. This arrest, I soon learned, was no joke. It seemed ridiculous at first, and it was. It lacked the glamour of a civil rights arrest. It was unlikely that it would garner the attention of Movement leaders or a US Attorney or the Justice Department. We might lose. As the weeks went by, this seemed more and more possible.

Mississippi did not allow consorting in jail. So our group of small town radicals was split up. I was put in a six-foot by eight-foot cell where I lived for a moment with a very drunk older white man. As soon as he sobered up a bit, he was moved. Sheriff said I was bad for the morale of other whites and he didn't want me advocating for N----- rights in his jail.

What we were sure of, at first, was that we would be out soon. Surely this was just a matter designed to scare us. As one week turned into another, we became exactly that — more and more scared. What we learned much later was that our case was being argued from Oxford to Washington before we ever went to trial. Were these boys involved in activities that threatened harm to persons and property yet unknown? Were they plotting to bomb something on campus? Who were they and what were they up to? Were they undermining Mississippi's states rights?

"States rights" was a code word for white supremacy. This was never exactly said, but one grew up in it and eventually figured it out. Mississippi had a Sovereignty Commission, a sort of state-controlled HUAC/FBI, *whose purpose was to keep track of any person or organization or activities that might threaten Mississippi's strict segregationist way of life. We had certainly violated the white supremacist codes, so we had to be dealt with.*

It was almost a year before this matter was resolved. My mother says while we were being held in jail, FBI *agents called her and were very curt and intimidating to her. They asked her a lot of questions about my friends and associates at Ole Miss and around Oxford, Mississippi. When they asked her about "the theft," she was outraged. She told me sometime later, "If they had said you had gone to jail for protesting or speaking out against the war, well, I might have believed that. But stealing? Never! You weren't raised like that."*

The decision of the court went this way for all of us: ONE: *We were found guilty of grand larceny, a felony, and sentenced to three years in Parchman State Prison —* SUSPENDED, *with three years' probation;* TWO: *A fine of $2,500 was levied (which matched exactly the amount in my bank account) —* PAID; THREE: *Agree to leave the State of Mississippi for two years.*

Now, all of this had its upside. I finished Valley of the Dolls *and two other pot-boilers which I otherwise would never have read. My Aunt Peggy put me up in New York City while I was out on bail and I witnessed civil rights activist James Forman receive a $15,000 check from Washington Square United Methodist Church in New York City's Greenwich Village as the first reparations received from US churches for his Black Reparations Fund. Finally, I enrolled at New York Theological Seminary to study for the ministry, something I had not planned to do. One day while at NYTS, I walked along with another student named John Lane to Union Seminary uptown, a distance of at least three miles,* *to meet the controversial theologian, Dr. James Cone, whose book,* Black Theology, *had just rocked white theologians' world. This was new stuff for me even though Cone couldn't really mesh with us and dismissed us after only a minute or two. There was more. One of my professors for a class I cannot remember the name of was the even-more-controversial Dr. Julius Lester, who had just published* Look Out, Whitey! Black Power's Gon Get Your Mama! *All of us were terrified, long suspecting that this was what it was really about after all. I returned to Mississippi in September for the trial, fortified now with a reputation in some small circles in New York City as a freedom fighter against Southern white racism. I had arrived.*

The Civil Rights Movement was growing and gaining strength through the 1950s and '60s. The federal government's Great Society was opening up new opportunities for expanding the social contract but at the same time, a national counter-movement was organizing itself. This counter-movement would prove just as determined and just as skilled in organizing as those it opposed; eventually it would be better funded than the social change forces it sought to defeat. It stood ready to silence the shouts of "Freedom Now!," "Ain't Nobody Gonna Turn Me 'Round" and ultimately the shouts of "Black Power." Many of these counter measures evolved during school desegregation struggles. Others focused on fear of communism or fear of "creeping socialism" or "one-world-ism." The right began to consolidate all the currents opposing social change into one interlocking network to uphold and defend the "American Way of Life." This included the free enterprise system, states rights in the South, opposition to government regulations, support for the sanctity of private property, gun ownership, and individual freedoms. Those who opposed Roosevelt's New Deal as socialist and a class-based "share-the-wealth" ideology, who saw the United Nations as a step toward One World government, and who feared integration as a tactic in the spread of worldwide communism, were ripe to oppose the "social engineering" being orchestrated by "radicals" symbolized by the Warren Court.

All of this had to do with race. Whiteness was a propertied right. It was a promise this country had made to white people. Resistance to demands for racial equality percolated throughout this national counter-movement. In the Southern United States this opposition was overt, bigoted and violent. In other parts of the country opposition to "civil rights" was more muted, but just as committed to the separation of the races, especially in housing and education. Consistently, over the years, racism would be seen as a Southern phenomenon. From those associated with the "Knowing Class" as organizer Margery Freeman calls them, Northern progressives thought they were more sophisticated, better educated, and certainly more politically astute than the rest of America and especially the South. This arrogance showed up in white institutions and communities across the nation who "knew" that because they were against racism, we could all move on.

But racism is not confined to a certain region in the US. It is everywhere — without exception. New York City, for example, has been and is one of the most racially divided cities in America. Throughout its history race riots, police shootings and segregation in housing, education, wealth distribution, and certainly criminal justice have framed whatever else it might be. Its professional schools and corresponding social and educational service delivery systems refuse to address the racial inequities other than to say they exist. While more people may be willing to identify racism in Northern cities, entrenched racial realities are found everywhere, and few are prepared to organize to dismantle them. While outside the South individual opposition to racial equity may be more muted, everywhere the institutions' silence speaks loudly: We do not need to change.

The People's Institute "power analysis" plays out most dramatically in our property. Our homes have long been the cornerstone that upholds middle class wealth in America. The value of one's home was the bedrock upon which one's quality of life was built. In the US, any perceived threat to white property rights was a threat to one's livelihood and endangered white people's ability to transfer their wealth to future generations. Home assessments went down as black people were allowed to move into white neighborhoods. Many liberal-minded white persons hid behind these protective walls of real estate, leaving working class white people, often renters, to fight their racial battles for them. Working class whites were portrayed as the "racists," stereotyped as small-minded and narrow-thinking. In fact, all white people benefited from the arrangement.

Working class whites who had to face the challenge of civil rights as it played out in neighborhood, school, and work deeply resented those whites who espoused racial equity but did so securely removed from its direct impact. The swing to the right was rooted in the nation's historical race construct which was predicated on segregation, not only in the South, but in all sections and sectors of the country.

Progressive forces that had won the battle for civil rights should have led the nation for at least another generation. Yet the civil rights victories lasted less than ten years before resistance from both the right and the left began to undermine the liberal consensus forged in the 1960s. The galvanized counter movement, often underground and naively dismissed by liberals amid progress on civil rights, grew stronger year by year. Even the stinging defeats of conservative Presidential candidates between 1960 and 1968 helped build the resistance movement.

The right-wing counter movement to the Civil Rights Movement was a country club movement among the growing middle class of white people. Only a few years previous this aspiring middle class had been seen solely as working class laboring and living in America's great cities in the North and Midwest. They understood that their hard-fought battles with management now allowed them to move to the suburbs complete with front and back yards and a pension to boot. These long-ignored white bastions had benefited greatly from progressive social legislation enacted to bring the country out of economic depression. They were supportive of civil rights within sharply defined parameters usually ending at the intersection of city limits and their property lines. They voiced their support for "Negro rights" — always with the refrain, "as long as those rights don't infringe on mine." However infringement was everywhere — in the schools, in the factories, in the neighborhoods, in taxes necessary to fund these Great Society initiatives.

By the late fifties and into the sixties, in private white enclaves from Citizen Councils on one extreme to seemingly more polite and respected civic associations like the Jaycees, Rotary and Kiwanis clubs, questions were being raised as to "how far" this "civil rights business" was going to go. "How about our civil rights?" was the question first whispered and then shouted. The standard-bearer of these forgotten Americans was Arizona's Senator Barry Goldwater. Even though he suffered one of the most resounding defeats of a presidential candidate in the nation's history in 1964 at the hands of incumbent Democrat Lyndon Baines Johnson, Goldwater had a clear vision of the next generation of American politics. He was "holding the coats" for those conservative leaders whose ideological antipathy for a multiracial, fully integrated United States was sweeping the country. These leaders were determined to take back the presidency, appoint the Supreme Court, and "get the government off our backs." By 1968, this right-wing movement, fueled by growing class- and raced-based resentment about the direction the country was going and abetted by the left's growing opposition to the Vietnam War, would elect Richard Nixon as the next President. Lyndon B. Johnson would decide not to seek a second term as President. Few saw it coming except Allard Lowenstein and his "Dump Johnson" crusade; no one thought it had a chance at succeeding. Until it did.

The Republican Party, which had questioned its own future in the face of Goldwater's 1964 defeat, found itself returned to power after only eight years. When Richard M. Nixon lost the 1960 presidency to Senator John F. Kennedy and the 1962 governor's race to Edmund G. "Pat" Brown in California, he had been so thoroughly dismissed as a political force that some people thought he was dead. Yet in 1968, Nixon was elected the 37th President of the United States.

Nixon resurrected and "waved the bloody shirt," successfully tapping into white fears about the dismantling of the racial state. Appealing to what his advisors urged him to call the "Silent Majority," Nixon campaigned on a "Law and Order" theme which harkened back to old western movies and the legacy of a thousand Marshall Dillons coming down hard on horse thieves and gunmen who defied social norms and threatened the peace. Nixon's people knew the depth of resentment in white communities against black people who had been battering them psychically for the past twenty years. This resentment was especially directed toward those blacks who were blamed for burning down Detroit and Newark and the Watts section of Los Angeles. In living rooms across white America curses had rained down on the six o'clock news at King and his elite apologists like Cronkite, Huntley and Brinkley plus scores of invisible East Coast elites.

Nixon was recast as George Wallace, but without the direct, public race-baiting and without his slicked-back, oily Brylcreem look. Nixon never publicly uttered the N-word (only belied by tapes of his private Oval Office conversations released in 2010), but he might just as well have. White people had had enough, not just from blacks and Mexican Americans, but from Indians, too — parading around in war bonnets as if it were 1868 and not 1968. The resentment boiled over as their own children returned from college in all-out rebellion against everything their parents had been taught to hold dear and sacred. It seemed as though every college student was enthralled by "New Left" rhetoric. Their world was under siege and the "Silent Majority" seethed.

Although Nixon capitalized on the fears of white people to get himself elected, once in office he did not actually "turn back the clock" on civil rights in America or the legislative victories symbolized by the civil rights acts. He did not urge the Supreme Court to declare unconstitutional the civil right acts of 1964 and 1965. He did not try to nullify the 1968 Civil Rights Act that banned housing discrimination on the basis of race and had outlawed such common practices as redlining, steering, and refusing loans to people of color on the basis of neighborhood racial quotas. In fact, Nixon sponsored legislation that led to the passage of the Community Reinvestment Act of 1974, requiring banks to show that they were investing in neighborhoods previously excluded from financial and investment capital. He recognized, however, that opposition was mounting nationwide to such remedies as busing students to achieve racial balance in the schools of the nation. Opposition was rising to any efforts that appeared to use quota systems as a means of integrating the workplace or in college admissions and hiring practices, in either the public or private spheres.

Nixon was anathema to progressives and white liberals, but only because they had yet to meet Ronald Reagan or George W. Bush. Newt Gingrich's "Contract with America" was still twenty years in the future; the Republican Tea Party and "Trumpism" still a generation later. The 1968 Kerner Commission prediction of two societies, one white and affluent, the other black and poor, was coming true. Leadership was increasingly white for a host of reasons. Black folk's issues were becoming passé, melded into other forms of white-focused oppressions. Race talk was outlawed in the public sphere. Racism was said, largely by whites, to have been eradicated in the United States. The myth of a colorblind society was born.

CHAPTER 25

White Mainstream Response to the Civil Rights Movement

When did it all change? This is a question I have asked myself for the past thirty-five years. There is no exact date, but the nation's movement toward racial equity and civil rights was stymied. By 1980, when Ronald Reagan became President, organizing had fallen out of favor. This was certainly true in my case. In the eight years I directed St. Mark's community center, St. Mark's became a programmatic powerhouse, open twenty-four hours a day. Grants were now the answer. We opened the Tremé Junior High Street Academy in 1974 with a $5,000 donation from educational activist, Jonathan Kozol. Nelson and I had met Kozol at a party uptown hosted by Corinne Freeman Smith who had been a part of Mississippi summer in 1964 and was a strong activist in her own right. She was the sister of the woman who became my third wife in 1981, Margery Freeman, one of the original staff people at Tremé Street Academy and later with the People's Institute for Survival and Beyond. Small world. In 1977, St. Mark's was awarded $285,000 from the State of Louisiana Department of Education for the operation of our Street Academy. That same year we received forty slots in a government employment program; St. Mark's became one of the largest employers in Tremé.

When the Street Academy day ended at 3:00 each afternoon, a plethora of programs and activities kicked in. As St. Mark's began to be recognized for its successful programs, the National Division of the United Methodist Church funded a free health clinic called the HEAD (Health Emergency Aid Dispensary) Clinic and an Emergency Drop-In Center, an all-night soup kitchen and a youth hostel catering to the needs of the largely white young people from all over the country as they arrived in New Orleans often penniless and without a place to stay.

In retrospect, I realized that the euphoria I once experienced from participating in a successful community-based action was now reserved for the feeling that resulted from a successful grant application. I felt the same excitement when we received a grant from the National Endowment for the Humanities for an oral history project and a grant for artists in Tremé to paint murals around the neighborhood. I was now a social entrepreneur. Yet with each program accomplishment, I found that I felt less and less accountable to community residents and more to my private and public funders. It was as if all the organizing victories achieved since 1954 were done and over with and programs like St. Mark's were called to implement what had been accomplished. The Civil Rights Era, which had seen some of the best community-based organizing in the nation's history, had done its job.

But had it? Racism had not ended. When I took a hard look at what we had accomplished, I realized those in power had not ceded even a fraction of real power to the people most impacted by their policies. Militarism was as threatening as ever. What happened? I, and so many thousands like me, had become professional managers of community programs. We had abandoned organizing in exchange for direct services that brought more money to our organizations and didn't require accountability to the people we served. We mothballed our critique of power and substituted a strategy that depended on our assessing community deficits. Our careers had no time or room for community leadership. We told ourselves that in order to meet the community's needs, we would sacrifice working against racism which had no money in it in order to get government and foundation grants that had plenty. By 1980, this transition was complete.

In the last quarter of the twentieth century, white people reasserted control of what constitutes social change and how it would best be carried out, regulated and evaluated. Ironically, most of those who made the various movements happen no longer qualified to work in the very arenas they had helped to create. They lacked the credentials.

It would take thirty years in some parts of the United States for whites to begin to adjust to the new realities that outlawed overt racism. By then whites had built another country, a private culture in defiance of government dictates. Across the country, white people withdrew from the "public" sphere and migrated to "whites only" suburbs to evade racial integration. As People's Institute organizer Barbara Major explained, the word "public" preceding words like "housing," "hospital," "health care," "transportation," "defender," "schools," and even "swimming pool" in some parts of the country, became code words that meant poor and most often black and Latino. Whites retreated more and more into the private spheres of influence. The word "private" began to mean "better." Abetted by a media eager to promote and patronize a growing white middle class, the ideal family in American life became one who owned private property, sent their children to a private school as a step toward entrance to one of the elite private colleges; who of course had one or — preferably — two private cars; who had access to private health care and legal services. Whites have been the only people in the US able to "privatize" themselves as a collective and with government support and cultural permission.

Whites took to the courts and to state legislatures to oppose busing kids from the "inner city" to the suburbs and vice-versa. All the while increased property taxes swelled suburban coffers to support building new suburban schools. Progressive urban whites called for "magnet schools," designed to keep their children in the public schools by offering special academic and arts programs in "safe" environments where they would not be subject to "lower standards" or "cultural isolation" occasioned by the presence of black children. The process of privatization and re-segregation was so extensive that today it is still possible to grow up in small towns and big cities in America with no social or educational interaction between whites and people of color, particularly African Americans, because of housing patterns and segregated school systems.

The contemporary battle about health care reform demonstrates the racialization of the private/public dichotomy. Anti-racist writer Tim Wise explains:

> [T]here is evidence that many whites may perceive [President Obama's] efforts in racialized terms, no matter how universal the rhetoric...This could even be due to his rhetorical use of the term "public option" to describe the part of the reform initiative that would fall to the government. After all, use of the term "public" conjures images of other public amenities, like public transportation, or public housing, both of which are so often seen as urban or "inner city" institutions utilized by people of color.[1]

Tragically, the very Civil Rights Movement participants who had sparked hope among millions of impoverished black and Latino people became the televised visage of "public welfare." Blacks, especially black women, became the lasting image of poverty in America, one that Ronald Reagan used to his political advantage during his first campaign for President in 1976 when he spoke from the political stump about Cadillac-driving welfare queens buying steaks with food stamps. Reagan failed to get the Republican nomination in '76, but he used race as a prod to electrify his followers. He built a constituency on the time-honored American political tradition of blaming those least powerful and by raising the race flag to mobilize those white people who felt left out of the Great Society. Ron Chisom characterizes this period as having two great fears: one, that all black women are welfare cheats, and two, that the Russians are coming. Scapegoating black people has always been a staple of Internalized Racial Superiority.

In 1980, Ronald Reagan's successful campaign for the Republican nomination was launched at the Neshoba County Fair outside Philadelphia, Mississippi. This Philadelphia conjured the ghosts of slain civil rights workers Goodman, Schwerner and Chaney. The other Philadelphia (PA) might have called up the ideals of the founders, yet unfulfilled, but still a part of King's Dream. Reagan wasn't lost. He knew exactly what he was doing. So did white people.

Government assistance or "welfare," as it would popularly be called, became seared into the psyche of the nation as a metaphor for race. Although there were always more white people "on welfare" than blacks or Latino/as, the program itself would take on a racial cast. It would be associated with those who would rather be taken care of by Uncle Sam than work for a living. Despite its gross mischaracterization of the majority of black and brown people who were still, as always, largely shut-out of decent private sector jobs, access to private housing and equal education, the stigma took hold. This stereotype still exists today.

Ironically, in many cities legal segregation had actually aided black community self-determination by providing some buffers for black doctors, lawyers, funeral homes and finance institutions from the brutality of Jim Crow discrimination. Integration on the other hand often destroyed these protective barriers. While many black individuals prospered after integration, they did so largely by leaving black-owned enterprises and organizations. White institutions grabbed up much of the black professional class, leaving the vast majority of poor African Americans behind. This was how it was meant to be. The construct of race required it. The anti-social contract remained in force.

The phenomenon of black poverty was severed from its historic racial roots, now systemic in nature, and tied to individual attributes and behaviors. Blacks were characterized as having an "innate" proclivity for laziness, dependency, too many babies, lack of a work ethic, even criminality. Whites, millions of whom were poor and also depended on government assistance, hid their poverty, telling themselves that "bad luck" had put them in this "temporary" situation. No media sought them out and dramatized their stories as it did with black families on welfare. Once again race trumped class in the United States. Rather than a War on Poverty, as the Johnson administration tagged it, one that required foot soldiers organized across race lines, a chance for genuine social change was missed. The War on Poverty had by 1968 become a skirmish, and by the mid-70s, it was over. The real war in Vietnam smashed Johnson's vision for the nation and his own political legacy. It would within a few years destroy Nixon's, too.

Mistrust of the government in Washington, DC that had pervaded and colored every aspect of life in the white South spread into white communities of the North as well. For black people, it was just the opposite. Federal intervention was that for which one hoped. What blacks feared was anything that led off with "states rights."

The downward spiral of America's great cities by the late 1960s had spread across the United States. Cities were associated with criminal behaviors and violence. These realities were associated with race. White flight caused quakes all along these infrastructural fault lines. Life had never been easy or welcoming to blacks in any of these arenas. While cities expanded job opportunities and cultural enrichment activities in ways that rural areas did not, this did not mean urban settings guaranteed or encouraged advancement for its "colored inhabitants." People were pushed into ghettos: Chinatowns, Mexican and Puerto Rican barrios. Urban Indians were crowded into parts of the city where liquor stores and police precincts became social control mechanisms that filled city jails every weekend.

The "riots" of the 1960s were not seen by most white people as being caused by the oppressive environments created by white-controlled institutions and culture as the 1968 Kerner Commission had determined, but by blacks themselves. In New York City, blacks and

Puerto Ricans were targeted; in Newark much the same; blacks were blamed in Detroit. In Los Angeles, blacks, Mexicans, and other Latinos, even Asians were at fault. Everywhere, people of color were to blame for their own circumstances and conditions. Whites were never held responsible for theirs.

As segregation hardened throughout the cities and suburbs, the public arenas of the nation became those areas where civil rights were played out, guaranteed, and put on display. Private arenas, be they country club or business associations, were where policy was determined, money raised and money made, candidates chosen and elections won. In New Orleans, just one example among many, blacks became the majority population and with their large numbers helped to elect Ernest "Dutch" Morial mayor in 1976. The Mayor's office in New Orleans was held by an African American for the next thirty-three years, even after Hurricane Katrina in 2005. By 1980, every elective position, except for the office of District Attorney and certain judgeships, was held by blacks. The School Board, City Council, Police Chief — all were black. But control of the economics of the city remained in the hands of rich white men and their families. By 2013, though blacks represented over 60% of the city's population, they owned less than 7% of businesses. Demographic change had impacted electoral politics but had made little difference in who had and controlled the money and the power that came with it.

Like New Orleans, cities like Detroit; Newark; Camden; Gary, Indiana; East St. Louis, Illinois and Cleveland, Ohio all elected black mayors in the 1970s. All immediately faced a dwindling tax base as whites accelerated their flight to the suburbs, abetted by tax policies that built new infrastructures, highways, and services such as shopping malls and gated communities. "Follow the money" led from downtown to the suburbs.

The cities' inner cores began to resemble a patchwork quilt with boarded up buildings, abandoned and burned housing. Graffiti-scarred walls and street signs became emblematic of inner cities across the nation, populated more and more by poor, disaffected and, too often, hopeless black and brown families. Private investment dried up; banks and finance companies refused to invest in cities whose infrastructure was failing and whose crime rate was skyrocketing. The cities, like many of their residents, came to depend on government subsidies to survive. Suburbs attracted not only white people but white resources as well. Huge malls, making it possible to shop where one lived, meant that many whites returned to the inner cities only to work, further depleting the city coffers of much needed resources and fostering a sense of profound alienation between white suburbia and the "inner city." City schools declined along with property taxes. City services lagged behind residential needs. City government increasingly became a primary employer of blacks who remained in the city.

Detroit was the greatest example of the nation's abandonment of its cities by whites. It had been the fifth largest city in the United States, home to the mighty automobile industry with all its tributary effects under-girding the economy of heartland cities like Akron, Toledo, Youngstown, Cleveland, and Flint. By 1970, Detroit had lost over one million residents, mostly white working class people. By 2010, the city had shrunk to 713,777 and ranked 18th in population among cities in the United States. This decline in Detroit's numbers and stature as one of America's great cities has continued. In the summer of 2013 with Detroit facing civil bankruptcy, the State of Michigan took over the city and named a special master to run it until the crisis could be overcome, i.e. creditors paid. Today, depending on who you ask, there is rebirth in Detroit going on, which almost always means whites are returning to the city and gentrification is taking place.

The cities of the US had not been built with people of color in mind. As they filled with large and growing populations of black and brown citizens, the practices of redlining, lack of access to credit and financing and overall discrimination against people of color caused urban infrastructures to collapse. None of the institutions — schools, health services, churches, universities — were prepared for such a radical change in demographics. As white people fled, the taxes, real estate, property appraisals, jobs, and small businesses that they owned and operated went with them. Universities and school systems remained in the cities, but these un-taxed entities were founded in the context of the dominant white culture and often had no real relationships with communities of color in their midst. White people who worked in these institutions were not prepared to address these new realities. Whites continued to be both in charge and over-represented in all areas of decision-making in all sectors of the society. While white men controlled the private sectors of business, finance and capital to be sure, the helping professions such as social work and teaching became bastions for white women.

During the 1970s and '80s, large cities became places that white people avoided if they could. Most would drive to work, park in the employees' garage, eat in the employees' cafeteria and reverse their steps on the way home. One could work in an all-white environment in an all-black city.

Gov. Nelson Rockefeller of New York, ironically, is credited with first calling the systemic assault on the black communities of the US a "War on Drugs." It was more a war on black people. Yet no one opposes efforts to rid communities of drugs. Rockefeller was always cast as part of the liberal wing of the Republican Party. Today this wing no longer exists, but in 1972 it did. Rockefeller wanted to be President and his closest advisors warned him he was seen as too liberal. He had to "get tough." Thus the War on Drugs announced to the party that Rockefeller was no pansy and was more than an East Coast liberal. He was "tough," too. Drugs were bad news and were ravaging the inner cities of the United States. Clamping down on black communities where the drug trade was fast becoming the primary economic engine in the aftermath of white flight was genius. Much like the convict-leasing system that followed the Reconstruction era, the War on Drugs was a primary social control mechanism that followed the Civil Rights Movement. Both were built on lies. The black community was never the center of the drug trade, nor did it have more drug addicts than other communities. It was, however, a way to use racial stereotypes and fear-mongering to make it seem real. Associating the black community with drugs and their after effects knocked the moral underpinnings from under the black community's fight for equality in the still racialized American state. By 1972 the black dope dealer was beginning to take root in the dominant white cultural mindset. The proud black man of *Eyes on the Prize* and the Memphis garbage strike was being replaced in white people's eyes by the depiction of black men on television and in the movies as violent, child- abandoning, drug-pushing, urban get-over artists. "J. J." on *Good Times,* a popular TV show premiering in 1974 which ran for six years, was portrayed as unambitious, amusing — a throwback to the era of minstrel shows much like the characters in *Amos and Andy.* Funny he was, as were the Kingfish and Algonquin J. Calhoun on *Amos and Andy,* but they played handsomely to white people's stereotypical images of black people and black men. The Superfly movies of the same period, the first opening in 1972 and a second in 1973, drove this home. Black men were hipsters, ex-cons, drug couriers who lacked a moral center and any ties to family and home. Since relatively few white people knew black men (or women, for that matter), this depiction hit all the right buttons. The truth, as chronicled persistently by the Drug Policy Alliance, yet unknown then and still now, is that most drugs are sold by whites and more white people use drugs than black people. But the media barrage sent the opposite message. White people knew that drugs dealers were black. Drug users were black. The War, we were told, was not against black people, but against black people who bought and sold drugs. The prisons of the nation began to fill up with black and brown. The strategy worked: Take young black men off the street, lock 'em up, and we will all sleep easier. Michelle Alexander calls it the "new Jim Crow." Out of sight, out of mind was the result. Alexander writes:

> We tell ourselves they "deserve" their fate, even though we know — and don't know — that whites are just as likely to commit many crimes, especially drug crimes. We know that people released from prison face a lifetime of discrimination, scorn and exclusion, and yet we claim not to know that an undercaste exists. We know it and we don't know at the same time.[2]

Mass incarceration of black men in this country is seen by millions of white people as their just desserts: "If you do the crime, do the time." But not all of us. Just some of us. The criminalization of black people, especially in the cities, became a self-fulfilling prophecy. As resources emptied out the "ghetto," crime began to rise. Drugs were among the few resources the community did not lack.

By the end of the 1980s, boarded up buildings, closed down movie theaters, vacancy signs, razor wire fences, check cashing emporiums and graffiti made up the prototypical urban landscape. Street corner profiteers replaced those who once had their offices forty stories high; the car dealership that once had showcased the newest model Cadillac now housed a job training center. The problem was that Cadillac had left town. Black and brown people were being trained for non-existent jobs.

The inability of institutions to change their fundamental white cultural framework to better serve people of color gave rise to systemic failure. Racial disparities grew as disproportionate numbers of black and brown persons began to constitute the constituencies of these systems. More blacks went to jail, including adult women whose children would enter foster care; more children of color dropped out of school; fewer went to college and fewer graduated. More and more became unemployed and underemployed; more died younger. The list goes on.

Racial disparities are as striking today as they were in 1954 when the Supreme Court overturned "separate but equal." This country remains in every way an apartheid nation. In the education system black and Latino children suffer in over-regimented and underfunded segregated schools. In the criminal justice system with its profiling, police brutality, sentencing disparities and post-release second class status, the structural outcomes are as predictable today in Arkansas as in New York City.

According to a 2013 report by the Pew Research Center, in 1984, the median net worth of black households was 9% that of white households. By 2011, the black-white wealth gap had widened: black household wealth was 7% that of white households. Similar trends are evident for Latinos who in 1984 had 13% of white wealth; by 2011 that percentage had widened to 9%. Translated into actual dollars: In 2011, white families were worth $91,405. Black households were worth $6,446. Latino households were worth $7,843.[3]

These institutional disparities devastate black and Latino communities. Home ownership, the primary source of wealth for people of color, was decimated by the "housing bubble burst" of 2008 that was compounded by predatory lending practices that created loans impossible to pay off. Meanwhile, the systemic "cradle to prison pipeline" chokes community's efforts to achieve equity. To challenge these structural inequities, the roots of white supremacy have to be recognized as still alive and visible within white-dominant cultural institutions. These historical tentacles are the structural veins of the nation's bloodlines.

Ironically, even as the racial wealth gap increases, poor white people continue to fall further behind. Yet the nation's racialized version of poverty, which resurfaced with a virulence after President Obama's Affordable Care Act was passed in 2011, prevents poor white people from recognizing their common ground with poor people of color. The poorest white person, who would benefit from the Act, is swept up in a resurgent resistance movement: "Obama can't make me do nuthin' — he doesn't have the right." Read: I don't have to listen to a black man.

CHAPTER 26

Internalized Racial Superiority — Updated

In New Orleans where I lived for thirty-five years, the home Margery Freeman and I bought in 1997 was valued much higher because of this mid-city neighborhood's racial makeup. In a city where African Americans made up over two-thirds of the population pre-Katrina, the neighborhoods where whites still lived had home appraisals dramatically higher than those in neighborhoods where few whites lived. This initial advantage, based on racially-steered housing patterns, made it easier for us to obtain flood insurance. When the levees broke after Hurricane Katrina hit and the city was flooded, our home was covered. This was true even though our house was ruined because it was located close to the 17th Street Canal whose flood wall was breached. The insurance paid off and we were able to use the payment to buy a co-op apartment in 2006 in the Bronx. This was approximately two years after we moved to New York City in 2004. The Bronx co-op required much renovation to make it comfortable for us, but upon completion, we asked our friend and colleague with the People's Institute, Shadia Alvarez, what the neighbors had to say. She gave us a "thumbs up" and said "the price just went up." It was a good example of how we could not run from the privileges that come with the status of being white. We experienced first-hand that we benefitted from being white even as we worked to "undo racism." Our presence, regardless of our politics, altered the racial dynamics. Over the years this has happened many times while hailing a taxi, checking into hotels, crossing borders, even being handed the check in restaurants after dining with fellow anti-racist trainers.

Benefits of being white are intergenerational. Our son Nathan bought an early nineteenth century home in Tremé in 2004 on a handshake. He had cash on hand from a prior house he'd also bought on a handshake. The following year, when Katrina hit New Orleans and the levees broke, he was able to collect insurance and Road Home money and use them both to fix up his house (which hadn't flooded much) and buy another. And another. In 2007, he and his wife sold their Tremé home (now worth a great deal more than they had paid for it) and moved into a triplex in the St. Roch area of town. Both their new home and the neighborhood were pretty run down, but they knew that with thousands of young white people coming to New Orleans post Katrina needing places to live, St. Roch would soon become an up-and-coming hip neighborhood. While Nathan is a committed community activist, progressive in heart and action, he understood the conundrum of gentrification — better services and safer streets, but higher rents and mortgages. His presence, regardless of his politics, altered the racial dynamics of the neighborhood.

In the 1990s, cities like New York and San Francisco, even Los Angeles and Atlanta, began to experience the beginnings of an economic turn-around. Crime rates began to decrease, cheap rents became available in certain parts of town, and digital jobs opened up for internet-savvy young people. Younger white people as well as some young black professionals began returning to the city, eager to combine work in information systems and finance in the dot.com age with an urban lifestyle built around access to the arts, health clubs open most of the night, music venues, gourmet coffee houses, bicycle paths and restaurants on every corner.

Gentrification (a term first used in 1964 by British sociologist Ruth Glass) has led to the rebirth of some cities' central business districts. The boom years of the dot.com era made it possible to rent space and renovate old warehouses, buy once beautiful houses downtown at low prices either to "fix-up" or to live in with eight to ten others sometimes sleeping in shifts and paying exorbitant rents to live in the city. Cities are becoming those places where poor and even medium income wage earners can no longer afford to live unless, as recent immigrants have always done, they squeeze several families into smaller homes and apartments.

Ironically, Internalized Racial Superiority has made this movement of reverse white flight possible. White people have internalized messages given to us over generations that say we are entitled to all we are and all we have, that we are individuals with good intentions who have worked hard to achieve our successes. Because we are a-historical, we don't know that our systems and institutions were created with a bias in our favor. We are "normal," measuring those persons and cultures around us by our own rules. Individual young white people often declare that it is the urbanity that attracts them back to the city's core. Dismissive of the bland white suburban culture in which many have been raised, they enjoy the night life and specialty store existence cities afford them. Many of the cities have one or more large universities around which this new lifestyle develops. Cities like New York, Boston, San Francisco, Chapel Hill, and Austin attract the newly-graduated, becoming a permanent residence for young professionals — at least until their children reach school age. In 2007, Manhattan for the first time in generations had a net gain among the number of white children being born compared to children of color.

With gentrification, however, comes entitlement and white entitlement is the cornerstone of race privilege both historically and in the present day. Over the past three decades, improvements have been made in the quality of life for city dwellers. Police departments have begun once again "to protect and serve," at least for white residents of gentrifying neighborhoods. City services have begun to streamline and operate more efficiently. Schools that had been "dumping grounds" for its black and Latino students since the 1950s are now required — in certain neighborhoods — to provide more diverse and academically-rewarding environments for their students. Especially in the early years from pre-K to third grade, changes in the demographics have meant improvements in the schools. The Institute for Children & Poverty reported in 2009 that in New York City, a new school initiative closed the lowest performing institutions and replaced them with smaller, more specialized schools, squeezing more children from the former schools into other schools in their district.[1] Privatized charter schools share building space with traditional public schools, the children segregated by floors — often by class, ethnicity, language, or race.

Whites often do not recognize the potentially adverse effects of gentrification on people of color and even some poor white people. Because they have internalized for generations the messages of being superior and blameless, white professionals look at their actions only in terms of their individual effort, not evaluating the systemic results.

Internalized superiority often prevents whites from seeing what has happened and to whom, and from establishing any collective connection to the process. If they are made aware of the effects of gentrification, whites often respond, "It happened before I came here so it is not anything for which I can be held responsible."

This is the history of the US. A first generation encounter with indigenous people allowed a second generation to remove them from the land. By a third generation, "settlers" move in, making no connection to the process, yet benefiting from it. Today, white people rarely feel any responsibility for the enslavement of African peoples or recognize the corresponding wealth accumulation by the white collective. "I didn't do it" is a common refrain from a people socialized to be individuals. Socialized as individuals and acculturated in the "I," whites in the race-constructed society do not see themselves as actors in this race drama of the US.

Present day Harlem is a good example. Whites, especially younger whites who are often attracted to the city because of its "diversity" and its "urban feel" — both US code words for race — have, for more than two decades, been moving into Harlem because it has been the cultural hub of the black nation for the past 100 years.

This "urban pioneering" was rare before 2000. But just as in the move westward, once whites arrived, things began to change. African American and other black stores began to close, national chain stores moved in, rents skyrocketed, and restaurants that catered to the black residents had to change their menu or face bankruptcy. Whites don't necessarily notice that we and others like us are now the predominant clientele. "I was eating there before others moved in." This inherent right of discovery is deeply-embedded in our psyches.

If questioned, most whites would express love for Harlem and all that it represents to them. What we do not take responsibility for in this "new Harlem Renaissance" are the people who have been moved out so that we might move in. We claim innocence because we were not directly involved in the eviction process. Our institutional intermediaries did that for us. Like the Army and the Indian agents before us, the land was cleared by the time we arrived.

One well-publicized example of the impact of gentrification is the fight for control of Marcus Garvey Park in West Harlem. Since 1969, African American and black drummers from all over the world have claimed Marcus Garvey Park as being uniquely theirs. Every Saturday, drummers have drummed and in so-doing have given recognition to the African diaspora and its roots. The park is a spiritual and cultural symbol. Now the neighborhood is changing. New white homeowners complained that the constant drumming every Saturday ruins their weekend and invades their privacy. The drums had to move.

The story is repeated over and over in cities across the country. When gentrification began in New Orleans' Tremé neighborhood in the 1980s, a fight developed quickly between new white residents and the local music clubs, some of which had been in the community for generations. Although the history of Tremé and its association with New Orleans music was one of the reasons new, often white, residents wanted to live in that neighborhood, a noise ordinance was invoked. White individual property rights take precedence. In Tremé's Lil' Sisters club, just as in Marcus Garvey Park, it is the same. Complaints from a few white people override a community of color's cultural prerogatives. Even in Harlem, the cultural capital of the black United States, and in Tremé, the birthplace of jazz.

Gentrification is a conundrum. Without it entire sections of America's great cities would be left to fester. The national will is not there to rebuild through use of federal dollars nor would such federal programs likely lure middle class buyers back. It must happen through the private sector. At first the process attracts young people willing to live ten to a house and split the rent. Predictably, young people begin to create their own neighborhood venues for music, outdoor cafes, and specialty jobs. This pushes poor people, usually black or brown, to what are now called first ring suburbs. Today a majority of poor people live in those suburbs, once a haven for whites fleeing the city, now for poor people who cannot afford to live in their former neighborhoods. Ferguson, Missouri, made infamous by the police killing of Michael Brown in 2014, is typical. Two thirds of the city is now black; 25% live below the poverty level. Money and investment in the race-constructed society follows white people. That's the way it was set up years ago.

Racism keeps its hold on the American psyche. It is as deeply-embedded in the American reality as ever. Systemic outcomes across the broad range of society demonstrate that black and brown people fare far less well than whites. There is not one quality of life indicator in the US where race is a neutral factor nor one that has people of color faring better than whites. The gaps along the racial divide are in most cases growing wider with the passage of time rather than diminishing.

While the nation makes some progress and each new generation of young people is heralded as the one that will finally end racism's scourge, the structural inequities have not been remedied. Without these fundamental changes — without overcoming white supremacy — the heartbeat of racism remains strong and deadly.

Probably the most important example of racism's holding power is what has happened to voting rights. The 1965 Voting Rights Act represented the apex of the Civil Rights Movement. While other acts passed by Congress addressing housing discrimination, redlining, and even affirmative action have allowed significant advances for people of color in the US, the Voting Rights Act has had the most profound impact, assuring the power of the vote for African Americans and other people of color that is central to the achievement of racial equity in the country. Key to the Voting Rights Act has been the provision that allowed voters immediate access to the US Department of Justice when any of the eleven Southern states attempted to blunt the ability of people of color, especially blacks, to be fairly represented in the electoral process. This law hung over the white South like the sword of Damocles. Then, in 2013, the Supreme Court ruled in *Shelby County v. Holder* that particular provision, requiring Justice Department approval of any change to voting procedures, was no longer necessary in the states of the old Confederacy. The ruling effectively gutted and neutered the most important part of the act.

Immediately upon the Court's decision, states began to enact policies guaranteed to lessen the influence of so-called minority groups in statewide and even federal elections, especially in the Deep South. Voter ID laws have been passed in thirty-four states, ostensibly to prevent voter fraud, even as voter fraud is almost non-existent anywhere in the United States. But voter ID laws disproportionately impact those voting blocs with the highest rates of illiteracy, discouraging senior citizens and high school dropouts unable or unwilling to read the details of the law's various provisions. While states reassure residents that they will provide access for anyone who wants a photo ID, those policymakers well understand that people of color, especially those on the margins of mainstream society, are least likely to obtain the photo ID. As if the ID laws weren't discouragement enough, the Supreme Court even considered (*Evenwel v. Abbott*) a challenge to the historic "one man - one vote" principle fundamental to our democracy. While the Supreme Court did affirm (on April 4, 2016) that all residents will be counted in determining voting districts, forces opposed to expanded voting rights will likely continue to pursue other avenues to reduce those rights, particularly for those most marginalized — black and brown people.

Today, white supremacy retains its hold on white people without referring to race at all. Don't speak about race or people of color. No race talk, no racism. Allow the institutions of the state to function as they were constructed to do. Trust that those opposed to racial equity will pick up the codes and symbols of racism without ever mentioning the word. Each president of the United States from Lyndon Baines Johnson to George W. Bush has walked this "colorblind" racial tightrope. Bill Clinton, beloved in many ways by black voters, agreed to welfare reform knowing full well that more stringent welfare rules would disproportionately and negatively impact poor and jobless black people. Even Barack Obama has been constrained from speaking about race. Such irony!

De-regulation, privatization, and the demonizing of the federal government have been the strategies underlying a transformed Republican party into a virtually all-white party. This appeal to whites, however, crosses party lines and even ideologies. People on the political left charge President Obama with being a centrist politician who does not do enough to pass progressive legislation and change US foreign policies so that such policy no longer supports despotic and undemocratic regimes. The political right wing, however, opposes Obama's every move, all the while calling him a socialist, a radical, an anti-American Islamist.

White supremacy is a psychological state as well as an ideology or political platform. White people find it difficult to follow black leadership or take directions from people of color in general, yet most of us deny this is so. White supremacy is a cultural phenomenon expressed most dramatically through our institutions and our understandings of what constitutes truth and societal norms. Yet many if not most whites deny that white culture even exists. Thus white supremacy persists.

So what must we do and where are we headed as a nation? Will we see another black president? I think not for a long time. The nation has proved itself not ready. It wasn't prepared to invest the time and political capital to ensure President Obama would get the support he needed to be effective. Election night 2008 was such an opportunity and such a sign of hope. Obama received 43% of the white vote, more than any Democrat in a two-man race since 1976. Yet his opponents quickly made the time and invested their political capital in making sure Obama would not be successful. By the midterm elections of 2010, the initial hope was shattered by the surge of forces that wanted to turn America back to some past time. A similar pattern emerged in the 2012 and 2014 elections: Elation at Obama's re-election, then an outraged white electorate rises again — this time with unlimited cash — to say NO! Perhaps it might have been different had those of us who believed a new day had arrived stuck together and held fast against the reactionary agenda of those who wanted to take the country back to their racial "normality." But we didn't want to talk about race and we didn't want to understand racism.

EPILOGUE

A Whole Lot of People is Strong

— JIM DUNN, PHD THESIS TITLE

Jim Dunn and Ron Chisom believed in community organizing as the only way racism was to be "undone." They felt, however, such organizing must be led by people of color. What I would learn over the years is that whites in charge meant that racism would ultimately not be addressed. Whites would change the subject. Why? Because we always have throughout history. Denial takes many forms. Some of us insist that racism has nothing to do with us or is an artifact of this nation's racial past. Others, to deflect being implicated in the racial arrangement, insist that racism be part of a broader analysis of gender, class, and other dynamics of oppression. This risks false comparisons and dilutes the reality of racism. Denying the centrality of white supremacy in racism, we expand the analysis to something with which we are more comfortable.

I met Jim Dunn for the first time around 1980, but I had heard about him from Ron a couple of years before. I knew he taught at Antioch College in Yellow Springs, Ohio. I knew he was a folksinger and a poet because Ron told his story and brought a book of his poems home to New Orleans. I knew he had a white wife and together they led a group in Yellow Springs called HUMAN. (Help Us Make a Nation). Sign me up. It was the best acronym I had ever seen or heard about. Jim and Diana along with other organizers in Ohio sponsored HUMAN Day each August so I began to attend whenever I could. It was powerful stuff with poets and artists and singers from all over the US. I met Emmett Till's mother, Mamie Till Mobley, at HUMAN Day. Also Pete Seeger and Holly Near, even Odetta had been there, all of whom were legendary to me. I first met Dr. Michael

Washington and the Rev. Daniel Buford there, both of whom would impact me in many different ways, but especially my understanding of history and power arrangements. I met The Reverend Frederick Douglass Kirkpatrick, a poet and folksinger himself and a friend of Margery Freeman's from anti-war organizing days in Houston, Texas in the mid-1960s. Kirkpatrick was a founder of the Deacons for Defense and Justice in Jonesboro and Bogalusa, Louisiana. Another legend. It was heady times and I was there, blown away.

Jim was a great teacher, preacher, and storyteller through poetry, history and song. He was humorous, deadly serious, and in 1989 dead himself from cancer. Diana would say his death was brought about by racism. For years the pain in his shoulder and arm was falsely labeled as a form of "tennis elbow." Had he been diagnosed earlier he might still be living today, she would say, but as a black man in the US, his treatment by the medical institutions he frequented was dismissive and ultimately lethal. By the time anyone knew, his cancer was too far along. He still lived another four years or so. He passed on in February 1989, while the Institute's national gathering was in progress. Diana said the last few weeks he struggled to survive until PISAB's national gathering was happening. Then he could pass.

Jim was a MENSCH. The tag team of Jim Dunn and Ron Chisom was powerful. In their presence was greatness. You just knew it. What they began in 1980 still goes on strongly today with a new generation of trainers/organizers primed to take the work forward into a new phase whenever the inevitable transition takes place.

Ron Chisom, like Jim Dunn, is also a MENSCH. He is probably the most charismatic person I have ever known. People flock to him, bond with him, and remain loyal to him even when they fall out with him. Ron is the real deal. He is straight out of Tremé, bypassing college and most formal training. He embodies the People's Institute understanding of culture as a way of life and as the lifeblood of a people. Ron always shows up. He has criss-crossed the country for forty years or more now, yet remains rooted in New Orleans, rhythms and all. He has taken the Institute to new heights into places maybe only he and a few key Institute leaders might have envisioned. From gatherings of incarcerated men and women to philanthropic boardrooms, from homeless shelters to UN international conferences, the Institute has brought a consistent analysis of power, history and culture. It has been criticized but never taken off course. I believe that is because Ron has insisted on its grounding in community, especially in the New Orleans Tremé community.

From its birth in 1980, the People's Institute for Survival and Beyond has kept up a steady drumbeat against racism across the United States and in several countries around the world, always with an emphasis on community organizing as the key to "undoing racism." This emphasis on organizing is often lost among participants in the "Undoing Racism®/Community Organizing" workshops offered by the Institute. Yet little by little, over the decades, the anti-racist principles and analysis taught by People's Institute organizers have significantly impacted systemic structures in many cities and states around the US. Notable examples are found in Greensboro, North Carolina; New Orleans, Louisiana; New York City and Seattle, Washington. In Greensboro, organizers with the Racial Equity Institute have become a force in the county's health care institutions, in area universities, and in the Guilford County School District. In the latter, a People's Institute trainer, Monica Walker, heads the school system's Diversity Office and another former trainer, Deena Hayes, sits on its school board. Their work, with others, led to the district adopting a "racial justice audit" to inform decisions not just about hiring and curriculum but about building contracts and vendors. Another Institute trainer, Bay Love, today holds the prestigious position as Director of the Greensboro Civil Rights Museum. His use of mega-data demonstrates irrefutably the depth of structural racism in the US and brings the hope of "undoing racism" ever closer.

In New Orleans, home base for the People's Institute, tenant leaders in public housing and health care workers from area clinics and hospitals have participated in Undoing Racism® workshops for thirty-five years. In the aftermath of Hurricane Katrina, People's Institute staff and board suffered great personal losses and its offices and institutional archives were drowned in nine feet of flood waters. Yet Institute organizers like Diana Dunn, Barbara Major, Kimberley Richards, and Derek Rankin, along with a new generation of white European Dissenters, including Renee Corrigan, Lauren Holtzman and Bridget LeHane, still managed to work with hundreds of young volunteers whose enthusiasm and will to help ironically threatened to overwhelm much of the city's history and culture. Because so many community leaders had been taught by the People's Institute, locals insisted that volunteers bring an understanding of racism, culture and history into their rebuilding efforts.

In New York City, a call went out in 2004 to the People's Institute initiated by a core group of social workers representing many of the area's schools of social work. The social workers asked the People's Institute to school them in the basics of community organizing and in how to use anti-racism as the lens through which to approach their work. Mary Pender Greene (2011 President of the National Association of Social Workers – New York City), Sandy Bernabei (2015 NASW-NYC President), and Mimi Abramovitz (nationally known Bertha Capen Reynolds Professor of Social Policy at Hunter College School of Social Work), put their reputations and relationships to the test with deans, professors, funders, boards and staff of human service organizations, insisting not only that the profession was not preparing students for their future work, especially with families of color, but that they were not prepared to prepare them. To date, many thousands of social work students, academics and non-profit professionals, equipped with an anti-racist analysis, are active in the city's five boroughs and surrounding counties and states, working with constituents whose daily lives are impacted by structural racism.

The story is similar in Seattle where in the mid-1990s a core group of organizers, notably Ven Knox, Mary Flowers, Dwight Mitzoguchi, Martin Friedman, Sili Savusa, and Dustin Washington, began to push city departments, school systems and the state prison system to develop a greater understanding and knowledge of how their policies and practices negatively affect the lives of people of color. Especially effective has been the multiracial organizing that has forced city and state officials, including police chiefs, prison wardens, and district attorneys, to use an anti-racist lens in their work.

The common thread among all these cities is organizing within an anti-racist framework. The power of structural racism can only be met through the organizing efforts of key constituents both within and without the various systems. The People's Institute exemplifies the importance of longevity in the nation's struggle against racism. The key leadership has remained largely intact and today is nurturing the next generation of anti-racist organizers. It has also retained its focus on racism as the fundamental divide among the nation's people. The Institute believes that other oppressions are best confronted with an anti-racist strategy, with people of color providing leadership and the historic stamina necessary to keep the efforts going. If people of color are not guiding anti-racist efforts, internalized racial superiority is likely to redirect the organizing toward ends more palatable to white people and less liberating for people of color.

Today there are more efforts around the country dedicated to the eradication of racism than at any other time in the nation's history. The number keeps growing. This gives us great hope, particularly if the various groups find ways to work together, support each other's efforts, and resist the inevitable tensions that threaten to splinter the movement. Anti-racist organizing is found on college campuses, within city and state governments, professional associations and systemic specialties including health care, education, human services, and criminal justice work. National, community-based movements such as Black Lives Matter, Within Our Lifetime, Nation of Islam, together with immigration rights groups such as the DREAMers, supported by anti-racist white groups like European Dissent, Challenging White Supremacy, Catalyst, and Showing Up for Racial Justice, together with multiracial anti-racist organizing efforts like the White Privilege Conference, Race Forward, and the Center for the Study of White American Culture, will undo racism.

In fact, undoing racism is inevitable. White supremacy can't last. This is probably the primary reason white people must get on board as anti-racist organizers. History demands it and the future requires it. Claiming the moral imperative to end racism and defeat white supremacy is not enough. The need many white people have to reclaim our full humanity stolen now some five hundred years and counting can only be achieved by destroying the beast that dehumanized us in the first place. It won't be easy. As Deacon Kenneth L. Radcliffe writes, the pull of white supremacy is like a narcotic coursing through all white people's veins. It addicts us regardless of class or economic status and is passed from one generation to the next with no clear antidote.[1] Recovery from our addiction to white supremacy will not be without relapses, to be sure.

But racism cannot last. In fact, as a vital belief system it is already dying. The myriad changes at work in the world today — from the rise of China and India as world economic powers to the changing demographics in the United States — already signal that the hegemony of the United States and Europe will not dominate the future world as they have for the past 500 years. These changes will not happen overnight; the hold white supremacy has on the world's psyche, most particularly white people's, will not simply vanish. Organizing to eradicate racism and white supremacy must continue and strengthen in the US and worldwide.

Despite the current reality that racism continues to permeate the national consciousness and its structural arrangement, we must keep striving for the elusive goal of racial equity. There is no other choice. Either we challenge and transform these current white-dominated institutions so our nation can become one in which everyone's humanity is recognized and affirmed, or racism will destroy us. As longtime New Orleans activist Barbara Major says, the United States is a multicultural nation but our systems remain mono-cultural.

What must we do? We must stand and organize. This country changes when organizing reaches a critical mass of people pushing for the right kind of change. This has been true throughout the nation's history. As many resources need to be applied toward organizing as are now given to direct services to poor people. We must organize with an analysis of power, as the People's Institute says. A needs-directed strategy will not "undo racism." During other great periods of change such as the Civil Rights Movement, the needs of racially-oppressed communities were great, yet it was the organizing of those communities for a singular purpose that was the key to change. The same has been true of other periods of genuine transformation in this country: during abolition, the struggle for women's rights, the rise of labor from the 1880s to the 1930s, and present day immigrant rights efforts and gay, lesbian, bisexual and transgender organizing. The key is organizing to build and sustain mass movements.

Our hope stems from this history — we have done this before. Because of the race-constructed society in which we live, movements are most successful when led by people of color. It is this fact that made the Civil Rights Movement one of the most transformative times in the nation's history. We must do "big tent" organizing that doesn't require that all people see and agree on everything. Progressive forces in the US must stop fighting each other, while regressive forces organize and carry the day.

We can "undo" racism when we find ways to work together across lines of class, gender, language, geography and organizations. There is not just one way to do it. One group can't do it. Single-issue organizing will fail. We must organize across lines of oppression and understand how this effort creates both opportunities and challenges. We must understand how white people have internalized white supremacist perspectives and people of color have internalized a sense of inferiority. If we do not understand the impact of this double whammy, our movement-building will be impossible.

We can "undo" racism if we recognize and organize within systems. We cannot overcome structural racism only through community-based organizing. We must acknowledge and reach out to potential allies who work within systems, bringing them together with constituents so that we can better understand how the systems function to keep communities down. The work to "undo" racism currently being done within the criminal justice system, as well as in human service, educational, and health care systems, gives us examples that fuel our hope.

Finally we can "undo" racism when we recognize that the work is rooted in culture and spirituality. However one defines these two powerful forces, they cannot be ignored. For most people, culture is found in the various forms of spirituality whose power wards off the demonic and materialist influences that threaten to kill the spirit. "Undoing racism" is not just a technical nor solely a secular process. We must recognize there is something within oppressed communities that has allowed them to survive as cultural peoples. We must tap into this strength. Ultimately racism and white supremacy are by-products of an age which prides itself on being "beyond" any ties to the world outside the intellect and the rational. It is a worldview that has no need for something larger than itself. This view of the world will destroy it.

Notes

Introduction

1. Y. N. Kly, *The Anti-Social Contract* (Atlanta: Clarity Press, 1989). "...apart from the written portion of the social contract (the U.S. Constitution), there is an unwritten portion, which for lack of a better word we may call the anti-social contract..." p. 2.
2. Rakesh Kochhar and Richard Fry, "Wealth inequality has widened along racial, ethnic lines since end of Great Recession" (Pew Research Center, 2014) 1.
3. Ira Katznelson, *When Affirmative Action Was White: An Untold History of Racial Inequality in Twentieth-Century America* (New York: Norton, 2005).
4. *Annals of Congress,* 1st Congress, 2nd Session, 1505–8, quoted in Winthrop Jordan, *White Over Black: American Attitudes Toward the Negro, 1550–1812* (Chapel Hill: University of North Carolina Press, 1968), 545.
5. Quoted in Tim Wise, *Colorblind: The Rise of Post-Racial Politics and the Retreat from Racial Equity* (San Francisco: City Lights Books, 2010), 63.

Part I

Chapter 1

1. Thomas F. Gossett, *Race: The History of an Idea in America, New edition* (New York: Oxford, 1997), 134.

2. Gossett, *History of an Idea,* 137.
3. Winthrop D. Jordan, *White Over Black: American Attitudes Toward the Negro, 1550–1812* (Chapel Hill: University of North Carolina Press, 1968), 94–95.
4. Leon C. Higginbotham, *In the Matter of Color: Race and the American Legal Process: The Colonial Period* (New York: Oxford University Press, 1978), 44. The earliest known earlier usage of the term "white" took place in the Maryland colony in 1681, also in anti-miscegenation legislation.
5. Y. N. Kly, *Anti-Social Contract,* 30.
6. Higginbotham, *In The Matter of Color,* 54.
7. Meizhu Lui et al., *The Color of Wealth: The Story Behind the U.S. Racial Wealth Divide* (New York: New Press, 2006), 233.
8. Kly, *Anti-Social Contract,* 36.
9. Jordan, *White over Black,* 80.
10. Quoted in Gossett, *Race: History of an Idea,* 35.
11. Quoted in Jordan, *White Over Black,* 275.
12. Quoted in Jordan, *White Over Black,* 223.
13. Ronald A. Takaki, *A Different Mirror: A History of Multicultural America* (New York: Little, Brown & Co, 1993), 80.
14. Karen Farquharson, "Racial Categories in Three Nations: Australia, South Africa and the United States," in *Proceedings of 'Public sociologies: lessons and trans-Tasman comparisons," the Annual Conference of The Australian Sociological Association (TASA),* Auckland, New Zealand, 04-07 December 2007. http://researchbank.swinburne.edu.au/vital/access/manager/Repository/swin:16944.
15. Quoted in Jordan, *White Over Black,* 143.
16. Quoted in Kly, *Anti-Social Contract,* 2.
17. Quoted in Jordan, *White Over Black,* 547.

Chapter 2

1. Jordan, *White Over Black,* 575-6.
2. Lui et al., *Color of Wealth,* 237.
3. Jordan, *White Over Black,* 229.
4. Quoted in Patricia Sullivan, *Lift Every Voice: The NAACP and the Making of the Civil Rights Movement* (New York: New Press, 2009), 66.

5. Robert Tignor, Jeremy Adelman, Peter Brown, Benjamin Elman, Xinru Liu, Holly Pittman and Michael Tsin, *Worlds Together, Worlds Apart: A History of the World: From the Beginnings of Humankind to the Present,* 4th edition (New York: Norton, 2015), 274.
6. Ronald Chisom and Michael Washington, *Undoing Racism: A Philosophy of International Social Change* (New Orleans: People's Institute Press, 1996), 34.

Chapter 3

1. James Webb, *Born Fighting: How the Scots-Irish Shaped America* (New York: Broadway Books, 2004).
2. W. J. Cash, *The Mind of the South* (New York: Vintage Books, 1960), 40.
3. Douglas A. Blackmon, *Slavery by Another Name: The Re-enslavement of Black Americans from the Civil War to World War II* (New York: Anchor Books, 2008), 110.
4. Gossett, *Race: History of an Idea,* 254.
5. James W. Loewen, *Sundown Towns: A Hidden Dimension of American Racism* (New York: New Press, 2005), 4.
6. Eric Foner, *Reconstruction: America's Unfinished Revolution: 1863–1877,* Francis Parkman Prize edition (New York: HarperCollins, 2005), 604.
7. Matthew Frye Jacobson, *Whiteness of a Different Color: European Immigrants and the Alchemy of Race* (Cambridge, MA: Harvard University Press, 1998), 92.
8. Lui et al., *Color of Wealth,* 248.
9. Joseph Healey, *Race, Ethnicity Gender and Class: The Sociology of Group Conflict and Change* (Thousand Oaks, CA: Pine Forge Press, 2006). Quoted portion cited from Donald L. Noel, "A theory of the Origin of Ethnic Stratification," *Social Problems* 16, no. 2 (1968): 163.
10. David R. Roediger, *How Race Survived U.S. History: From Settlement and Slavery to the Obama Phenomenon* (New York: Verso, 2008), 136-37.
11. Lui et al., *Color of Wealth,* 251.
12. Roosevelt, Theodore, "Fifth Annual Message, December 5, 1905," The American Presidency Project, accessed June 20, 2016, http://www.presidency.ucsb.edu/ws/?pid=29546.

13. Gossett, *Race: History of an Idea,* 188.
14. Healey, *Race, Ethnicity, Gender and Class,* 539.
15. Gossett, *Race: History of an Idea,* 329.
16. Bryan N. Massingale, *Racial Justice and the Catholic Church* (Maryknoll, NY: Orbis Books, 2010), 112.

Chapter 4

1. Gossett, *Race: History of an Idea,* 83.
2. Isabel Wilkerson, *The Warmth of Other Suns: The Epic Story of America's Great Migration* (New York: Random House, 2010).
3. Blackmon, *Slavery By Another Name,* 359.
4. Wilkerson, *Warmth of Other Suns,* 274–5.
5. Quoted in Paul Dickson and Thomas B. Allen, *The Bonus Army: An American Epic* (New York: Walker & Company, 2005), 118.
6. Benjamin Rich, *Searching for Whitopia* (New York: Hyperion, 2009), 187.

Chapter 5

1. Racial Equity Institute, LLC, "History of White Affirmative Action and the Legacy of Racism," presentation at Undoing Racism® and other workshops, 2011–present.
2. Jordan, *White Over Black,* 582.
3. Toni Morrison, *Playing in the Dark: Whiteness and the Literary Imagination* (New York: Vintage Books, 1993), 9.
4. Drug Policy Alliance, "New York's Rockefeller Drug Laws: Explaining the Reforms of 2009," accessed June 16, 2016, http://www.drugpolicy.org/docUploads/Explaining_the_RDL_reforms_of_2009_FINAL.pdf.
5. Michelle Alexander, *The New Jim Crow: Mass Incarceration in the Age of Colorblindness* (New York: New Press, 2010), 2.
6. Thomas C. Schelling, "A Process of Residential Segregation: Neighborhood Tipping," in *Racial Discrimination in Economic Life,* ed. Anthony H. Pascal. (Lexington, MS: Lexington Books, 1972).

Part II

Chapter 6

1. Ford Foundation, *Report on the Study for the Ford Foundation on Policy and Program* (Detroit, MI: The Ford Foundation, 1949), 9.

Chapter 7

1. Kenneth J. Cooper, "Letters from Thurgood: Segregation Is Un-American, Too," *Westside Gazette* (Broward Cty., FL), January 25, 2011, http://thewestsidegazette.com/letters-from-thurgood-segregation-is-un-american-too/

Chapter 8

1. Paul Keith Conkin, *Tomorrow a New World: The New Deal Community Program* (Ithaca: Cornell University Press for the American Historical Association, 1959).
2. Schelling, "A Process of Residential Segregation."
3. Lui et al., *Color of Wealth,* 257.
4. Rakesh Kochhar and Richard Fry. *Wealth Inequality Has Widened Along Racial, Ethnic Lines Since End of Great Recession* (Pew Research Center, 2014).

Chapter 9

1. bell hooks, *Rock My Soul: Black People and Self Esteem* (New York: Simon & Shuster, 2003).
2. Eric Foner, *Reconstruction: America's Unfinished Revolution: 1863–1877,* Francis Parkman Prize edition. (New York: HarperCollins, 2005), 530.
3. Bruce Watson, *Freedom Summer: The Savage Season that Made Mississippi Burn and Made America a Democracy* (New York: Viking, 2010), 48.
4. Juan Gonzales and Joseph Torres, *News For All the People: The Epic Story of Race and the American Media* (New York: Verso, 2011).

Chapter 10

1. Frances Cress Welsing, *The Isis Papers: The Keys to the Colors* (Chicago: Third World Press, 1999), 9.
2. Watson, *Freedom Summer,* 51.

Chapter 12

1. Randall Robinson, *The Debt: What America Owes to Blacks* (New York: Penguin Putnam Inc., 2000), 3.
2. Luke Tripp, "Black Working Class Radicalism In Detroit, 1960-1970," Industrial Workers of the World, 2009, accessed June 16, 2016, www.iww.org/en/node/4622.
3. Wilkerson, *Warmth of Other Suns,* 131.

Chapter 13

1. Patricia Sullivan, *Lift Every Voice: The NAACP and the Making of the Civil Rights Movement* (New York: New Press, 2009), chapters 8–9.
2. Sullivan, *Lift Every Voice,* 333.
3. Sullivan, *Lift Every Voice,* 425.

Chapter 15

1. Charles E. Cobb Jr., *This Non-Violent Stuff'll Get You Killed!* (New York: Basic Books, 2014).
2. Andrew Ferguson, "The Boy from Yazoo City: Haley Barbour, Mississippi's Favorite Son," *The Weekly Standard,* December 20, 2010.

Chapter 16

1. Diane McWhorter, *Carry Me Home: Birmingham, Alabama, the Climactic Battle of the Civil Rights Revolution* (New York: Simon & Schuster, 2001).
2. Civil Rights Movement Veterans, "History & Timeline, 1963 (Jan-June)," accessed June 16, 2016, http://www.crmvet.org/tim/timhis63.htm.
3. Quoted in John Dittmer, *Local People: The Struggle for Civil Rights in Mississippi* (Champaign, IL: University of Illinois Press, 1995), 205.

4. Dennis Sweeney, tragically, would later be charged with the murder of Congressman Allard Lowenstein, declared mentally ill and confined for life in a New York State mental facility.

Chapter 17

1. Peter Jan Honigsberg, *Crossing Border Street: A Civil Rights Memoir* (Berkeley: University of California Press, 2002), 105.
2. Ferguson, "Boy from Yazoo City."

Chapter 18

1. Elaine Allen Lechtreck, "Southern White Ministers and the CRM." PhD diss., Union Institute, 2007.
2. Lechtreck, "Southern White Ministers."
3. Hodding Carter, *So The Heffners Left McComb* (Garden City, NY: Doubleday, 1965).
4. George Lipsitz, *The Possessive Investment in Whiteness: How White People Profit from Identity Politics* (Philadelphia: Temple University Press, 1998), 7.

Chapter 19

1. Toni Morrison, *Race-ing Justice, En-Gendering Power* (New York: Pantheon Books, 1992), xxviii.

Chapter 20

1. Frances Fox Piven and Richard A. Cloward, *Poor People's Movements: Why They Succeed, How They Fail* (New York: Vintage Books, 1979), 36.

Chapter 21

1. Ian Haney López, *Dog Whistle Politics: How Coded Racial Appeals have Reinvented Racism and Wrecked the Middle Class* (New York: Oxford University Press, 2014).

Chapter 22

1. Michael Harrington, *The Other America: Poverty in the United States,* (New York: McMillan, 1962), 9.
2. Lena Bae, "Why You've Never Heard of Community Action: Civic Participation and Poverty," *Harvard Political Review,* April 10, 2011. http://harvardpolitics.com/united-states/civic-participation-and-poverty-looking-back-on-the-community-action-program/.
3. Mary K. Capps, "Community Decision-Making: A Study of the Board of Directors of Total Community Action, Inc." PhD diss., Tulane University, 1970, 14.
4. Capps, "Community Decision-Making," 150.
5. Rose M. Garrity, "The Cooptation of the Battered Women's Movement," *The Voice, the Newsletter of the National Coalition Against Domestic Violence,* 2000.

Chapter 25

1. Tim Wise, *Colorblind: The Rise of Post-Racial Politics and the Retreat from Racial Equity* (San Francisco: City Lights Books, 2010), 145.
2. Alexander, *New Jim Crow,* 177.
3. Pew Research Institute. "Race in America: Tracking 50 Years of Demographic Trends," accessed June 16, 2016. http://www.pewsocialtrends.org /2013/ 08/22/race-demographics/.

Chapter 26

1. *Pushed Out: The Hidden Costs of Gentrification: Displacement and Homelessness* (New York: Institute for Children and Poverty, 2009).

Epilogue

1. Kenneth L. Radcliffe, *Applying Alcoholics Anonymous Principles to the Disease of Racism* (Xlibris Corporation, 2012).

References

Alexander, Michelle. *The New Jim Crow: Mass Incarceration in the Age of Colorblindness.* New York: The New Press, 2010.

Allen, Theodore W. *The Invention of the White Race: The Origin of Racial Oppression in Anglo-America. Volume 2, The Origin of Racial Oppression in Anglo-America.* New York: Verso, 1997.

Ani, Marimba. *Let the Circle Be Unbroken: The Implications of African Spirituality in the Diaspora.* New York: Nkonimfo Publications, 1980. 7th printing 2004.

Bae, Lena. "Why You've Never Heard of Community Action: Civic Participation and Poverty," *Harvard Political Review,* April 10, 2011. http://harvardpolitics.com/united-states/civic-participation-and-poverty-looking-back-on-the-community-action-program/.

Banks, Dennis W. *Ojibwa Warrior: Dennis Banks and the Rise of the American Indian Movement.* With Richard Erdoes. Norman: University of Oklahoma Press, 2004.

Benjamin, Rich. *Searching for Whitopia.* New York: Hyperion, 2009.

Blackmon, Douglas A. *Slavery by Another Name: The Re-Enslavement of Black Americans from the Civil War to World War II.* New York: Anchor Books, 2008.

Brodkin, Karen. *How Jews became White Folks and What That Says about Race in America.* New Brunswick, NJ: Rutgers University Press, 1999.

Brown, Dee. *Bury My Heart At Wounded Knee: An Indian History of the American West.* Rev. ed. New York: Henry Holt & Company, 2007.

Capps, Mary K. "Community Decision-Making: A Study of the Board of Directors of Total Community Action, Inc." PhD diss., Tulane University, 1970.

Carter, Hodding. *So The Heffners Left McComb.* Garden City, NY: Doubleday, 1965.

Case, Carroll. *The Slaughter: An American Atrocity.* Asheville, NC: FBC, Inc., 1998.

Cash, W. J. *The Mind of the South.* New York: Knopf, 1941. Reprinted by Vintage Books, 1960.

Chang, Iris. *The Chinese in America: A Narrative History.* New York: Viking, 2003.

Chisom, Ronald and Michael Washington. *Undoing Racism: A Philosophy of International Social Change.* New Orleans: People's Institute Press, 1996.

Cobb, Charles E., Jr. *This Non-Violent Stuff'll Get Your Killed!* New York: Basic Books, 2014.

Conkin, Paul Keith. *Tomorrow a New World: The New Deal Community Program.* Ithaca: Cornell University Press, 1959. Published for the American Historical Association.

Cooper, Kenneth J. "Letters from Thurgood: Segregation Is Un-American, Too." Westside Gazette (Broward Cty., FL), January 25, 2011. http://thewestsidegazette.com/letters-from-thurgood-segregation-is-un-american-too/

DeGruy, Joy. *Post Traumatic Slave Syndrome: America's Legacy of Enduring Injury and Healing.* Portland, OR: Joy DeGruy Publications, 2005.

Deloria, Vine, Jr. *Custer Died for Your Sins: An Indian Manifesto.* London: The Macmillan Co, 1969.

Dickson, Paul and Thomas B. Allen. *The Bonus Army: An American Epic.* New York: Walker & Co., 2005.

Dittmer, John. *Local People: The Struggle for Civil Rights in Mississippi.* Champaign, IL: University of Illinois Press, 1995.

Drug Policy Alliance. "New York's Rockefeller Drug Laws: Explaining the Reforms of 2009." Accessed June 16, 2016. http://www.drugpolicy.org/ docUploads/Explaining_the_RDL_reforms_of_2009_FINAL.pdf.

Editorial. "Inching Closer to States' Rights." *New York Times,* May 30, 2011. http://www.nytimes.com/2011/05/30/opinion/30mon1.html?_r=0

Egerton, John. "Homegrown Progressives," *Southern Changes* 16, no. 3 (1994): 4-17.

Enck-Wanzer, Darrel, ed. *The Young Lords: A Reader.* New York: New York University Press, 2010.

Fanon, Franz. *Black Skin, White Masks.* Translated by Charles Lam Markmann. New York: Grove Press, 1967.

Farquharson, Karen. "Racial Categories in Three Nations: Australia, South Africa and the United States." *Proceedings of "Public sociologies: lessons and trans-Tasman comparisons," the Annual Conference of The Australian Sociological Association (TASA),* Auckland, New Zealand, 04-07 December 2007. http:// researchbank.swinburne.edu.au/vital/access/manager/Repository/swin:16944

Fehrenbacher, Don E. and Virginia E., eds. *Recollected Words of Abraham Lincoln.* Palo Alto: Stanford University Press, 1996

Ferguson, Andrew. "The Boy from Yazoo City: Haley Barbour, Mississippi's Favorite Son." *The Weekly Standard,* Dec. 27, 2010.

Ferling, John. *The Ascent of George Washington: The Hidden Political Genius of an American Icon.* New York: Bloomsbury, 2009.

Ford Foundation. *Report on the Study for the Ford Foundation on Policy and Program.* Detroit, MI: The Ford Foundation, 1949.

Foner, Eric. *Reconstruction: America's Unfinished Revolution: 1863–1877.* Francis Parkman Prize edition. New York: HarperCollins, 2005.

Formisano, Ronald. *Boston Against Busing: Race, Class and Ethnicity in the 1960s and 1970s.* Chapel Hill, University of North Carolina Press, 2004.

Fredrickson, George M. *Big Enough to be Inconsistent: Abraham Lincoln Confronts Slavery and Race.* Cambridge, MA: Harvard University Press, 2008.

Galeano, Eduardo. *Open Veins of Latin America: Five Centuries of the Pillage of a Continent.* New York: Monthly Review Press, 1973.

Garrity, Rose M. "The Cooptation of the Battered Women's Movement." *The Voice, the Newsletter of the National Coalition Against Domestic Violence,* 2000.

Gonzalez, Juan. *Harvest of Empire: A History of Latinos in America.* New York: Penguin Books, 2000.

Gonzales, Juan and Joseph Torres. *News For All the People: The Epic Story of Race and The American Media.* New York: Verso, 2011.

Gossett, Thomas F. *Race: The History of an Idea in America.* New edition. New York: Oxford University Press, 1997.

Guglielmo, Jennifer and Salvatore Salerno, eds., *Are Italians White? How Race is Made in America.* New York: Routledge, 2003.

Handlin, Oscar. *The Uprooted.* Philadelphia: University of Pennsylvania Press, 1973.

Hanes, W. Travis, III and Frank Sanello. *The Opium War: The Addiction of One Empire and the Corruption of Another.* New York: Barnes & Noble, 2002.

Haney Lopez, Ian F. *Dog Whistle Politics: How Coded Racial Appeals Have Reinvented Racism and Wrecked the Middle Class.* New York: Oxford University Press, 2014.

Haney Lopez, Ian F. *Racism on Trial: The Chicano Fight for Justice.* Cambridge, MA: The Belknap Press of Harvard University, 2003.

Harrington, Michael. *The Other America: Poverty in the United States.* New York: McMillan, 1962.

Healey, Joseph. *Race, Ethnicity Gender and Class: The Sociology of Group Conflict and Change.* Thousand Oaks, CA: Pine Forge Press, 2006.

Higginbotham, Leon C. *In the Matter of Color: Race and the American Legal Process: The Colonial Period.* New York: Oxford University Press, 1978.

Higginbotham, Leon C. *Shades of Freedom.* New York: Oxford University Press, 1996.

Hitler, Adolph, *Mein Kampf.* New York: Houghton and Mifflin, 1938. Vol. 1, Ch. 9.

Honigsberg, Peter Jan. *Crossing Border Street: A Civil Rights Memoir.* Berkeley: University of California Press, 2002.

hooks, bell. *Rock My Soul: Black People and Self Esteem.* New York: Simon & Shuster, 2003.

Horseman, Reginald. *Race and Manifest Destiny: The Origins of American Racial Anglo-Saxonism.* Cambridge, MA: Harvard University Press, 1981.

Ignatiev, Noel. *How the Irish Became White.* New York: Routledge,1995.

Institute for Children and Poverty. "Pushed Out: The Hidden Costs of Gentrification: Displacement and Homelessness." Spring 2009. Accessed June 16, 2016. http://www.icphusa.org/PDF/reports/ICP%20Report_Pushed%20 Out.pdf

Jacobson, Matthew Frye. *Whiteness of a Different Color: European Immigrants and the Alchemy of Race.* Cambridge, MA: Harvard University Press, 1998.

Jordan, Winthrop. *White Over Black: American Attitudes Toward the Negro, 1550–1812.* Chapel Hill: University of North Carolina Press, 1968.

Kamara, Jemadari and Tony Menelik Van Der Meer. *State of the Race: Creating Our 21st Century: Where Do We Go From Here?* Boston: Diaspora Press, 2004.

Katznelson, Ira. *Fear Itself: The New Deal and the Origins of Our Time.* New York: Liveright Publishing Corporation, 2013.

Katznelson, Ira. *When Affirmative Action Was White: An Untold History of Racial Inequality in Twentieth-Century America.* New York: Norton, 2005.

Keith, LeeAnna. *The Colfax Massacre: The Untold Story of Black Power, White Terror & The Death of Reconstruction.* New York: Oxford University Press, 2008.

Kelley, Robin D. *Hammer and Hoe: Alabama Communists during the Great Depression.* Chapel Hill, NC: University of North Carolina Press, 1990.

Kly, Y. N. *The Anti-Social Contract.* Atlanta: Clarity Press, 1989.

Kochhar, Rakesh and Richard Fry. *Wealth Inequality Has Widened Along Racial, Ethnic Lines Since End of Great Recession.* Pew Research Center, 2014.

Kochhar, Rakesh, Richard Fry and Paul Taylor. "Wealth Gaps Rise to Record Highs Between Whites, Blacks and Hispanics Twenty-to-One." Pew Research Center: Social & Demographic Trends, July 26, 2011.

Kluger, Richard. *Simple Justice: The History of* Brown v. Board of Education *and Black America's Struggle for Equality.* New York: Knopf, 1976.

Lehman, Nicholas. *The Promised Land: The Great Black Migration and How It Changed America.* New York: Knopf, 1991.

Lechtreck, Elaine Allen. "Southern White Ministers and the Civil Rights Movement." PhD diss., Union Institute, 2007.

Lewis, Gordon K. and Anthony P. Maingot. *Main Currents in Caribbean Thought: The Historical Evolution of Caribbean Society in Its Ideological Aspects, 1492–1900.* Lincoln, NE: University of Nebraska Press, 2004.

Lewis-Colman, David M. *Race against Liberalism: Black Workers and the UAW in Detroit.* Urbana, IL: University of Illinois Press, 2008.

Lind, Michael. *What Lincoln Believed: The Values and Convictions of America's Greatest President.* New York: Double Day, 2004.

Lipsitz, George. *The Possessive Investment in Whiteness: How White People Profit from Identity Politics.* Philadelphia: Temple University Press, 1998.

Loewen, James W. *Lies My Teacher Told Me: Everything Your American History Textbook Got Wrong.* New York: Simon & Shuster, 1996.

Loewen, James W. *Sundown Towns: A Hidden Dimension of American Racism.* New York: The New Press, 2005.

Loewen, James W. and Charles Sallis, eds. *Mississippi: Conflict and Change.* New York: Random House. 1974.

Lui, Meizhu, Barbara Robles, Betsy Leondar-Wright, Rose Brewer, and Rebecca Adamson. *The Color of Wealth: The Story Behind the U.S. Racial Wealth Divide.* New York: New Press, 2006.

Martinez, Elizabeth. *De Colores Means All of Us*. Cambridge, MA: South End Press, 1998.

Massingale, Bryan N. *Racial Justice and the Catholic Church*. Maryknoll, NY: Orbis Books, 2010.

McKenzie, Phyllis. *The Mexican Texans*. San Antonio: University of Texas Institute of Texan Cultures, 2004.

McGreal, Chris. "A $95,000 Question: Why Are Whites Five Times Richer than Blacks in the US?" The *Guardian* (UK), May 17, 2010. Accessed June 16, 2016. http://www.guardian.co.uk/world/2010/may/17/white-people-95000-richer-black

McWhorter, Diane. *Carry Me Home: Birmingham, Alabama, the Climactic Battle of the Civil Rights Revolution*. New York: Simon & Schuster, 2001.

Morgan, Edmund S. *American Slavery, American Freedom: The Ordeal of Colonia Virginia*. New York: Norton, 1975.

Morrison, Toni. *Playing in the Dark: Whiteness and the Literary Imagination*. New York: Vintage Books, 1993.

Morrison, Toni. *Race-ing Justice, En-Gendering Power*. New York: Pantheon Books, 1992.

Navajo Code Talkers. http://www.navajocodetalkers.org.

Neiwert, David A. *Strawberry Days: How Internment Destroyed a Japanese American Community*. New York: Palgrave MacMillan, 2005.

Newman, Richard S. *The Transformation of American Abolitionism: Fighting Slavery in the Early Republic*. Chapel Hill: University of North Carolina Press, 2002.

Newton, Huey P. "War Against the Panthers: A Study of Repression in America." University of Santa Cruz, 1980. https://archive.org/stream/WarAgainst ThePanthersAStudyOfRepressionInAmerica/WATP_djvu.txt.

Noel, Donald L. "A Theory of the Origin of Ethnic Stratification," *Social Problems* 16, no. 2 (1968): 157-172.

Oliver, Melvin L. and Thomas M. Shapiro. *Black Wealth/White Wealth: A New Perspective on Racial Inequality*. New York: Routledge, 1995.

Palen, J. John and Bruce London. *Gentrification, Displacement, and Neighborhood Revitalization.* New York: SUNY Press, 1984.

Parascandola, Louis J., ed. *Look for Me All Around You: Anglophone Caribbean Immigrants in the Harlem Renaissance.* Detroit: Wayne State University, 2005.

Perry, Jeffrey B. *Hubert Harrison: The Voice of Harlem Radicalism, 1883–1918.* New York: Columbia University Press, 2009.

Pew Research Institute. "Race in America: Tracking 50 Years of Demographic Trends." Accessed June 16, 2016. http://www.pewsocialtrends.org/2013/08/22/race-demographics/

Pharr, Suzanne. *Homophobia: A Weapon of Sexism.* Inverness, CA: Chardon Press, 1988.

Piven, Frances Fox and Richard A. Cloward. *Poor People's Movements: Why They Succeed, How They Fail.* New York: Vintage Books, 1979.

Pushed Out: The Hidden Costs of Gentrification: Displacement and Homelessness. New York: Institute for Children and Poverty, 2009.

Racial Equity Institute, LLC. "History of White Affirmative Action and the Legacy of Racism" Presentation at Undoing Racism® and other workshops, 2011–present.

Radcliffe, Kenneth L. *Applying Alcoholics Anonymous Principles to the Disease of Racism.* Xlibris Corporation, 2012.

Ransby, Barbara. *Ella Baker and the Black Freedom Movement: A Radical Democratic Vision.* Chapel Hill: University of North Carolina Press, 2003.

Reid, Omar G., Sekou Mims and Larry Higginbottom. *Post Traumatic Slavery Disorder: Definition, Diagnosis and Treatment.* Charlotte, NC: Conquering Books, 2005.

Rich, Benjamin. *Searching for Whitopia: An Improbable Journey to the Heart of White America.* New York: Hyperion, 2009.

Robinson, Greg. *By Order of the President: FDR and the Internment of the Japanese Americans.* Cambridge, MA: Harvard University Press, 2001.

Robinson, Randall. *The Debt: What America Owes to Blacks.* New York: Penguin Putnam Inc., 2000.

Roediger, David R. *How Race Survived U.S. History: From Settlement and Slavery to the Obama Phenomenon.* New York: Verso, 2008.

Roosevelt, Theodore, "Fifth Annual Message, December 5, 1905," The American Presidency Project, accessed June 20, 2016, http://www.presidency.ucsb. edu/ws/?pid=29546.

Salaff, Stephen. "The Diary and the Cenotaph: Racial and Atomic Fever in the Canadian Record." *Bulletin of Concerned Asian Scholars* 10, no. 2 (1978): 38-40.

Sandbrook, Dominic. *Mad as Hell: The Crisis of the 1970s and the Rise of the Populist Revolt.* New York: Knopf, 2011.

Schelling, Thomas C. "A Process of Residential Segregation: Neighborhood Tipping." In *Racial Discrimination in Economic Life,* edited by Anthony H. Pascal. Lexington, MS: Lexington Books, 1972.

Shin, Yuna, "North Carolina Provides Insight into Changing Southern Politics," *Huffington Post,* November 30, 2008. Accessed June 16, 2016. http://www.huffingtonpost.com/yuna-shin/north-carolina-provides-i_b_139515.html

Sinsheimer, Joseph A."The Freedom Vote of 1963: New Strategies of Racial Protest in Mississippi." *Journal of Southern History* 55, no. 2 (1989): 217–244. doi:10.2307/2208903.

Skates, John Ray. "German Prisoners of War in Mississippi, 1943–1946," Mississippi Historical Society, 2001.

Skloot, Rebecca. *The Immortal Life of Henrietta Lacks.* New York: Broadway Paperbacks, 2010.

Smith, Lillian. *Killers of the Dream.* New York: Norton, 1949.

Smith, Lillian. *Strange Fruit.* New York: Reynal & Hitchcock Publishers, 1944.

Steffen, Jordan. "White House Honors Japanese American WWII Veterans." *Los Angeles Times,* October 6, 2010. Accessed June 16, 2016. http://articles.latimes.com/2010/oct/06/nation/la-na-veterans-medal-20101006.

Stroupe, Nibs and Inez Fleming. *While We Run This Race: Confronting the Power of Racism in a Southern Church.* New York: Orbis Books, 1995.

Sullivan, Patricia. *Lift Every Voice: The NAACP and the Making of the Civil Rights Movement.* New York: New Press, 2009.

Takaki, Ronald. *A Different Mirror: A History of Multicultural America.* New York: Little, Brown & Co, 1993.

Takaki, Ronald. *Strangers from a Different Shore: A History of Asian Americans.* New York: Penguin Books, 1990.

Taylor, Paul, "Wealth Gaps and Perception Gaps: A Paradox of the Great Recession," Pew Research Center, July 29, 2011. Accessed June 16, 2016. http://pewresearch.org/pubs/2076.

Thomas, Piri. "Puerto Rican Paradise." In *Worlds of Difference: Inequality in the Aging Experience,* 3rd edition, edited by Eleanor Palo Stoller and Rose Campbell Gibson, 44–46. Thousand Oaks, CA: Pine Forge Press, 2000.

Tignor, Robert, Jeremy Adelman, Peter Brown, Benjamin Elman, Xinru Liu, Holly Pittman and Michael Tsin. *Worlds Together, Worlds Apart: A History of the World: From the Beginnings of Humankind to the Present,* 4th edition. New York: Norton, 2015.

Tripp, Luke, "Black Working Class Radicalism In Detroit, 1960-1970," Industrial Workers of the World, 2009. Accessed June 16, 2016. www.iww.org/en/node/4622.

Turner, Frederick Jackson. *The Frontier in American History.* New York: Holt, 1921.

Van Sertima, Ivan. *They Came Before Columbus: The African Presence in Ancient America.* New York: Random House, 2003.

Washington, Harriet A. *Medical Apartheid: The Dark History of Medical Experimentation on Black Americans from Colonial Times to the Present.* New York: Harlem Moon, 2006.

Watson, Bruce. *Freedom Summer: The Savage Season that Made Mississippi Burn and Made America a Democracy.* New York: Viking, 2010.

Webb, James. *Born Fighting: How the Scots-Irish Shaped America.* New York: Broadway Books, 2004.

Welsing, Frances Cress. *The Isis Papers: The Keys to the Colors.* Chicago: Third World Press, 1991.

Wikipedia contributors. "Brownsville Affair." *Wikipedia, The Free Encyclopedia,* https://en.wikipedia.org/w/index.php?title=Brownsville_Affair&oldid =714075900 (accessed June 16, 2016).

Wilkerson, Isabel. *The Warmth of Other Suns: The Epic Story of America's Great Migration.* New York: Random House, 2010.

Wise, Tim. *Colorblind: The Rise of Post-Racial Politics and the Retreat from Racial Equity.* San Francisco: City Lights Books, 2010.

Wyman, David S. *Paper Walls: America and the Refugee Crisis 1938–1941.* Amherst, MA: University of Massachusetts Press, 1968.

X, Malcolm. *Malcolm X Speaks: Selected Speeches and Statements.* Edited by George Breitman. New York: Merit Publishers, 1965.

INDEX

I

J

K

L

M

N

S

T

U

V

W

X

Y

Z

About the Author

David Billings has been an anti-racist trainer and organizer with the People's Institute for Survival and Beyond since 1983. Billings has worked with anti-racist organizing groups across the country, including AntiRacist Alliance and New York Education Equity Alliance. He currently consults with Citizens for Economic Equity in New Orleans.

Rev. Billings is an ordained United Methodist minister. He also is an historian with a special interest in the history of race and racism. Over the years, Billings' organizing work has been cited for many awards including the Westchester County chapter of the National Association of Social Workers "Public Citizen of the Year;" the New Orleans Pax Christi "Bread and Roses" award; the Loyola University of New Orleans "Homeless and Hunger Award"; the 2010 Martin Luther King Social Justice Award from the New Orleans Jazz Foundation; and the National Alliance against Racist Oppression's Angela Davis Award for community service. He was the Whitney Young 2006 lecturer at the Westchester County NASW symposium.

David Billings was born in McComb, Mississippi and grew up in Helena, Arkansas. He has a BA from the University of Mississippi, a Masters of Divinity degree from New York Theological Seminary, and a Doctor of Ministry (ABD) from the University of Creation Spirituality (now Wisdom University). He is married to Margery Freeman and has three children, Nathan and Noah Shroyer, and Stella Billings, and six grandchildren, Jonathan, Abigail, Isaiah, Sofia, Twain, and Whipple Ann. David and Margery currently live in McComb, Mississippi.

CPSIA information can be obtained
at www.ICGtesting.com
Printed in the USA
LVOW13s0339240718
584734LV00011B/221/P